The Queen is D

DATE DUE

Also by Mark Simpson
Male Impersonators
It's a Queer World
Anti-Gay (ed.)
Saint Morrissey (forthcoming 2001)

Also by Steven Zeeland
Barrack Buddies and Soldier Lovers
Sailors and Sexual Identity
The Masculine Marine
Military Trade

The Queen is DEAD

a story of jarheads, eggheads, serial killers and bad sex

Mark Simpson and Steven Zeeland

A ARCADIA BOOKS
LONDON

Arcadia Books Ltd
15–16 Nassau Street
London W1W 7AB

www.arcadiabooks.co.uk

First published in Great Britain 2001
Copyright © Mark Simpson and Steven Zeeland 2001

A catalogue record for this book is available from the British Library.

ISBN 1–900850–49–4

Designed and typeset in FF Scala and Scala Sans by
Discript, London WC2N 4BN
Printed in England by The Cromwell Press, Trowbridge, Wiltshire

Arcadia Books distributors are as follows:
in the UK and elsewhere in Europe:
Turnaround Publishers Services
Unit 3, Olympia Trading Estate
Coburg Road
London N22 6TZ

in the USA and Canada:
Consortium Book Sales and Distribution, Inc.
1045 Westgate Drive
St Paul, MN 55114–1065

in Australia:
Tower Books
PO Box 213
Brookvale, NSW 2100

in New Zealand:
Addenda
Box 78224
Grey Lynn
Auckland

in South Africa:
Peter Hyde Associates (Pty) Ltd
PO Box 2856
Cape Town 8000

Contents (39)

Acknowledgements

They know who they are.

To Randy F.

We have seen what the beloved gains in playing his role: he is magnified in the lover's heart. He is sheltered, saved. But what of the lover? Why does he demand disgust and rebuffs, the other's indifference, the tortures of jealousy and, in the end, the despair that comes from the certainty of not being loved? And yet he must have something to gain by this. What is behind it all?

– Jean-Paul Sartre

A homosexual is not a man who loves homosexuals, but a man who, seeing a soldier, immediately wants to have him for a friend.

– Marcel Proust

Pickup Lines

London, 4 March 1995

Dear Steven Zeeland,

I have just finished reading your latest book, *Sailors and Sexual Identity*. If you have come across my book *Male Impersonators: Men Performing Masculinity* you'll know why I read it greedily in one sitting.

Back in 1990, when I was twenty-five and bumming around Southern California for a year, I happened to be having my hair cut in the Military YMCA in San Diego – they did a mean flat-top and I was still in my post-rockabilly Elvis-joins-the-Army phase. A small, very confident, slightly ovoid thirty-something Puerto Rican introduced himself as 'Stan' and declared he was a Captain in the US Navy (a lie, as it turned out, but like all Stan's lies, one delivered with such confidence and élan that it seemed almost churlish not to believe him). He had mistaken me for USMC issue. Disappointed, he grasped at straws: 'Are you Australian?'

Not having been in Southern California very long, and being only twenty-five years old, I hadn't yet understood the basically rhetorical nature of such questions, and I unkindly disabused him of that idea too.

But Stan generously decided that he liked me anyway and even more generously introduced me to his harem of military boys, which was comprised of several sailors and Marines – but mostly, for some reason, Marines – none older than twenty; none less attractive than say, a young Sean Penn; and none less friendly than an abandoned Collie pup. (Stan, in typical military chicken-hawk *modus operandi* had found these young men on his nightly sweeps of the streets, Navy bars, and dirty bookstores of San Diego.)

Actually, while I'd like to say that I ravished a battalion or two of studly jarheads during my stay, the embarrassing truth is that I mostly just hung out with them, played a lot of pool and got very drunk. My stupidity in the cupidity dept. cost me a lifetime of once-in-a-lifetime opportunities. On one dismally remembered occasion, I was putting a particularly cute and particularly drunk Marine to bed who kept telling me, over and over, 'Man, I'm like . . . *totally fucked up!'*

Like a fool that does not deserve the use of his genitalia I *tucked* him in and said, 'Night-night. See you tomorrow.' I think I may even have put my hand on his forehead.

The next day Stan called me up to laugh at me. The bewildered Marine had told him what had happened. Or what hadn't happened. 'Don't you know,' exclaimed Stan, 'that "Man, I'm totally fucked up!" is standard Marine code for "Please jump me *now*!"'

I enjoyed my San Diego furlough, but I think it may have spoilt me. Since my return to London I've been daydreaming about becoming one of those legendary old queens you hear about who own a house near Oceanside: full of pool tables, Bud on tap and, of course, hordes of 'totally fucked up' Marines.

Care to join me?

Yours sincerely,

Mark Simpson

A Spy in the House of Marines

San Diego, May 17, 1995

Dear Mark,

Your letter of April 7 was a pleasant surprise, and well timed. The night before its arrival I had visited the Oceanside home of a Marine Corps lieutenant, and there met eight young enlisted Marines, several of whom had some interesting stories to tell me. I returned to Hillcrest with renewed enthusiasm for completing my third volume of interviews with military men, tentatively titled *The Masculine Marine*.

Two months before I had bought and read *Male Impersonators*. I found it fun, stimulating – and inspiring. I had already planned to write to you as a potential pre-publication reviewer for *Marine*.

Two ideas in your essay 'Active Sports' seem to me especially relevant to Marines: 'All that running around produces a physical reassurance against the possibility of penetration' (and excites us to want to do just that). And of course the idea that the performance of masculinity in war is about the repudiation of penetrability.

Have you read Leo Bersani's *Homos*? In 'The Gay Presence' he theorizes that:

> the most serious danger in gay Marines being open about their gayness is that they might begin, like some of their gay civilian brothers, to play at being Marines ... In imagining what he presumably already is (both gay and a Marine), the gay Marine may learn the invaluable lesson that identity is not serious (as if what he is imitating never existed before it was imitated). Nothing is more inimical to military life than that lesson ... The gay soldier letting out his gayness may begin to see its theatricalities as incompatible with the monolithic theatricality of military masculinity. Gays might then begin to abandon the armed forces by the thousands – which could sap the morale of their deserted straight comrades and furnish recruits for a new type of anti-militarism

(yet to be defined), one somewhere "between" or "outside" both pacifism and guerrilla terrorism.

What do you think of this idea?

Elsewhere, Bersani makes clear that he has no special interest in, attraction to, or experience with Marines, gay or otherwise, and even suggests a 'continuity between a sexual preference for rough and uniformed trade, a sentimentalizing of the armed forces, and right-wing politics.' But if Bersani is too removed from this subject to speak with authority, I may be too close to form a larger abstract picture.

Lance Corporal 'Ted', USMC, with Zeeland, in the barracks at Camp Pendleton

I appreciated your regret about the cute drunk 'totally fucked up' Marine. I'll bet it remains all that much more intense a fantasy for being unrealized! You can empathize with a story of mine included in the next book: a gay Marine, Keith, introduced me to his straight buddy Ted (photo enclosed), whom I promptly developed a powerful crush on. Ted ended up sleeping over, and (because Keith was on my living-room floor getting fucked by sailor Anthony) sharing my bed with me. Unfortunately, only a few hours previous I had conducted an interview with Ted in which he had clearly positioned himself behind the gay/straight boundary, and confided in me all of his absent-father issues. So I couldn't, in good conscience, do what I wanted, and lay torturously awake the whole night listening to these other two growling and moaning like dying steers.

I had less scruples in the (almost mirror) case of a gay Army infantryman I knew in Frankfurt who once brought his straight buddy (cute, dumb, virginal, and so butch that, as a result of a farming accident, on one foot he only had two toes) out to the bars with him. The gay guy was supposed to baby-sit the straight guy and protect him from predators, but met up with another gay GI and asked if they could sleep in my hallway. 'Two-toe' (by now very drunk) agreed to bunk down with me – reluctantly, he wanted it to be known. But as I scratched his bristles he asked me: 'If I pass out, do you want me to lie on my stomach or on my back?'

I fully sympathize with how the taste of Marines has spoiled you. At thirty-five (today) I find that the only men capable of arousing me on sight any more are Marines. I am thoroughly bored with the vapid sun and freeway culture of San Diego, and often contemplate leaving it, but how much more tedious life would be without the daily opportunity to admire the god-like beauty of young Marines, to say nothing of more corporeal forms of worship.

After a visit to the Del Mar Enlisted Men's Club at Camp Pendleton last week I instructed my roommate Alex (himself a recent ex-Marine) that upon my death I want my ashes poured into the piss trough there.

And so, I must accept your offer and join you in the House of Marines.

Yours,

Steven

Boys Who Marry Dad

London, 20 May 1995

Dear Steven,

So your next opus probes the private world of the Marine, does it? Well, my lawyers will be in touch with you very shortly. That's *my* book your writing!

Seriously, I know it will make fascinating reading, and there isn't anyone better able to write it. All the same, a part of me can't help but wonder if this isn't one murky, fuzzy area of human desire and sexual identity which would be better off left in the shadows. As I'm sure you're well aware, your work, like mine, navigates the boundaries between 'hetero' and 'homo', trying to blur them but perhaps only succeeding in redrawing them even more strongly. Maybe this is an area of human activity where language not only falls short, but actually corrupts the idea and ultimately undoes the act even before it's done. The timeless straight-boy line 'oh man, was I drunk last night' is considerably wiser than all the books you or I might write.

Yes, I have read Leo Bersani's *Homos*, and found the passage you quoted particularly interesting. And yes, I think it's true that the performance of masculinity that the military requires is not allowed to be at all ironic – after all, these men have to be persuaded to engage in highly irrational, plainly dumb behaviour: running across a minefield at a machine-gun emplacement is not something most people, or even most of the sort of people that become Marines, would do 'ironically'. Killing and being killed can't be put in quotation marks. *Esprit de corps*, the dear love of comrades, is not something you can afford to have a distance on. Which of course, is precisely why someone like me who has too much of a distance on everything is drawn to military boys.

And then Bersani betrays how seriously he himself takes identities here by talking of the 'gay soldier letting his gayness out'. Bersani is really trading in essences, not wanting to allow for the possibility that a soldier might be homosexual in behaviour, even exclusively so, and not be 'gay' at all (the

'Samurai' model of homosexuality, if you like) and thus have no 'gayness' to 'let out'. Identity is 'not serious', in other words, unless it is the *gay identity*.

Personally, I don't find the idea of 'gays' abandoning the armed forces in their thousands such an encouraging vision as 6os queen Bersani seems to. Maybe I'm just illustrating the 'continuity between a preference for rough and uni-formed trade, a sentimentalizing of the armed forces, and right-wing politics', but I think something would be lost if there was no other place for the homosocial/homoerotic than the gay disco. Not least because I'd have to abandon all hope of getting a good lay ever again.

I have to say that I understand entirely your crush on the young Marine whose picture you kindly sent me. Isn't it fun-ny how the paternal/filial relationships get all jumbled up? By the way, my not-so-original theory about boys in the mili-tary – especially the Marines – is that they are lost boys who probably had poor relationships with their fathers (if they had any at all). Joining the military is a second chance. A kind of marriage to Dad number 2.

I may be in S. Cal at the end of June, beginning of July, so perhaps we'll be able to meet. I'll be travelling with my 'best mate' Jason.

Oh, he's a Sergeant in the Royal Marine Commandos.

Yours,

Mark

PS I enclose a picture of myself that Bersani would no doubt find highly revealing, taken a few years ago out-side Camp Pendleton USMC after spending the night there in the Military Police barracks...

'Wannabe startin' something'

Foucault's Scrotum

San Diego, June 1995

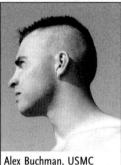

Alex Buchman, USMC

Dear Mark,

Thanks for your letter of May 20. I must warn you that Alex, my roommate, lusts for your flesh (his photo is included as Figure 12 in *Sailors*). Please do give me a call if you are going to be in Southern California this summer; it would be great to meet a fellow heretic of your stature.

I was never really much of a believer in the gay religion. For years I quarrelled with proselytizing friends who insisted that my attraction to military boys must be a manifestation of my internalized homophobia. My half-hearted and rather unfortunate attempts at ingratiating myself with these people show up in bits of *Barrack Buddies and Soldier Lovers*.

Being a queer theoretician was never my aspiration. At heart I am a frustrated novelist (and failed musician). My first manuscript was rejected by publishers who told me that it did not meet the marketing requirements of gay fiction. A German friend suggested that I produce a manuscript of interviews with the GIs I knew from the Frankfurt bars; this, he said, would sell. I resisted the idea at first, but reasoned that I could always use the material so accumulated for my second novel. Of course once I got going, I recognized that the real-life transcripts were more strange and wonderful than any narrative I could distil from them, and here I am. Luckily, I landed with a smart editor who was able to help me understand the significance of my own research, and appreciate the extent to which my old intuitions seem to have been on target.

In writing these books I am of course answering my own riddles – but at a price. I know only too well (as the anecdote I wrote you in my last letter reminds) how talking about sex imposes as many barriers as it eliminates. *Sailors* ends with me clapping my hand over the mouth of some video booth trick who wants to tell me his story.

I had misgivings about doing a book on Marines, who, as I wrote in my last book, probably deserve to keep some of their secrets. Then again, my work doesn't seek to impose much explanation, but mostly just catalogues personal experience and leaves it open to interpretation. Very few of my readers are as perceptive as you, Mark. I hope that my Marine interviews might serve as useful source material for your commentaries. I expect you will positively feast on several of the interviews I have thus far gathered, which affirm your father theories with almost embarrassing bluntness. But what delights me most are the confusing, irreducible contradictions in the individual lives of uniformed men. It is in my interest, too, to leave the Marine mystique intact. (Surely no book anyone writes could seriously impair Marines' powerful seductive aura. I am certain that they, and we, will still make the leap of faith to our respective turn-ons.)

I've further pondered over *Homos.* I understand that Marines are expected to take their masculinity very seriously, but I'm not sure that coming out inclines Marines to view Marine masculinity ironically, or that non-gay Marines are all necessarily so thick as to not, with time, on some level, come to understand themselves as butch drag performers. I think the biggest problem for gay Marines is that in conceptualizing their desire as fundamentally different from non-gay Marines, they may cut themselves off from physical and emotional closeness with Marines. And the problem for non-gay Marines is of course the simpler truth that (Bersani again): 'the homoeroticism inherent in military life ... risks being exposed to those who would at once deny and enjoy it when self-confessed homos from within the ranks go public.' Gay activists in the US campaigned for a policy to allow service members to come out publicly with the proviso that they never actually engage in sex. The reverse would probably serve the Marine Corps better: continuing to ban gay identity (a bogus and potentially divisive distinction) but eliminating penalties for sexual acts which, after all, sometimes proceed as an expression of the masculine bonding the military prizes. (After all, Marines who insist on calling themselves gay could always be transferred to 'pogue' units. Or to the Navy.)

I think you're right that Bersani contradicts himself when he states that 'identity is not serious' and that gayness is an essentially anti-communitarian Genet-rimming Nazi 'kind of meta-transgressive *dépassement* of the field of transgressive possibility itself'. Possibly I'm jaded, but the vision of Foucault strung up by his scrotum in a South of Market loft seems to me as mundane as a trip to the mall.

I hope all three of my military-boy books serve to underscore the truth behind the 'oh man, I was so drunk last night' lie. The residue of my Christian slave morality impels me to point out that it is a lie. But I think you are right: it is wise, for in telling it, the Marine who has had sex with another man may be showing not just his fear that what he has done will be called 'gay', but his recognition that it is dishonest and unfair to call what he has done any significant departure from what any other man might feel or do. Maybe he recognizes the bigger lie of the only socially accepted explanation for what is in many ways the mundane exercise of just another human potential.

I wonder how the full integration of women into the combat arms will impact on the homoerotic bond. My liberal bad conscience prompts the observation that, because differences (gender, racial, etc.) are mostly constructed, people of all stripes can and do bond. But then I think of my Marine interviewee Jack, who explains the masculine Marine mystique in terms of smell: 'You know what Mom smells like. And you know what Dad smells like.'

I thought you would like that.

Yours,

Steve

II

Marine Rodeo

London, 7 August 1995

Dear Steve,

It was good to meet you and Alex during my and Jason's all-too brief stay in SD. I'm sorry that we couldn't link up on the last night, but it was bound to prove an anticlimax after Saturday night's adventures in Camp Pendleton. I thought I'd died and gone to Heaven when I was watching the Marine Rodeo – all those Texas jarheads in too-tight Wrangler jeans (Marine masculinity squeezed into the Cowboy).

As if this wasn't enough for a bum-bandit Brit tourist, there was the 'YMCA' moment later that evening on the dance floor at the Del Mar Enlisted Men's Club. All those *friendly* nineteen-year-old lads just in from an exercise in the field, sunburnt and still in their combat fatigues, doing the full Village People 'YMCA' routine. Complete with hand gestures.

Now I *knew* I'd died and gone to Heaven.

Having Alex act as our tour guide, showing us where he used to live on camp, added a certain poignancy. He certainly still has a military bearing. Has he readjusted to being beaten into a ploughshare, or does he still miss the days when he was a sword? As you know, Jason is still 'in', in both senses. I think he found the whole experience very alarming, for all sorts of reasons.

The Marine life theme continued the following day. Before leaving SD we visited Sea World. In spite of my Ren-like cynicism I actually found myself impressed by the dolphins' Broadway routines and the unfeasibly acrobatic killer whale, and whooped and cheered in all the places I was supposed to. Sometimes it's nice just to relax and let the American pleasure machine work you over. Jase's obvious enjoyment of it all helped to defuse my killjoy instincts. When he smiles or laughs at something I can't help but see it from his point of view (the emotional vampirism of the jaded?). Besides, Jase keeps his feelings so screwed down most of the time that it feels churlish not to root with him when he lets something out (now I'm beginning to sound like a gayist). All in all, I found travelling *with* someone to be a revelation, after having spent so long travelling alone.

On the way back up to LAX we stopped overnight in Laguna Beach, played pool in the Boom Boom Room, drank too many frosted beers, enjoyed a oversized Mexican meal and wandered along the beach, watching the surf catch the moonlight, before going to sleep on top of the bedcovers in our motel room because it was so warm.

Our last night in California was just as banal as I could have wished it to be.

On the way to the airport Jason bought a California State Lottery ticket. 'If we win,' he declared in that deep Glaswegian brogue that so perplexed most of the Americans we met that they would look to me with a mixture of pleading and panic in their eyes, 'we'll never have to go home!'. And he was only half-joking. I know it's easy to be generous with money that you haven't won and a future that isn't going to happen, but I was touched by Jason's offer to share his with me all the same. And in California it's possible to believe, just for a few days, that anything is possible, if you have enough money. Even me and Jason.

When does your Marine book come out?

Sorry there are no profound/pretentious quotes or observations in this letter. I suppose that it must be because I'm in a good mood. No doubt by the next time I write, things will be back to normal and I'll be reaching for Freud again.

Best,

Mark

PS Sorry if I was short with you on the way back from Pendleton that night. It had been a very long day. Rows with Jason in the morning, the beach in the afternoon, the drive to Pendleton, and then an evening of visions which probably only dying men should see. And, to be brutally honest, you were talking far too much. Don't you realize that like most writers, I prefer the sound of my own voice?

Talkshow Exhibitionism

San Diego, September 13, 1995

Dear Mark,

Tonight is the first cool evening we've had for some time. It was a hot August in San Diego, and my brain has been running at a seriously reduced capacity. Did I mention how much I hate summer? Anyway, I am seven-eighths done with the Marine book. The last bit may take me a couple of months yet. I want the finished work to be more disciplined and leaner than my Navy book (for which a little excess seemed appropriate). The only problem has to do with that elusive 'almost mystical' quality of Marines, which, I think you suggested, talking about can only spoil. So although I'm calling my Introduction 'Penetrating Marine Machismo', really I only rim it some.

In aspiring to new heights of perversion, I even interviewed two lesbian Marines, relishing the prospect of force-feeding my gay male readership images of women masturbating in the boot camp showers. The experiment, of course, failed; I had to concede that I was out of my depth. (And, really, what pleasure would it bring to alienate my audience? I've received a few genuinely touching letters of late from ex-sailors and lonely old military chasers thanking me for bringing some joy into their lives. Also, I see from the Internet that there are copies of *Sailors* in the official US Navy library in D.C., and at the Naval Academy in Annapolis – a few feet over from Clausewitz on the military science shelves. Does this mean it's time to change my address?)

Please apprise me if you know of anyone who might provide me with a photograph of naked recruits shaving each other.

On return visits to the Area 51 enlisted club Alex and I established that 'YMCA' is a regular highlight of that DJ's program. I

Camp Pendleton US Marines dancing to 'YMCA'

even managed to get a proper photograph (enclosed). We noted that the dance floor emptied, however, upon fulfilment of one Marine's request for Gloria Gaynor's 'I Will Survive'.

I've just finished reading Craig Cameron's *American Samurai: Myth, Imagination and the Conduct of Battle in the First Marine Division, 1941–1951*. He talks about the Marine Corps' prescient 1911 recognition of the importance of self-promotion, about the kinds of men who were attracted to the mythic images so propagated, and about how their efforts to live up to those nebulous ideals in turn generated new mythic images. I think that must sometimes even be true of sexual stereotypes. A Marine Corps major I've interviewed tells me that when he gets in bed with some guys he just doesn't have a chance to topple their expectations. But who knows what he really wants in the first place, right? Like you said, sex is a nightmare.

I think you'll enjoy Alex's interview – it's the best. (And I'm not just writing that because I know he's going to read this before I send it off.)

Alex started school at San Diego State University this week. At twenty-three, he is the grand old man of his freshman English class. It's a big adjustment for him, but I remind him that if ever he feels defensive on campus, he need only remind himself that he has been trained to kill with his bare hands and can dispatch any smug brattish eighteen-year-old or insolent professor as he deems necessary. (A caption to an illustration in the *Marine Battle Skills Training Handbook*: 'Execute a heel stomp to your opponent's skull, ending the encounter.') This always makes him smile.

How are your own two new books coming along? I look forward to your next missive replete with quotes from your Viennese hero.

Yours,

Steve

Useless Illusions

London, 1 October 1995

Dear Steven,

I'm currently in the process of finishing the introduction to a book of collected journalism, based on my 'It's A Queer World' columns in *Attitude*. Somewhat bathetically, I'm attempting to introduce/justify this money-for-old-rope project by explaining the sexual history of the Western world in twenty pages, and I don't even have the benefit of a French accent, a shaved head and a polo-neck jumper.

I do, however, share Foucault's genius for fucking up life.

We also had some very warm weather during July and August, and I found that my brain was completely cooked. Mind you, the onset of cooler weather a few days ago didn't exactly clear my brain and bring me back to the land of the sane – I caught a nasty dose of the flu and spent a week in bed having feverish dreams of all the nasty things I'd like to do to Jason – if I ever see him again.

Things between me and Jason are slightly in limbo at the moment: he hasn't returned my messages left on his mobile phone voicemail and has maintained radio silence for over two months. I've written him a couple of times, but have received no reply. Which is probably a bit of a hint, but one I'm studiously not taking. Alas, the only satisfactory explanation for his behaviour – that he's dead or has been posted to the Falklands – has been eliminated by British Telecom's confirmation that he has been receiving his voicemail messages.

Part of my attraction to Jason, and probably to military trade in general, is down to a baseless fantasy I have that they are somehow more likely to possess that priceless pheromone called 'integrity'. Of course, part of the appeal of the military to those that shelter behind its fortress walls is that it actually protects its boys from 'real life' and its dreary responsibilities; that's the trade-off you get for handing over your freedom. Jason knows I'm not the sort of dreary responsibility to turn up at the gate of his camp demanding to see him, so he can literally just switch me off. As a gay friend of mine would say: he's relying on me being big so that he can be small. (My gay friend is not someone who could ever be accused of that particular failing: he was dumped by a guy, now a major fashion magazine editor, who apparently used to shout 'Go!' before he came; in revenge Paul told everyone in town his humiliating secret and then went up to his ex at a party and shouted 'Go!' in his face loud enough so that everyone in the room heard him.)

In a suitably military metaphor, I'm hoisted by my own petard. Mr Bersani would be very pleased, but he'd probably be even more pleased to see me hoisted by my scrotum in a Castro leather bar.

I'm glad to hear that you have been putting the finishing touches to *The Masculine Marine* and I can hardly wait to see you rim Marine Machismo in your introduction. I am also looking forward to reading Alex's interview; I hope that his first term at SD State University is going well and that he hasn't stamped on anyone's head yet. (Though I think that if you could find time to send me a copy of *Marine Battle Skills Training Handbook,* I might be able to put it to some practical use myself.)

Best wishes,

Mark

PS No Freud, I'm afraid. Oh, all right, just one quote: 'Illusions make life more tolerable, and the first duty of all living creatures is to tolerate life. But illusion becomes valueless if it makes this harder for us.' You'd never guess I was feeling sorry for myself, would you?

Viva Hate

San Diego, October 31, 1995

Dear Mark,

The same morning I received your letter with its melancholic closing quote from Freud I read the following on the op-ed page of *The New York Times*, under the headline: 'The Millennium Approaches: What to Do?'

> The historian Hillel Schwartz's study, 'Century's End,' includes a January 1900 letter that Sigmund Freud wrote to Wilhelm Fliess, full of edgy anger: 'The new century, the most interesting thing about which for us may be that it contains the dates of our deaths, has brought me nothing but a stupid review in *Die Zeit*.'

May I be so lucky as to get even a stupid review of my Germany novel, working title *Blood Sausage Hymn*, in *Die Zeit* in 2000.

I'm sorry to hear about your troubles with Jason. As you can imagine, I've had my share of experiences with boys who used the transience of military life as an excuse to shirk responsibility to friends/lovers/*me*. There were many times when I found it helpful to lie on the floor, taking a certain joy in disconsolately moaning along to a few select songs (Morrissey's 'I Don't Mind if You Forget Me' comes to mind, with it's 'Rejection from a fool is cruel' refrain; and, in really dark times, Lou Reed's 'Berlin'. I'm sure you have your own favourites), cursing the bastard who'd done me wrong (anger is so much more constructive than hurt). There was John P, who said goodbye on the eve of supposedly being sent back to the States for setting fire to his commanding officer's desk (that he probably did do), who cowardly ran away from me when I saw him on the street with some other queen about a month later. And Brad M, the paratrooper, who never said goodbye at all. There was Jimmy G, who on our third date emerged from a toilet stall in the Blue Angel with some unforgivably ugly German. I remember sweetly telling the bunny-like Jimmy that I hoped he got syphilis. But I said it with a laugh. It became my policy to be ridiculously forgiving – out of vanity. Condescension, I believed, would etch kinder lines on my face than bitterness.

And I could tell you a few stories about life with Alex that would make your hair stand on end. But of course that's something different, since the two of us haven't had sex with each other, or even slept together, in over a year. Most of our friends find this odd. But as Gore Vidal says in the current *Advocate* of his forty-five years with Howard Austen, 'As the relationship is not sexual, we continue. I do my best to observe my own law: no sex with friends if you want to keep the friend. A sexual partner can become a friend. But a friend in the bed is either an enemy in the making or, simply, heartbreak. A poignant subject that I leave to all the other writers.' More and more, sex for me seems only possible with no words spoken. At least not until afterwards . . .

It looks as though my book will indeed be called *The Masculine Marine*. Having posited an alluring archetype with the main title, I'll need something subversive for the subtitle. It should be out in September, and I hope to have the galleys to you by March.

Both of my two last trips up to Oceanside searching the streets for that one final interviewee ended with me meeting a (to all appearances) stereotypical Marine who turned out to be a gay sailor. Since this happened on two occasions, with two different men, it's hard not to see it as some kind of lesson.

Yours,

Steve

Boys Who Marry Dad Instead of Me

London, 11 November 1995

Dear Steven,

You and I, Steven, are doomed, so long as we date military boys, to be only ever the 'other woman', whilst they get on with the serious business of being married to their military 'dad'. Then again, maybe we're just doomed.

Mind, I can't complain. Jason, being in the military and living 250 miles away, was perfect for me because he was never *real*. There was no chance of him turning up on my doorstep with his belongings and hang-ups at 2 a.m. asking me to organize the rest of his life for him. The Forces did the serious business of looking after him – I just played at it during leave and the occasional weekend. That's why I take my hat off to you, Steven: your sterling community service in 'civilianizing' these military boys, persuading them to leave and then counselling, supporting, loving and feeding them, requires far more dedication, patience and patriotism than I could ever hope to muster. Really, the Pentagon should give you a grant – after all you probably save the taxpayer millions in court/prison/rehabilitation/hospital fees.

In the end, Jason's problem is just the same as mine, and probably everyone else's: he didn't want what he wanted.

For the historical record Jase and I've had some communication of sorts since I last wrote to you, but it hasn't exactly been worthwhile. I've reassured him that I don't want an explanation for what happened and that I hope that we can remain friends, etc. He's agreed wholeheartedly with all this and promised to call me. Needless to say, he hasn't. Obviously he has more sense than I do.

Nevertheless, I think (hope?) it is possible if not admirable to remain more than friends but less than lovers. You and Alex seem to have succeeded, though perhaps I will yet read of one or both of your bloody ends, *à la* Orton, in the *National Enquirer*.

But Jason is right in detecting too much desperation on my part. I'm like an investor worried about losing all his capital in a high-risk venture he should never have considered in the first place (but the weekly dividends looked so *good*).

Much better to be the chased than the chaser. Being looked after by someone is always preferable to looking after someone because you can always find someone *else* to look after you. Attention is easy to find; it's the *giving* of it that is easy to lose. Boys are like cats – who knows how many saucers of cream and stroking hands are waiting for them around the neighbourhood? Human happiness is an immeasurably fragile thing – but how much more immeasurable is that fragility when your happiness depends on the happiness of another? Which, I suppose, is the point. True happiness, if it exists, is only possible when the stakes are at their highest. Gore Vidal obviously decided a long time ago not to play the emotional top table/and stick instead with one-dollar whistdrives – separating sex and emotion is tidy, sensible and well-mannered, but also perhaps cowardly, mean and timid; an indication that *amour propre* cannot tolerate or afford the possibility of injury by *amour impropre*.

Much as I'd like to believe otherwise, I suspect he's right. Sex, because it makes fools of us all, is something best shared with people you'll probably never see again.

The Masculine Marine, eh? How about *Boys Who Marry Dad Instead of Me* as a subtitle?

I loved your Oceanside story about the 'stereotypical' Marines who turned out to be sailors. I think the lesson is fairly obvious. It's always the wannabes that pay most attention to appearances. And proof – as if it were needed – that people like us eroticize an ideal that doesn't exist.

All the best,

Mark

Embracing the Wholesome

San Diego, December 4, 1995

Dear Mark,

I'm not sure I'm looking for the same kind of 'integrity' you seek. Certainly I relish a middle-American wholesomeness, but I probably take just as much pleasure in spoiling it (by helping to liberate my boys of their unselfconscious simplicity) as in celebrating it. My eroticization of military men was political in origin, just like my recent transformation from meat-eater to vegetarian. (I spurned any and all vegetables already at age two. At age ten, after the notorious 'creamed corn' incident, my parents abandoned their attempts to force me to be healthy, throwing up their hands in despair, much as I just had the creamed corn). Of course, my politics is all about liberal guilt, which in a predictably perverse way comes from my conservative, religious parents, which –

But is there a sexual theory that properly acknowledges the potential for personal weirdness?

You are right on the money when you say that boys are like cats. I just read William S. Burroughs' *The Cat Inside*, in which he recognizes the boys of his past in neighbourhood strays.

Alex and Samantha, Casa de las Pulgas, San Diego

The Masculine Marine should be out in September. Alex will be on the cover. It would be great if you are able to jot down a few lines for the back.

Please accept my apologies for taking so long to write these letters. I do take great pleasure in reading yours.

Yours,

Steve

Kill the Thing You Love

London, 8 January 1996

Dear Mr Zeeland,

Thank you for your letter, which I was very pleased to find on my return from the Canaries, where I spent Xmas with my ex-ex.

Yes, inevitably, tragically, I'm back with Jason. After all the self-pitying I've subjected you to/we've gone and made up. If my life is beginning to resemble a badly dubbed foreign daytime soap, I hope you don't feel inclined to change channels. If it's any consolation, I should state that I don't treat all my friends like this – just you. This is because you understand me so much better than the others, because our relationship is so much closer, more intimate and more *honest*.

And because you live thousands of miles away and I don't have to look you in the face.

I'm sorry that I suggested that you were looking for a kind of 'integrity' in your military boys. That was an uncalled-for slur. I'm sorry that I suggested that I was looking for it myself. I realize now that in fact I was hoping that my quarry would (mis)recognize integrity in *me*. As for your confession of wanting to spoil the middle-American wholesomeness you find in your boys, it reminds me – cornily, perhaps – of Oscar Wilde's lines from 'The Ballad of Reading Gaol':

> *Yet each man kills the thing he loves . . .*
> *The coward does it with a kiss.*
> *The brave man does it with a sword!*

And the queer studies writer with a tape recorder.

Whatever your reasons for spoiling middle-American wholesomeness, Steve, please leave some for me. (I'd be *proud* to write a few lines extolling your corrupting influence for the back of your book.)

Best,

Mark

PS   I recently started an article about the difference between straight men and gay men with the epigram: 'the problem with straight men is they're repressed; the problem with gay men is they're not.' It must be more than just a clever formulation of mine, because after I'd written it I found I couldn't write anything else.

Desert Porn Shoot

San Diego, February 6, 1996

Dear Mark,

Thought of you today. I opened my phone bill! Another, oh, eight or nine such calls and I could just as well buy a round-trip ticket to London. But it was well worth it to talk with you . . . a second time.

I feel as though I know you better than would seem likely after only two conversations. Of course that's because of your letters, which are so much more satisfying than anyone's e-mail, which is all that anyone in this country seems to want to write any more. Besides you the only other literate and reliable correspondents in my life these days are Germans – two men and one woman from my Frankfurt days who obstinately persist in seeing friendship as some sort of sacred bond.

And, recently, Scott O'Hara, the legendary porn star and editor and publisher of *STEAM*. Have you heard about the rather awful play based on some of his experiences, 'Making Porn'? I saw it when I was up in San Francisco in September. The charming, gentlemanly O'Hara played the nasty, poisonous porn producer (some of his spittle actually hit me, sitting as I was in the front row. Thankfully I missed the torrent of milk thrown in the simulated come shot). I only knew him from a few of his videos (perhaps you've got a copy of *Sergeant Swann's Private Files* somewhere yourself?). Sadly, *STEAM* is going under. It was to have featured my début as a magazine contributor. But much more painful is the thought that, with the demise of *STEAM*, the world can't help but become a more sanitary place ... On our last trip up to Pendleton Alex and I discovered that my beloved piss trough at the Del Mar E-club is being replaced by individual porcelain urinals with vanity partitions. For Marines! I told Alex, 'I'm starting to really hate the 90s.'

'The problem with straight men is that they're repressed; the problem with gay men is that they're not' is not only a great start for a magazine piece, I think it's a brilliant opening salvo for your next book.

Within a few weeks Haworth should be supplying you with a copy of my embarrassingly raw, unedited manuscript for *Marine*. It's odd; whenever I sit down and look over the manuscript, I feel very good about it. Certainly some of the interviews are the best I've done. But then, as weeks go by and I brood on it some more ... I don't know. I think it's the problem we talked about before: how can you both celebrate and dissect a mystique?

I repeated your Wilde quote to my editor. I pointed out that I began my research with adoration of my military man icon, decided he had to be sacrificed in the interest of my study, and now seek to revive him in the ether of my fantasies. He pointed out the obvious, in his best yawning Gore Vidal impersonation: 'You're terribly Christian.'

But much as I wrote you before that in this book I do not penetrate but only rim Marine masculinity, I don't think I've exactly killed the thing I love. It's just slightly trickling blood.

Both of the military guys I met on photo shoots this past weekend ended up bleeding, but not from my research. I have a new intermittent part-time job – assisting beefcake photographer David Lloyd.

Andy, the first model, was a handsome and stupid Coast Guardsman who blathered incessantly on the two-hour ride to the desert (it takes that long because Lloyd, who is elderly, drives 45 miles an hour on the freeway, changes lanes without noticing and almost never remembers to turn off his turn signal). Andy told us that he hates Arabs and wants to go to wherever it is they have that big black stone and blow it up; that he wants to do a stand-up comedy act based on the humour he sees in picturing his ex-wife defecating (we were treated to samples); how much fun it is to use a night stick on small-time drug users, etc.

At last Lloyd delivered us to a ravine very close to, and in clear view of, the highway and its near-constant parade of confused retirees in RVs who, because of the fork in the road there, moved as slowly as Lloyd himself. Andy whined. We climbed farther back into the scrub.

Lloyd handed him a faded male–female skin magazine and with me retired behind some cacti, partially out of view. When Andy called out 'Ready!' Lloyd rheumatically scurried forward, and I leapt upon a rock brandishing a shiny hoop of metallic fabric, directing a shimmering golden orb onto the brawny Coast Guardsman's flawless body. But at twenty-eight, Andy is older than most of Lloyd's models, and his (immense) erection fell like a second-hand with each heartbeat. He had to be left alone with the magazine another half-dozen times.

After almost an hour, Lloyd finally collected a roll's worth of hard-ons. He opened the camera and discovered that there was no film in it. We had to do them all over.

Oddly enough, the hard-ons came easier the second time. Andy began to relax and tell his awful jokes again. He declared that he felt 'really comfortable' with me, that Lloyd had told him I was a decent guy and he could see that, and maybe we would work to-gether again because he felt –

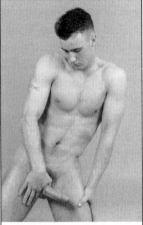

Nude Marine photographed by Zeeland's late friend and mentor

'really comfortable' with me. He repeated this twice more.

On the ride back he dropped the name of a straight club he would be visiting later that evening. I considered seeking him out, if only to see how much he would tease me. But though I would have liked to have sucked his dick, I really didn't want to listen to him any more. Plus which I had to get up early again the next morning.

As we were packing up to leave the ravine, Andy got some horrible cactus thing embedded in his foot and made a big deal of stoically yanking it out, for my benefit.

Early the next morning Lloyd and I returned to the desert with a slender blond Marine of Swedish ancestry. Kris fitted certain of the stereotypes (both Marine and Swedish?): he had little to say, never joked, and showed an utter lack of inhibition. Lloyd handed him the magazine, and the three of us stood right there as Kris casually masturbated. Later, he clambered grinning onto a high rock and swung about his hard-on (eight and three-quarter inches long; Lloyd produced a ruler and measured it) in plain view of passing cars. (Being naughty and rebellious seems to be part of the point; when on the ride home I asked him, in so many words, if he thought being a Marine made him more likely to want to model, he said, 'No, you can get into a lot of trouble doing this.')

Mid-way through the shoot Kris excused himself. After he returned, we noticed a horrible laceration on his ass. He muttered, sheepishly: 'Guess I got that when I went to the bathroom.' The Marine happily complied when Lloyd asked him to lay on his back and throw his legs in the air. Picture David Lloyd: wispy grey hair blowing, arms scrunched close to his body to still his trembling hands, stooping, inching crab-like ever closer to the anus, only to look up from the camera with a sour expression and intone, 'Oh, that's not a good shot.' With the Marine barely out of earshot he speculated that the problem was the result of the trip to 'the bathroom'.

Pleased with the $500 he was paid for the session, Kris was slightly more loquacious on the way back. I asked him for his opinion on 'controversial issues, like – women in the military'. He said that he didn't have any objection to them serving, but didn't feel they should be in combat: out in the field you have to go for many days without showering, and women would smell too bad. I asked him if he had been in the military during the gays-in-the-military debate.

'Yeah.'

Silence.

What did the Marines he served with have to say about that?

'Uh, they don't think they should be there.'

Silence.

Was that his opinion, too?

'Yeah.'

Long, tense pause. David Lloyd shot me an admonitory look in the rear-view mirror, so I quit without advancing to the obvious next question: why? It would have been too perfect had he answered, 'I don't want some gay guy looking at me naked.'

But I'm guessing you'll concur that, having just been paid to appear nude in what he knows, but does not want to admit that he knows, to be a gay magazine (Lloyd says he shows them – but never hands them – copies of the magazines he sells to) the guy would be unlikely to share his true opinions, even if he could articulate them...

Does this sound like a fun part-time job to you? My gay friends are predictably envious. But apart from the first few minutes of striptease I find the shoots to be rather mundane work. Part of my duty is to listen to Lloyd repeat the same anecdotes and jokes. I have to put up with his driving, sometimes lax personal hygiene, and frequent temper tantrums. But I was envious when he reported that, at the end of a second shoot, alone in his loft with the model, this same Marine asked for, and was granted, permission to come.

Lloyd finds his models by putting ads for 'physique models – no porn' in the free papers distributed on the bases...

However, he also knows, and wants me to meet, a legendary old pimp who is still active in procuring Marines for millionaires. I suppose there's some sort of book in the whole sordid scene of men whose obsessive desires become a long-term pursuit, or even a vocation. But would this be the best project for my mental health?

February 11

On Friday I went out to the desert on another shoot: another Marine, another exhibitionist. This one, though married, is the pimp's favourite, and is said to have earned $16,000 so far this winter. The boy is a buff, baby-faced strawberry blond with light red pubic hair and dark brown puppydog eyes. He kept giving me lingering stares. Toward the end of the shoot, as Lloyd was changing film, the Marine said: 'Sure you don't want to do this last roll for me?' I laughed: 'Noooo...' 'Why not? We're about the same.' Dumbfounded, I just grinned and looked away. Alex and Anthony tell me this was the moment to slip him my number.

But he had nowhere to put it. And I don't have $16,000.

Yours,

Steve

PS   Thought of your 'cats are like boys' idea again this past week as I ran myself ragged trying to find a home for an abandoned pregnant Siamese I'd been putting out food for. Who else but you could have enlightened me to the parallel between my eroticizing sailors and Marines and compulsively rescuing cats?! I'm serious. Could it be that I've reversed the Wilde aphorism? *Men Who Love the Things That Must be Killed.*

I'm finally reading *Palimpsest.* Vidal: 'Avoid admirable writers. Avoid writers.'

Alex started therapy this week. I did find a home for the cat. And tomorrow I'm assisting on a photo session with black body-builder twins from the Louisiana bayou.

Oprah Whitman

London, 6 March 1996

Dear Steven,

Your book is a rapturous delight. It's smart. It's funny. It's horny. And it will cause a scandal. In a word – it's perfect.

However, I do have one complaint. Your introductory preambles to each interview were so enjoyable that I was disappointed when they ended so quickly. You may disagree, but I think that you are much more interesting than your interview subjects and your words much more readable. You simply have to write a novel NOW or I will fly over to SD and box your ears or, worse, I'll hang around the dirty bookstores and steal some of your trade.

I faxed this review to your publishers. I hope it's useful:

> Not a book about 'gays in the military', but a book about being young, male, American and in love with masculinity in the 90s. Not a collection of interviews with jarheads, but pure poetry about desire, identity, longing and belonging, from men who are not supposed to dream.
>
> *The Masculine Marine* is a song of innocence and experience that speaks what should not be spoken in a world that doesn't want to listen. Steve Zeeland is a Walt Whitman for our times.

A touch melodramatic, I know. But deservingly so. I toyed with the idea of calling you an 'Oprah Whitman' for our times, but I'm not sure whether most readers would get it. More generally, yes, I still think it's a book that shouldn't have been written – or rather, a book that shouldn't *have to be* written. But it isn't you or I that have made sexual identity *the* preoccupation of the Western world in the final years of the twentieth century.

An East Coaster called Glenn Belverio, a.k.a. Glennda Orgasm, a cable-access neo-con drag queen friend of Bruce LaBruce, is staying with me at the moment. It's too early to tell how the visit will pan out; however Glenn is very smart and very cruel and very funny, so the auguries are good. Things did get off to a bad start, however, when Michelle, a convincing blonde transsexual friend of mine obsessed with *Star Wars* and Abba ('my gender is Swedish Wookie' she once declared to me after I made the mistake of letting her see a Kate Bornstein book) stood in the arrivals hall holding a card scrawled in magic-marker block capitals MISS ORGASM.

We waited and waited. No sign of Glenn (although, I've never met him before and have only seen him 'dressed' on video, so I wasn't exactly sure what I was looking for). Eventually a very tall, crop-haired, attractive, sensitive-looking Latin walked past us. Michelle did her unnerving trick of switching out of her femmey-tranny twitter and into her paint-peeling, fog-horn, East German shot-putting fish-wife voice she usually employs to attract the bewildered attention of some poor young man on the street whose only crime was possessing a penis and large hands: '*Look!*' she boomed, pointing at the sensitive Latin, '*There's one*, FOR SURE – *but not* OURS!'

About fifteen minutes later I was tannoyed to meet a 'Mr Glenn Belverio' at the Meeting Point. Sure enough, it was the man Michelle had yelled at. Apparently he's big pals with Ms Paglia, whom he's made some agit-prop vox-pop videos with, including the classic 'Glennda and Camille Do Downtown', in which 'Glennda' and Camille (verbally) punch their way into a picket of feminists protesting outside a dirty bookstore about how pornography degrades women. So I have to be nice to Glenn or else Ms P'll put a hex on me and I'll turn to stone (butch).

I really wish that I had some stories to tell you about Marines in the desert, or even just on Hampstead Heath, but alas no. My heart goes out to you when you tell me that your part-time job is mostly dull. That I should be bored in this way! However, I understand your dilemma over Andy completely. What is the point of a young man with a great meaty body, a great meaty dick, and a great meaty job, who insists on using *language* the whole time? Doesn't he realize his whole purpose is to represent something *less* than human – and thus something *more* than human – something ... *meaty*? You should have spanked his beefy ass.

By rabbiting on incessantly he was definitely trying to sub-
vert your whole project – trying to become a personality (e.g.
his ambitions to be a 'stand-up comic') instead of an erection.
I suppose, also, if I'm to get really absurd in my analysis of
your transaction, or lack of it, with the BiCoastal Guard, it
seems to me that his spouting of violent right-wing opinions
came from fear – an expression of his nervousness and his
desire not to be a victim but a victimizer, active not passive,
despite the fact that he was about to be probed by David's
lens and, as it turned out, a good deal of the desert vegetation
as well.

My Royal Marine, on the other hand, who is very much a
(difficult) personality despite my best efforts to reduce him to
something more manageable and less personal, is apparently
back from Norway, where he has spent the last two months
on exercise with NATO in –40°C temperatures defending the
freedom of the frozen fjords – in a tent. Perhaps this might
mean that he is keen to see me (he's left several messages on
my ansafone asking, 'Where are yoo? Are yoo seeing someone else?'). There are worse things to be loved for than your
body temperature.

We've just had a report published here which was conducted by the Ministry of Defence on the subject of homosexuality in the armed forces with the aim of justifying the
ban. Quotes from it have been excerpted in the press here –
stuff like, 'If there was a queer in my unit he'd be shot', or,
'If there was one in my platoon dying of hypothermia, I
wouldn't get in a sleeping bag with him'. Or (my favourite):
'In the Army, we don't like taking showers with men who
like to take showers with men'.

Which does somewhat beg the question: So why join the
Army in the first place?

But then, disavowal is a perfectly natural part of most
people's lives. Maybe it's only the brain-smart, life-dumb intellectual fags like us that insist on pointing up the difference
between surface and content here as if it were big news.

Best,

Mark

PS   I especially enjoyed Alex's testimony in *Marine* – although 'enjoyed' doesn't seem to be the appropriate word, given the harrowing details of his origins and the dramatically dysfunctional family romance . . .

Passionately Kiss'd

San Diego, March 22, 1996

Dear Mark,

> *What think you I take my pen in hand to record?*
> *The battle-ship, perfect-model'd, majestic, that I saw*
> *   pass the offing to-day under full sail?*
> *The splendors of the past day? or the splendor of the*
> *   night that envelops me?*
> *Of the vaunted glory and growth of the great city*
> *   spread around me? – no;*
> *But merely of two simple men I saw to-day on the*
> *   pier in the midst of the crowd, parting the parting*
> *   of dear friends,*
> *The one to remain hung on the other's neck and*
> *   passionately kiss'd him,*
> *While the one to depart tightly prest the one to*
> *   remain in his arms.*

These are the words I read to my managing editor, who had the temerity to ask me whether I thought you were sincere in your pre-publication review. It had been a long time, he admitted, since he'd read Whitman, and he thanked me (sincerely, I think) for being the first person to ever read poetry to him at the office.

I was very pleased and not a little moved by your review and the comments in your letter. I'm especially grateful for the compliment on my sense of humour. Of the three readings I did for *Sailors*, I drew the largest crowd, and sold the most books, in San Diego. But the experience was unsatisfying: no one laughed at my jokes. They all just sat there and stared at me, and then shuffled up with their books. I had a much better time in San Francisco, where my old friend Bart was sitting in the front row, crazily cackling away, and so clueing everyone in that it was OK to laugh. Then there was LA, where no one laughed or bought books.

Anyway, before I risk becoming maudlin: thank you.

Last week I was reminiscing about our summer's night

romp through Pendleton in your rented convertible. Alex and I played tour guide to a visiting East Coast painter, author, and junior professor, and his long-time companion. I resolved not to embarrass myself by too nakedly exposing my hunger for some intelligent conversation. This proved unnecessary: we had nothing to talk about. I was curious about the story behind the painter's article about the 'piss paintings' of Warhol and Demuth and Pollock via Havelock Ellis and Freud. I'd written to him because I loved that piece and the sections in his book on Demuth's and Paul Cadmus's paintings of sailors. I was disappointed to be told that his interest in these subjects is coldly academic, and that he doesn't even like Paul Cadmus's sailors. I guess I shouldn't be surprised that an Ivy League professor would be ... a little snooty? He kept emphasizing the necessity of distinguishing between high art and the vulgar.

Oh well, at least the visit provided evidence of Alex's increased tolerance. It used to be that whenever we drove onto the Marine Corps Recruit Depot and I so much as looked at a Marine for more than a half-second, he would clench his teeth and snarl: 'DON'T. STARE.' He was remarkably composed as we stood with our visitors by the parade deck and the painter kept gasping 'Oh my God! Maaaaaaarvellous!' and his companion, apropos of the DI's shouts, shriekingly demanded, 'Is he calling them PUSSIES?!?'

I hope Glennda Orgasm's visit went OK.

With this letter I'm sending you a copy of *Barrack Buddies and Soldier Lovers* (the increasingly rare first printing with the hideous chocolate cover; it was supposed to be green). Skip the introduction: it's an outdated and uneven blend of what I wanted to say and was told I should say. But I do still like most of the conversations; my favourites are (of course) the rougher boys (John and Scott and Kyle); Doc, a middle-class wannabe punk; and Jeff. If you read Jeff's interview, you might be interested to know the omitted conclusion of the 'story about the dog'. Jeff and his little sister were in their playhouse encouraging their dog to mount them when their mother happened by and saw what was going on. She returned with a rifle and, right before their eyes, shot Snoopy. His body was thrown behind a shed on their New England farm. Jeff told me that he and his sister used to go and look at it every day, and for the longest time it never decayed.

And then there's my interview with 'Randall'. The worst-yet book on 'gays in the military' has to be Lois Shawver's *And The Flag Was Still There*. This well-meaning liberal straight woman argues that there is no danger in queers and straights serving together because there is no homoerotic charge to military life: what people do in shower rooms and toilets is disgusting and embarrassing, and no one gets turned on by it. She quotes Randall as an example of the good queer who unfairly gets forced out of the service because he is too trusting. And he never had sex before he enlisted, so he didn't lie when he signed the papers. In my book, Randall tells how his first-ever sexual experience did indeed occur before he enlisted – in the office of the football coach he worked for at a Big-10 university. And he explains that he told the Army he was gay so they would kick him out – because he was sick of the anti-gay Army and didn't want to get sent to the Gulf War.

The passage that readers most often incorporate into their erotic fantasies seems to be Rolando's account of how as a medic he was responsible for treating 'hot' soldiers for sexually transmitted diseases.

Also enclosed is an advertising flyer for *Good Morning, Marines*, a video filmed in Camp Pendleton locker-rooms with hidden cameras.

*

I haven't read that book you asked about in your telephone message, *Boys of Boise*. It's long out of print. I am curious about it, too. I'll look for it in used bookstores.

I'm sorry that I don't have any good new photo-shoot stories – yet. The last session I did was with the body-builder twins from Louisiana. (They claim to be civilians, but I find it suspicious that they bank with a Navy credit union.) It was the least noteworthy experience so far. This was my first indoor shoot. The light cage in David Lloyd's loft lent the proceedings a clinical air. The equation two nude black brothers v. two clothed white men seemed to generate even more distance than usual. Reading the model releases, the twins initially balked at signing away their rights. Classic: 'But if we sign this, it means we won't ever be able to be in politics.' Trying to be helpful, I pointed out that Schwarzenegger did nude modelling as a young man, and is still spoken of as a potential candidate. The guy looked at me and pronounced, with gravity: 'Well, I would never want to be in Congress anyway.'

The next hurdle came when the twins scanned Lloyd's notepad, upon which was listed the shots he needed, usually followed, in a spidery hand, by the notation HARD.

Frowning: 'Do all these "hard"s mean what I think they mean?'

Lloyd: 'Well, yes, of course. I told you we have to have hard cocks. That's the name of the game in this business!'

'Oh. We forgot about that.'

'What? Well, you sure didn't have any trouble in the test session!'

'We *forgot* about that.'

Lloyd didn't seem to understand this business about the wilful forgetting. Another uncomfortable moment: Lloyd hoped to re-enact a shot he had clipped from some magazine: one nude man seated on another, kneeling man's shoulders. The twins were sceptical. 'We each weigh two hundred pounds.' They suggested that once they had got into position, I should step into the light cage and hold them in place. The loft was not warm that morning, and I felt odd about having to rub my hands together. I don't even remember where exactly I applied them. But as soon as I stepped aside, the twins, laughing, toppled.

To my horror, Lloyd took me aside and said, 'They're just trying to get back at whitey.'

Next week it's back to the desert.

Just now I got a phone call. A rival photographer wants Lloyd to let him photograph one of his models, supposedly just for one session. Lloyd is adamant: 'I'm not about to let anybody steal my models! I go to enough trouble to find the little fuckers!' Maybe there's a short story here: 'David and the Little Fuckers.' But meanwhile, yes, I am struggling along with my novel. I appreciate the threat to box my ears.

Yours,

Steve

Rubber Pussies

London, 30 March 1996

Dear Steven,

Every time I see that handwriting and an American post-age stamp, my heart skips a beat or two. Arrhythmia never felt so good. I think I'm falling for you. Perhaps the best thing about an affair between correspondents is that it is un-likely to ever turn into an affair between co-respondents.

I found Alex's interview very moving. His openness about his ambivalence towards the USMC and his own sexuality are quite touching and quite a lot more endearing than, say, 'Keith', who, for some reason I can't quite put my finger on, I took a dislike to. In fact, I almost wish that you hadn't begun the book with Keith's interview, since his story is in many ways (i.e. to me) the least interesting and at the same time the most stereotypical. But all the same, I can see why you began with him and why, in fact, you probably had to.

Perhaps my irritation – predictably trying to finger one that I have just claimed to be unfingerable – is something to do with the way in which Keith seems to be locked into a state of 'being for others'. He appears to want to be misrecognized by other men as the kind of man that he himself wishes he were. We both know that Marine-ness and masculinity itself has a great deal to do with wanting to be taken for what you are not, and hoping in that mis-take that you will mis-take yourself for what you would like to be. And somewhere along the line, if the line is long enough, you *become* what you imitate.

All the same, I can't help asserting that the 'performance' of masculinity is all very well and good – just so long as it doesn't become an *operetta*. This, in addition to an aversion to conversation about antiques and how women 'smell like fish', is why I don't have any time for leather clubs. Perversely, leather queen Keith talks about 'fags' and 'queens' contemp-tuously (not something I'm inclined to condemn in itself, I hasten to add) but appears to have embraced their identity and politics more zealously than most of *them*. I suppose that

Keith's 'crime' in my eyes is in bringing Marine-ness *too* close to the gay world – symbolized by that (to my mind) fascinating but ultimately tasteless USMC tattoo incorporating a pink triangle.

That Alex had the advantage of trusting you a great deal more than the other interviewees must have helped; but on the other hand, the fact that he knew you and lived with you could have worked the other way, making him less frank and more inhibited. It's a testament to you and your relationship with him that it didn't. The passage where he talks about blowing his step-dad – because he 'wanted to make him like me' – has extraordinary pathos. This is the homo trap – sex is the way we try and get close to men, but it's what finally pushes them and 'it' (the phallus) away.

Gay men are hidebound by their social function and designation – men who fuck with other men – to embody *all* sex and desire between men; which is an intolerable burden to bear, even if you work hard every day at the gym to broaden your shoulders. Plenty of gay men go along with this, saying that any man who has sex with another man is 'really gay'; but plenty of gays make the same error but apparently hold the opposite opinion: whatever two men might do in bed, only a *gay* man can fall in love with another man. This latter idea is, in addition to being insulting and diminishing to straight men, terrible news for gay men. I mean, how many of them *really* want to spend *the rest of their lives* in the company of other gays, tormented all the while by the knowledge that *gay love is the only kind of love they're ever going to get?*

Or is that just my own personal torment?

*

I thought your description of the 'Bobby' vids was shit-your-pants hilarious. Especially the paradox of 'Bobby' the predatory effeminate cross-dressing Hispanic queen who idolizes 'straight' Marine 'studs', angrily slapping away inquisitive/reciprocative wandering jarhead hands, busily 'impaling' them on latex vaginas, and generally ordering them about. If straights won't be as straight and studly as you would like, well, just shout at those pussies until they are! (I'm sure that it must have occurred to you that Bobby and the Marine Corps Recruit Depot drill instructor have a lot in common.)

I've finally got around to reading Mr Vidal's memoirs *Palimpsest*. Like all auto-fellatio it was enormously entertaining, frequently eyepopping, and not a little disturbing.

I have to say that I found the Jimmie Trimble (one-and-only) love-of-his-life narrative more than faintly comical. Naturally, I more than most can perfectly understand the attraction, not just on the basis of the plates depicting a blond all-American dream and star baseball player (who became a Marine), but also because of the nature of the boy. The passage where he quotes the last letter Jimmie wrote his Ma from the front line in the Pacific just before he died in battle and told her to take out more life insurance on him but 'not to worry', and by the way, she was 'the best Mom in the whole world', was so touching that it brought a tear to my cynical eye. It seems to me quite clear that Gore recognizes that Jimmie was just a better person than he – as well as better looking – so no wonder he repeatedly talks of him as his 'twin'. Jimmie is Gore's soul, one that, funnily enough, he appears to be disinterring when he is in what he calls 'the departure lounge of life'.

Reading that Gore has a portrait of Jimmie by his bed, I'm reminded of that wreck in a Tennessee William's play (or is it just a Tennessee play in my head? Everyone has one, you know) who carries around a picture of himself when he was young and attractive which he shows to people and says: 'This was me, once.' Gore advances his 'twin' theory with great enthusiasm, but dismisses any suggestion of 'narcissism' with the usual dig at Freud. And yet narcissism is plainly the name of the game. In *Palimpsest* Gore offers us the redrawn image of Jimmie Trimble as a better version of himself, and not so much as 'someone I used to love' as 'someone who used to love me'.

Perhaps Gore really is being more realistic than solipsistic, and he is merely – once again – the remorseless bearer of unwelcome news. (Though, if he does one more cameo role in a Hollywood movie expounding one of his duller conspiracy theories yet again, I think I might push his statue over and rename the place in my mind it stood in 'Truman Capote Square'.)

Palimpsest appears to have been, as many memoirs are and

indeed as Vidal himself more than hints at, a settling of scores and an extended opportunity to 'put the record straight'. However, just as his carping at Freud eventually convinces you that his problem with the Viennese dentist is exactly his insight, his splenetic dismissal of former friends like Anaïs Nin, who, quite reasonably, speculated that his monstrous mother had left him unable to love, makes you think to yourself, 'Well, now you come to mention it . . .'

*

Many thanks for the copy of your first book, *Barrack Buddies*, which I'm reading at the moment, and enjoying greatly. I'm particularly interested in Kyle. Probably for the same reasons you were. I've always had a thing for that Southern drawl. And lads who are like baked Alaska dessert: tough on the outside but soft and gooey on the inside.

Glenn or Glennda's stay was fine. He brought about five wigs, which were arrayed like dead cats in my flatmate's bedroom (he's away), surrounded by all the attendant powders, paints and lipsticks that I'm told girlies use. Watching the transformation was quite startling. Glenn is at least six one tall, even without heels and wig. I also found the smell of hair-spray etc. quite unsettling in my rigidly not to say paranoidly masculine flat environment. I was living with a *woman*! – OK only a simulacrum of one, but we're all simulacra these days. Glenn was actually very smart and very to the point. A breath of fresh air. He admitted to my face that he hadn't bothered finishing *Male Impersonators*.

I enclose a copy of *It's A Queer World* (which Glenn *did* like; I think. He described it as 'like drinking several dry martinis at high altitude'). I suspect a US book deal won't materialize. It's been to several American publishers, including St Martin's and Random House, who declared that it was 'too British' for the American market.

Which I suppose I should try to take as some kind of compliment.

Best,

Mark

Watch Queen

San Diego, April 29, 1996

Dear Mark,

The contention of St Martin's and Random House that *It's a Queer World* is 'too British' for US readers is bullshit. The idiocy of this notion should be obvious to anyone who's seen AbFab on the cover of *The Advocate*, ever watched an evening of PBS, or listened to rock radio sometime in the last thirty years.

Your subtle change in style also can't help make you more marketable to Americans. Though I kind of miss the 'heavier' tone of *Male Impersonators*, *Queer World* is deliciously more insidious. You pack a lot of prickly insight into deceptively sweet reading. I can only wonder at the scope of your vision, your energy in nailing such varied targets. Lest this sound too lofty, let me confess that I especially relish your intermittent bursts of cheap sarcasm – and sustained, gloriously wicked wit.

So far, the part I've most delighted in reading to friends is your take on *Ren and Stimpy*. (You might remember that in *Sailors* I described how Troy and I felt ourselves becoming Ren and Stimpy: more so, it seems, than I realized.) And thanks to your lovingly crafted piece on Morrissey (has he read it?) I'm feeling at least a little more charitable towards 'Southpaw Grammar.'

Congratulations, Mr Simpson.

*

That you were irritated with 'Keith' for some reason you couldn't quite put your finger on is superfluous further testimony to your keenness of perception. You didn't merely read between the lines, you seem to have intuited strategically omitted lines. Because, first of all, far more than his interview suggests, Keith can be an exceptionally irritating person.

Probably it's just that I've been staring at my computer screen too much, but these days whenever I think of Keith's tattoo, I picture it as two cascading Windows icons. You're right that his is the most plastic story in the book.

Keith's appearance might shock you. He's not at all conventionally attractive. But Keith did nonetheless have a steady stream of drop-dead gorgeous boyfriends. He really did seem to exude a peculiarly seductive energy and conviction that men at least bought as Marine-ness. (It took me a long time and, finally, great quantities of beer to confess to Alex that I had sex with Keith, once, two weeks after I interviewed him, capitulating in exasperation to the sort of pleas, repeated in daily phone calls, he uses at the end of Part One ('I just want somebody to hold me. Just a touch means a lot to me'). Manipulative, clinging, jealous, 'macho' yet somehow painfully vulnerable, Keith excelled at 'stray cat' boy tactics. Well, he was at least on par with 'Anthony', the sailor whose interview begins my previous book, and who was Keith's lover for a few months. (Alex, obviously, beats them both.)

To read part two of Keith's interview is to double-click on the rainbow triangle (itself a contraction of two logos) and see how much of the ink has seeped into his mind.

Keith's friends, me among them, were puzzled as to why being seen and admired as a butch Marine was not enough for him, why he had to keep trying on new costumes.

For a time, Keith lived with (actually, sponged off) a sort of mirror case, a brawny, giant, ex-Army Special Forces man, Mike Oboe. This was the biggest, butchest gay man you ever saw scowling down the other gym queens at West Coast and Rich's. The only immediately apparent queeny thing about Oboe was the lengths he went to not be queeny (e.g. the austere empty walls on his condo). Yet he too was comically anxious about his masculinity. He talked constantly about his work-out routine and the impossible crushing need to get bigger. He only wore shirts with horizontal stripes. Whenever he picked up guys he scared them off by going on and on about how he had been trained to kill.

The obvious explanation for guys like Keith and Mike is that they never got over being called sissies and fags. Our heterosexual system of male–female opposites tells these guys that sexual attraction to men is necessarily feminine, meaning that as long as they feel that attraction, they can never be masculine enough. The butcher they got, the more painfully elusive 'real' masculinity seemed.

Irritatingly, Keith never caught on that the Marine Corps is itself a little 'queer'. All Bersani's 'moving around inside his ever-hardening and ever-melting masculinity' did for him was turn him into a dourly devout leather queen. In fact, none of the Marines I interviewed, with the possible partial-exception of Jack, seems to have developed much of an ironic queer sensibility (Alex I disqualify for absorbing too much second-hand Judith Butler).

Another puzzle: Why was Keith, the effeminate boy ridiculed for his love of tap dancing, so much more convincing as a cursing, tobacco-spitting cartoon jarhead than he was in his later incarnation as cartoon gay leather Marine?

A month or two subsequent to Part Two of his interview saw Keith valiantly waving the leather flag in the San Diego Gay Pride parade – eliciting laughter from everyone I knew who knew him. (Not altogether unsympathetic laughter, I should add: Alex likened Keith to the little girl in the bumblebee costume in that Blind Melon video.) In part this had to do with his comical physical appearance. But what really did Keith in was his terrible sincerity. Talk about camp. If only he could have recognized and revelled in the contradictions his performance so glaringly exposed, maybe Keith could have really become the star he aspired to be. (My defining memory of Keith remains the *reverential awe* with which I saw him study a drag queen in Flicks.)

Judith Butler wrote me a half-page rave pre-pub review of *Marine*, and I wonder if she didn't like Keith best.

About a month after my interviews with 'Ted' and Keith, the gays-in-the-military debate crested. With exquisitely bad timing, straight boy Ted decided that he would lie and tell the Marine Corps he was gay so that they would kick him out. (Did Keith's revelation inspire him? Was he studying Keith, me, and others for research? I never got to ask.) Ironically, Keith, more stereotypically masculine than the soft-spoken Ted, became the subject of rumours and accusations, and was harassed by the other Marines and even by his own commander, while Ted's staged declaration met with sympathy and support. Ted was eventually discharged for medical reasons. Keith stayed in, but had less and less to do with other Marines.

Even back then I suspected that Keith's burgeoning 'sense of his own gayness' was, more than military homophobia, an impediment to his closeness with other Marines. But I didn't feel I could write that without talking to those other Marines. I did visit Ted a few more times, but he had grown wary of talking with me since Keith (jealous twice over) had taken it upon himself to inform the Kyle- (and Alex-) like 'straight' Marine that I was in love with him ...

*

Two years later Keith was getting out of the Marine Corps. He said it was because of troop cutbacks. (This is one of only two stories I ever caught him telling different versions of – and I did check up on him; the other was again Marine-stereotypical: whether he'd seen action in the Gulf War.) In any event, it wasn't a voluntary separation. As you read, he claimed that in the end he was still as gung-ho as he had ever been about being a Marine. But in a deleted, rather muddled passage he also confessed that other Marines didn't like him any more. This he vaguely attributed to their homophobia. I wasn't convinced. Sadly, I didn't like him too much any more myself.

You and I look on with Whitman's 'bitterest envy' at the buddy love of soldiers. Of course it's open to question whether such love has much shelf-life beyond boot camp, outside of combat. But Ted and Alex, though each felt ultimately excluded from the brotherhood, testify to the powerful sense they felt of barriers being broken down between men. My feeling is that his gung-ho gayness cost Keith his sense of belonging.

On the other hand, it might just have been that he's a pain.

*

I've since found a copy of *The Boys of Boise: Furore, Vice and Folly in an American City* (New York: Macmillan, 1966) by John Gerassi, on the infamous sex panic. It offers a liberal argument for greater tolerance of and improved mental hospitals for homosexuals. But Gerassi did point out that many of the teenage boys supposedly victimized by older Idahoan men were in fact experienced hustlers; a psychiatrist he cited recalled 'one child telling me how it made him feel important to stand there, with his arms crossed, while an "old man", as he called him, got down on his knees in order to – to – as the boys put it, "to blow me".' Also that homosexuality was common among the trappers and lumbermen who settled Idaho; and that mutual masturbation sessions were 'a ritual not only at Boise High but common to every high school, prep school, and boarding school in the country, not to mention colleges. Sometimes, not for personal gratification but only because it was part of the fun, one boy masturbated another for a few seconds.' As the homo scare spread, any meeting between males became suspect. 'One lawyer told me that the good old "night with the boys" disappeared. "You never saw so many men going out to the bars at night with their wives and girlfriends," he said. "I remember we used to have poker games once a week. Well, for a few weeks we cancelled them, then one of the guys got an idea: We'd invite a girl to play with us. You know, it's not very pleasant to play poker with women, not when you're in a serious game. But that's what we had to do."'

How the world has changed. I was shocked to learn from an article on the front page of the April 22 *New York Times* (copy enclosed) that, just in the last few years, American high school students have stopped showering together after gym class or football practice. The article speculated that the fear of same-sex public nudity might be due to increased modesty; to feelings of inadequacy generated by idealized images of the male body in advertising; or to discussion of homosexuality making students more fearful of being gazed upon desirously. A 1970s gay liberationist friend e-mailed me decrying the 'homophobia' of this last supposed reason. But so far no one has pointed out that male teenagers have long been afraid that a locker-room hard-on will mark them as queer. Increased discussion of gay identity would seem to inevitably strengthen that equation, and make teenagers more conscious of the locker-room as potentially homoerotic, indeed, as the classic gay porn backdrop. From my years of bathroom voyeurism I know that gay men are much more likely than straight men to piss in stalls instead of at urinals where other men might look at them.

My gayist correspondent may have made a good point

when I reported the story of Lloyd's model Kris, the Scandinavian Marine who didn't want to serve with gays but didn't mind appearing nude in gay porn: 'It is different. He's getting paid!' So maybe teenage boys who've been increasingly exposed to commercial images of male flesh have started to think of their bodies as commodities, and don't want to give it away for free?

*

A few weeks back Alex and I were looking for one of my old sailor friends at Shooterz, the San Diego pool bar at 30th and University. The sailor wasn't there, but the doorman, an ex-Marine of my acquaintance, told me about a couple who frequent the bar: a transgendered person with breasts and a penis and her twenty-two-year-old active duty Marine boyfriend. Apparently, all her boyfriends are Marines. Told that the doorman used to be a Marine, this boyfriend snarled 'What, that fag?' To which the tranny replied, 'Watch out who you're calling a fag. You suck my dick every night!' The doorman concluded, 'I guess he hasn't realized he's gay yet.' I asked him, 'How many gay men do you know who are attracted to trans people?' (To which Alex demurred, 'Well...' Aunt Ida-like (John Waters' *Female Trouble*) I've urged him to explore this attraction: 'I'd be so happy if you was to meet a nice tranny instead of these tired ghetto homosexuals. Come on, let's see who's in the AOL transgendered room right now!') Of course I wished that I could have met these two in time for inclusion in my book. But it sounds a lot like the story you were telling me when you were here about your London tranny friends, and indeed is probably a whole other book. (Yours? Today I'm thinking that my next non-fiction project might be a satirical sequel to Laud Humphries' infamous book *Tearoom Trade*. I want to be paid to cruise toilets.)

*

David Lloyd and I are supposed to resume outdoor shoots next week. I hope so. I need the money. Lately he has developed the habit of calling me and talking, sometimes for more than an hour, about projects he wants to pay me to help do, instead of actually paying me to do them. But I have to confess I've grown rather fond of the beefcake Nazi. Actually, that's an especially unfair thing to call him (and making fun of old people is already pretty unfair). In the 50s David braved getting blacklisted by joining the Communist Party. And all these years later he still behaves with surprising integrity, at least for someone in his profession.

David has some great stories. Every now and then he wakes me up with some amazing conversational nugget (which, for some reason, he never expects me to be interested in). About, for example, the party he went to in New York in the early 60s where 'There was that guy, that dreadful artist, oh, you know the one. Damn! I can't think of his name. Well, oh, it was disgusting! There he was, sitting there masturbating a cat with a knitting needle.' 'Artist?' 'Oh, you'd know who I meant. The one – the one who did those stupid paintings of soup cans!'

David has a theory that Gore Vidal possesses a terribly tiny penis, which has forced him to become a 'watch queen'.

*

Farewell Marine Corps Village People bonding ritual. On April 1, 1996, the Secretary of the Navy raised the on-base drinking age for sailors and Marines to twenty-one. Tonight, on this eve of Cinco de Mayo, my old cruising buddy Phillip and I will head to the San Ysidro border crossing. I'll be thinking of you. Also, I want to buy some Valium.

Yours,

Steve

Vidal Statistics

London, 21 May 1996

Dear Steve,

How marvellous that Judith Butler has written you a blurb. I often think that she would have made a good Marine, if she was clever enough to stop thinking.

I was interested to read your *NYT* cutting about showers. I'd read an edited version of this report in the *Guardian*, a liberal national newspaper here. It may or may not be significant that the part they decided to cut was the 'homophobic' speculation about homosexual anxieties. When I read the piece, I recalled your line on noticing that the piss-trough in the 'head' at Del Mar E-Club had been divided into politically correct modesty bays: 'I'm beginning to really hate the 90s.'

Perhaps people have just wised up to people like us, Steve.

Characteristically, though, I can't help but conclude that the implications are more depressingly generalized. The overt sexualization of media culture and the commodification of everything means that people can no longer trust themselves in their own nakedness; they feel that by taking off their Nike trainers, Calvin Klein boxers, O'Neil T-shirts that they are denuding themselves in ways which the mere absence of clothes never did to their fathers – that they are powerless and logo-less. Moreover, in a world where everyone has to wear a sexual identity, casual nakedness is not permitted (e.g. Keith's pink triangle USMC tattoo logo). I think your friend's point about Kris is pertinent here. To the younger generation it may be the case that unless they're being paid to take their clothes off, they're, *de facto*, being screwed.

I've a crudely Marxian theory that political correctness is, like late-twentieth-century feminism, merely a product of late capitalism. More precisely, political correctness sanctifies, *post hoc*, radical changes which have already occurred because they suited the material interests of late capitalism. Global capitalism has no need for nations or races any more – or, indeed, sexes. Attachments to these notions or 'prejudices' merely hinder capital's access to consumer and labour markets. In respect of bodies, capitalism decided that alienation was good for business – lonely anxious people use more goods and services – and so political correctness polices the body, giving us the right to be isolated and neurotic, making passive aggression a positive civic virtue.

Speaking of nakedness, I find your remark about David's theory about the size of Mr Vidal's *membrum virile* quite tantalizing. It is tempting to rewrite his entire career in the light of this (no doubt completely unfounded) idea. It would also explain his maxim that sex with strangers is fine, sex with friends not – because if you have sex with a friend, everyone you know will learn you are Princess Tinymeat by lunchtime the next day. Even Vidal's hatred of the Jewish Dentist suddenly makes sense. After all, a man with a paltry pee-pee is bound to be adamantly, opposed to the idea that *anatomy is destiny*.

Life, in the details rather than the abstract (which, as I'm sure you've noticed, I always feel much more at home with), goes on. I've been seeing a lot of Jason lately, as he's been doing a course at a military base not far from London. It's almost becoming a real 'relationship'.

What a terrifying thought.

Best,

Mark

Putting My Dick Where My Mouth Is

San Diego, June 1, 1996

Dear Mark,

I've just come back from a week in San Francisco. I can't imagine any place where campiness has more fully triumphed over camp, as you distinguish the two.

The most horrible thing is that every time I return there, it almost feels like home.

Boarding a Super Shuttle van at the airport, I took a seat in the third row against the window behind a taciturn Castro artefact. We were joined by a twenty-ish male–female couple who had been on my flight from San Diego but, with facial piercings and long sideburns, looked more San Francisco (though the distinction is not as marked as it was even a year ago). He climbed in back next to me; she sat beside the clone and stretched her arm over the back of the seat to hold the blond, stoned-looking boy's hand. After I told the driver where I was headed, the boy grinned and offered, 'I live about a block away from there.' I could only think to answer that I understood the address doesn't really belong to any official neighbourhood. 'That's right,' he nodded, 'It's not really in the Castro, or the Mission...' I commented that a friend of mine (Bart, of course) has dubbed it 'Upper Safeway', after the supermarket. He joked, 'Yeah, I call it "Mission Lite".' Without really thinking about it, I said, 'I've always liked places like that. Being in between.' Both boy and girl perked up. He: 'Um, yeah. It's a good place to get wherever you wanna go...' Nervously, I stared out the window, but saw, or imagined that I saw, the clasped hands advancing on my knee.

At last: a chance to put all this talk of sexual fluidity into personal practice. (To put my dick where my mouth is, I almost wrote, but my meetings with famous autofellator Scott O'Hara are another story.) But I just couldn't picture: what exactly would we do? The dalliance remained that. Needless to say, I could have easier imagined a threesome had the guy been one of the several military boys on the plane. And, finally, picturing Marines is a big part of why any feeling of belonging in San Francisco inevitably gives way to a temporarily renewed appreciation for boring San Diego.

(And anyway, one doesn't have to have actual sex with males and females to 'be' 'bisexual', any more than one necessarily has to change sex to be 'transgendered'. I've had two adult bookstore experiences so far this year with men who wanted to blow me while they watched images of 'lesbian' oral sex. I've come to realize that it can be silly even to talk of a specific sexual act when two practitioners can have such radically different interpretations of the 'same' act that it may not be the same act at all. Alex, for example, has confessed to me that he alternately conceives of fucking a man as sticking a steak knife into him, or impregnating him – two understandings I'd never had.)

But its pixillated marginality is precisely why we love our myopic fog-enshrouded queer Mecca by the Bay. (The city has installed restored antique streetcars to ferry tourists from Union Square to the Castro. I think it would make sense for all San Francisco neighbourhoods to be turned into sort of museum zones where, in accordance with strictly enforced municipal codes, time would stand still. I mean, more than it already does. Year after year, Haight-Ashbury would stay 1967: residents would be required to wear period clothes, drive VW buses, be prosecuted under 1967 laws, etc. – but of course pay current rent. In beatnik North Beach the calendar would be rolled back to the day On The Road was published. But I expect the queens of San Francisco would split into bitterly opposed factions over whether the Castro should be rolled back to 1977 – or 1976. Well, other people have made crazier proposals. You probably know that Dead Kennedys singer Jello Biafra once ran for mayor, and garnered six per cent of the vote, on a platform mandating that all SF city employees wear clown suits to work.) And so far the bookstore A Different Light on Castro Street is the only one I've seen that stocks It's a Queer World.

Do you ever get hate mail from readers excoriating you for writing things like 'for me personally the only attraction of going through all the trouble of changing sex would not be to become my own special transgressive creation but to leave

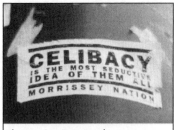

Flyer on San Francisco lamppost.

perverse sexuality and Pride marches behind'? I think you would in San Francisco.

Yours,

Steve

Scottish Accents

London, 29 June 1996

Dear Steve,

I also recently made a trip Northwards – to Edinburgh, for a bookshop reading.

Edinburgh is a lovely city – in the summer. In the winter it's colder than hell's gate, the wind just slams in from the North Sea, making you feel like you're wearing a kilt and no underwear, even when you've got asbestos thermals on. Becoming a whiskey alcoholic, like most of the Scottish appear to be, seems perfectly appropriate behaviour during these months.

But in the summer it's never too hot, and, after cramped, crowded London, its wide avenues and boulevards make a pleasant change. Edinburgh is more continental than British – I expect it's only a matter of time before the Scots get independence and stop having anything to do with us Sassenach southerners. The Scots are better educated and better looking.

The bookshop reading went OK. I read the pieces about a bingo hall and about the Motor Show, finishing with the essay on Mozza. People laughed in most of the right places and applauded at the end. By most objective measures it was, then, a success.

I have to say, though, that for the entire period I was reading I felt physically sick. It's one thing to open an old book of yours (and any book is by definition old) and scan a few lines, wince to yourself and shut it, hastily. It's quite another to read a whole chunk of it OUT LOUD and IN FRONT OF AN AUDIENCE. For twenty minutes. In the end I was editing it as I read, deleting words here, sentences there and whole paragraphs elsewhere. The questions afterwards went rather better, as I could extemporize and make things up as I went along.

After I'd finished, the first question was from a sharp, wiry young man with a blond flat-top in his early twenties put his hand up. 'Do you hate everyone?' [*Sharp intake of breath by audience.*]

'That's a pertinent question,' I said slowly, stalling for time. 'When it came to reading the proofs for *Queer World*, I was a bit taken aback seeing all my misanthropic journalism collected together. I asked myself: Am I really that bitter and twisted? I looked deep into my soul, into its darkest recesses, and the answer came back resoundingly: Yes, Mark, you are.' [*Sharp exhalation of in-taken breath by audience in laughter.*]

The bookshop manager, Jim, an affable, beefy young man who probably doesn't hate anyone, asked me if I thought that straight men and gay men could be friends. I replied that I wasn't sure that gay men and gay men could be friends. 'But,' I added, 'I hold out a certain amount of false optimism regarding the possibility of friendship between straight and gay men. You see, gay and straight men need one another to remind themselves of who they aren't. Gay men just remind one another of who they are, which is a recipe for resentment if ever there was one.'

Jim volunteered that he fancied straight men too and that he got a lot of stick from other gay men for admitting it. I congratulated him on having the courage to come out as a straight-chaser – a disposition which is, as you know, a matter of great shame in the gay faith. (Jim and I will be setting up a helpline shortly – for straight men who want to be chased, that is.)

Afterwards a bunch of us went to the pub and sank a few pints. As the evening progressed, the crowd thinned out until I was left alone with Jim and John, the wiry blond lad who'd posed the cheeky misanthropy question. As we got drunker, I felt warmer and warmer towards them. I really like the Scottish sense of humour, probably because, like me, it's a little bit melancholic, a little bit acid, and a little bit sour. And then there's the Scottish accent which, I have to say, gets me every time.

I also like the stroppiness of Scots – partly a product of their historical chips on their shoulders about being subjugated by a race that is less attractive than they are and which can't even hold its beer. Although John and Jim were 'fans', they were forever pulling me up on the sillier things I said and forcing me to explain myself (which, of course, I couldn't). After a while, and several more pints, I decided that they were *real pals* and that I might even move to such a city with such pals as these.

If my history with things Scottish wasn't already at miserable end.

Last weekend the Mad Jock in my life came to visit and a lot of things came to a pustular head and I more or less drove him out of the house. So now maybe I really do hate everyone. As I mentioned before, he's been staying every weekend for the past couple of months. Lately, I've been beginning to feel like a landlady running a free guesthouse. (Though I suspect such ladies get more affection; I *know* they get more sex.)

The night before, we performed our usual Saturday night ritual and went to see a crap action film – in this case *The Rock*, about some terrorists, led by an ex-Marine colonel avenging the deaths of his comrades in Vietnam, threatening San Francisco from Alcatraz with rockets filled with a hideous gas which causes the metal used in body piercings to rust. Or something. (The people of SF needn't have worried, however, since galloping to their rescue were Nicholas Cage and Sean Connery's Scottish accent.)

Before we went to the movie, we ate in a chain Mexican restaurant in the same tacky leisure complex off the North Circular. As we waited for the waitress to come and take our order, he hissed through gritted teeth, staring at his plate, his face all thunder and shame: 'Stop *looking* at me!'

Hope things are going better with you and Alex.

Best,

Mark

PS In answer to your question re hate mail: I don't get nearly enough, which is another reason why I should consider moving to the US. People are much more easily offended over there. Bless 'em.

Straight Chasers of the World

San Diego, July 13, 1996

Dear Mark,

Edinburgh sounds like a city I'd like. I belong somewhere much farther north than San Diego, and I think it's time I did something about it. Of course, not belonging has its advantages, too. Fitting in at all passes for an accomplishment, and I can always chuckle at the perversity of my ending up in a place largely defined by two of the things I most hate: sunshine and cars.

I, too, dread readings, though in my case it's more garden variety stage fright. My worst reading experience occurred at A Different Light, West Hollywood, in 1993. I'd never been to LA before, but had, and still harbour, some weird phobia about the famously non-place. I rented a small economy car and had a gay sailor interviewee/friend drive it for me (I allowed my Michigan driver's license to expire in 1984). Owing to various nerve-wracking complications, we got a late start. Anthony tore out of Coronado doing 90, pizza in one hand and a Coke in the other. On I-5 in downtown San Diego he lost control of the car. Suddenly we were skidding horizontally down the freeway, soda and ice cubes flying over both of us, me, with quiet (almost British?) restraint, repeating 'Anthony. Anthony. Anthony.' We came to a complete halt – in rush-hour traffic. Somehow we weren't hit. I don't remember how long it took us to get going again, but it was at least ten minutes before either of us spoke. Finally I said, 'What happened back there?' 'Oh, I just lost control of the car for a little bit, but everything's fine now.' Closer to LA, without warning Anthony screeched to a stop on the median, explaining that he was tired and needed to rest his eyes. Whenever I tried to change the radio station from screeching black dance music divas, he'd laugh and say, 'Change it back or we'll crash!' A few more miles down the road he veered off onto the median a second time.

I thought I felt all right when we got to the store and I began the reading, but only a few minutes into it I started trembling, stuttering, and found myself unable to continue. Muttering something about a close call on the freeway won sympathetic murmurs from the kindly old gentlemen who'd come to see me. Just when I seemed to have regained my composure, some homeless person staggered in off the street, ran up to me and began screaming incoherently.

After the reading, as Anthony and I were relaxing over a drink at Revolver, he said, 'You know, I'm feeling kind of tired. Would you mind driving?' With surprising ease I drove us all the way back to my Hillcrest apartment, and even parallel parked on the street out front. I haven't driven since. Two years later I returned to A Different Light, and it was almost as bad the second time.

First Time in LA: Zeeland at A Different Light, West Hollywood

As I reread your letter and write this one, I am faced with plotting bookstore appearances for *Marine*.

*

Straight chasers of the world ... As you know, my own credentials in the field are not unimpressive. After all, I did abandon higher education to chase one straight boy three thousand miles, and that wasn't even the most melodramatic chapter in my ten-year transcontinental pursuit of him.

Brent and I became best friends in 1977. The first time we had sex was a year later when we were eighteen. It happened in the dead of winter in the back seat of my clunky old Pontiac Catalina. We'd come from a friend's bachelor party, where a Super-8 fuck flick had been screened (multiple times, forwards and backwards). As it happened, the night before I'd confessed to Brent my nagging fantasies about neighbourhood boys whose sexual overtures I'd declined, and suggested I thought he might help to cure me of them. But I was thoroughly shocked and confused when, on our way home from the party, he made the overture. We made a bad, drunken, teeth-scraping attempt at sixty-nining.

That we had differing takes on the experience the next day I don't need to tell you.

Four years later Brent was a US soldier and married. Upon

consideration of my plea for a rematch, he assented, on the condition that I start going out to gay bars and finally get over him. He called me the day his wife was in the hospital delivering his baby. He insisted we do it in a hotel room, communicate only by written notes, and of course never kiss. I was surprised by his sexual readiness and the obvious intensity of his pleasure. We sucked each other off twice, he fucked me once (after cautioning that of course no way would he let me do that to him. Getting fucked hurt like hell. Though I tried playing bottom another three or four times over the years, I never learned to enjoy it). I kept my promise insofar as I did visit gay bars (and had three one-night stands, with three dull gay GIs), but of course the next time we went off together alone somewhere I tried to get Brent to put out again. A year later he was unexpectedly transferred back to the States. I stayed behind (it helped that he got sent to Oklahoma). Eventually, his German wife went through his uniform and found a letter from me declaring that I had abandoned all hope that our sexual adventures would be repeated; also, that I had written my last will and testament and was leaving her a necklace made of my molars. The very next day she packed up and returned to Germany, wailing as she left, 'And I don't want Steve's teeth!'

Of course I, the self-declared fag, had to be the homewrecker. Horndog Brent's many and varied liaisons with prostitutes and married female GI co-workers (and other men?) went undetected. But when Brent called and tearfully told me that his wife had left and taken his kid, he emphatically added that he did not regret anything we had done together.

I do think he fed off and encouraged my pursuit, at least for a long time. Maybe I made him seem more interesting to himself. When his next stupid wife was told the story, she intelligently forbade him to ever meet with me again.

When I finally stopped dreaming of Brent around 1987, I tried to write about him in my first attempt at a novel. I changed his name to Brad. Soon thereafter I met a straight GI in the Frankfurt red light district named Brad who was more handsome, more butch, and more willing than Brent. To my astonishment I discovered that, under just the right circumstances, it was sometimes possible to signal my interest and get straight men to chase me. (In my current attempt at a novel I am writing about Brad/Brent, and my out-and-proud gay friend Bart who voiced the requisite denunciations of my straight chasing, and, upon seeing Brad, bitterest envy.)

In 1991 I succeeded in getting a presumably straight sailor to chase me on Pier 39, but it wasn't much fun as his intention was pretty clearly to beat me to a bloody pulp (he'd caught me trying to photograph him drunkenly urinating in a public place). But I also met sailor Troy in San Francisco, and followed him a thousand miles up the Pacific coast to Whidbey Island, Washington.

Zeeland boyfriend Troy, US Navy, 1992

Here, however, is where my pre-queer theory queer theory confusion starts to get messy. Was Troy straight? As a teenager, he and his best friend were unusually intimate jack-off buddies. As a boy, he'd been sexually used by a teenager. But when I met him Troy was fucking a Navy chief petty officer's wife. He was utterly unselfconsciously butch. He liked to look at boys as well as girls, but claimed he never worried that this might make him queer. Among his CDs were Morrissey and Pet Shop Boys, but his favourite band was Judas Priest. He never worked out, and wore Navy-issue underwear with skid marks and holes.

Though I told him he could be 'bi', or 'just Troy', after a year of my companionship Troy pronounced himself gay, wore Calvins, and bought a rainbow flag keychain that he would sometimes flash to his shipmates ... Nowadays, he says he rejects any label. His friends are mostly straight. Unlike Brent and what I surmise of Brad, Troy now only has sex with men, but that's because his greatest pleasure is getting fucked. (His current [married, Mexican-American] lover has thanked me for 'breaking Troy in', but the slow business of negotiating Troy's rape terror/fantasy played a big part in killing my erotic interest in him.)

You write that 'most straight men still define themselves in terms of "not being queer"', and vice versa. But I wonder if we as straight-chasers don't have our own vital interest in maintaining exactly that polarity. Doesn't straight-chasing require space to chase? And if, in projects such as yours and mine, we become too successful in undermining straight identity, at least as we see it, what is left us but some more general 'same'-sex attraction? (Unless, I guess, it's exactly the act of undermining straight men's straightness that we eroticize.)

Since living in San Diego I've lost my edge as a straight-chaser, in part because I really can no longer quite believe in straight. For me, queer theory inescapably confirms what I learned from Brad and Brent and Troy and hundreds of other men I met in video booths and toilets: behaviour is an unreliable basis for sexual categories. Desire is messy. Identity is a joke.

Last winter I attended a 'military haircut party'. All the guests were a-twitter anticipating the reaction to a gay video on the TV by the one gorgeous 'straight' Marine in attendance. Only two or three years ago I would have shared their excitement, would have found the boy the most attractive in the room based solely on someone's pronouncement of his unavailability. Well, OK, given my pick of the men in the room I still would choose him over the gay guys. But, apart from his presumed freshness, now the only difference I could recognize was that so perfectly expressed in your own summation: the charming, seductive trouble with him was that he was (presumably) repressed; the trouble with them was that I could too easily have had them, as so many of them had had each other. This might still be difference enough, but it isn't the intra-'species' difference I used to get off on. Nowadays even my cigar-smoking, reptile-owning, blues, jazz and Stones-blaring straight downstairs neighbours, forever hooting at basketball on TV, just don't look straight enough.

Sadly, knowing that identity is fictive hasn't liberated me from the barrier of 'difference' I unthinkingly impose whenever some apparently non-gay man is friendly to me in public. In part I do this out of years of habit, and in part I guess because I still want to maintain that erotic distance, even though I know imposing it prevents me from making contact. And, naturally, my loss of faith in straight does little to make me more disposed to sex with gay men, from whom I still continue to feel increasingly different. By the way, on Saturday I had another adult bookstore encounter with a Marine. I was a little disappointed that he mostly wanted to blow me, but more so that he turned the channel to a military-theme gay porno. Someone told me that a new Dirk Yates *Private Collection* tape features an unfamiliar off-camera interlocutor who poses questions about the homoeroticism of military life. Though I haven't been able to confirm this, I find the prospect of having sex with a Marine to the uninvited accompaniment of some second-hand distillation of the public product of my desire to have sex with Marines more than a little irritating.

Am I just exaggerating? Living in what you termed Fagville, USA may be distorting my perspective. (Another reason I eroticized soldiers was that at the time I was living in Germany, where, by American standards, all men looked a little queeny.) It's also entirely possible that I've spent too much time in this apartment with my cats reading Judith Butler. (The cats and I were very interested to learn of her work-in-progress, *Politics at the Scene of Utterance*, said to deal 'with the political valences of hate speech, free speech, and pornography – including a chapter on homosexuality in the military'.) Will a fresh setting make it easier to suspend disbelief and chase anew?

The trips to Pendleton used to offer escape. Two weeks ago, for the first time since the Secretary of the Navy upped the drinking age, Alex and I returned to Area 51. On the drive up we speculated about what we would find. I said it would be sad; Alex predicted it would be so depressing as to preclude any future return.

Approaching the club, I recoiled at the sight of what I thought was the largest cockroach I had ever seen, on the front steps. Indicating its presence to Alex, I cringed again as some exiting uniformed heavy-booted MPs seemed destined to step on it.

The club was almost empty; the few boys there were all in the pool room. The room that Marines used to dance in was locked up. In a corner of the video game-room a DJ was set up, playing music to an audience of zero.

Leaving the club, anticipating Alex's reproaches for the hypocrisy of my being an animal rights supporter who hates cockroaches, I allowed that I could, queasily, recognize a certain beauty in insects. Alex answered that it was not a cockroach at all but a beetle. With his sometimes touching restrained passion/ he told me that what I had deemed its revolting size was probably, for its species, an accomplishment. He had moved 'the poor thing' to the bushes; it had already been stepped on and, though still living, was being devoured by ants ... Though we were quick to find something else to talk about, the beetle seemed somehow horribly significant. A few days later Alex mentioned that he found himself still pondering it, as I had been trying not to.

Probably I should move to Edinburgh, where people would call me on this silliness. Instead, Alex and I are moving to Seattle – maybe as soon as October.

Yours,

Steve

Rules of Engagement

London, 16 August 1996

Dear Steven,

Your account of your out-and-proud friend's envious reaction to the photo of the kind of unhealthy love-object you – and I – have a self-hating interest in made me laugh out loud.

Mind you, I've done something since my last letter that will probably make *you* laugh out loud: I've joined the British Army.

Or at least the part-time branch of it called the Territorial Army. I've almost convinced myself my interest is purely journalistic – the *Sunday Times Magazine* has commissioned me to write an article on it. But my motivation is probably more to do with mourning and melancholia. I mean: talk about incorporating the lost love-object! I suppose it's my equivalent to your following your soldier lover to Germany, losing him, and then taking on the whole US Army on the Rhine instead. My gay journo friend Paul, who is very hostile to anything in khaki that doesn't have a designer label, has encouraged me in this mad act, explaining that my joining the TA after Jason is a step in the right direction: 'like a heroin addict switching to methadone.'

In a few weeks' time I'll be going on the Selection Weekend, which involves forty-eight hours of assault courses, orienteering, sleeping outdoors, running with logs – the usual intellectual stuff. In the mean time, I have to turn up for Parade on Tuesday evenings. I simultaneously feel very much at home and slightly edgy, an inside–outsider (I have a double dark secret – a journalist *and* a poof). But everyone was so chummy on the Open Day I attended last week that I felt *dizzy*.

One chubby fair-haired lad called Gibbsy was especially friendly. He had one of those open, guileless faces that give out very direct looks. He kept cracking bad jokes and then checking to see if I was laughing. I was. Later he showed me how the GPMG (general-purpose machine-gun) worked and did his best to persuade me to opt for his outfit rather than the LSW (light support weapon) lads at the table next to him, which, I have to say, in addition to being a better-looking weapon, was operated by a better-looking squaddie whom I took an instant liking to, laughing even louder at his jokes and being even more interested in the gun parts than I was with Gibbsy (I'm so fickle). Green-eyed and chatty in a slightly wide-boy/Irish fashion (with a Norf Lahndahn accent), Dave had a lively cheekiness about him and twinkle to those eyes. I think that we might get on, become best bantering buddies, and name our boy-children after one another.

It was strange, though, to find my-self lying on the floor aiming the LSW, leg cocked, looking up at Dave while he rattled on about the firing procedure (firing setting, safety catch, etc.). This was the first time in a very long time I had found myself in the prone, learning position with another man. And I liked it.

USMC drill instructor and recruit

A thick-necked, incredibly butch Sergeant in his late twen-ties with cropped black hair giving us a talk about the TA solemnly informed us: 'It is an h'offence to be gay in the h'army,' he declared (his accent, peculiar to the British NCO, dropped 'h's and added them to words beginning with vow-els). 'I don't care what you do h'out there in civilian life, but in the h'army h'it's h'illegal. So that leaves you two h'options if you 'appen to be gay: either you don't join h'or you keep your mouth shut an' don't tell h'anyone about it – and don't come h'on to h'other squaddies in the shower!' (Sounds like an unofficial version of 'Don't Ask, Don't Tell' to me, and put a whole new light on the TA recruiting poster on the wall of one of the offices here: 'Lead a double life. Join the TA.')

Valiantly ignoring the palpable embarrassment in the room, he went on to tell us that he'd had, over the years, four recruits tell him that they were gay, 'when nobody 'ad h'asked them' – and they 'ad to be rejected. One bloke 'oo volunteered 'e was 'omosexual, well, that was the least of 'is worries, 'e was schizophrenic and had h'acute dermatitis h'as well.' (I think, Steve, that must have been one of my ex's.)

'But remember!' announced our Sergeant, finishing his 'omily on 'omosexuality with an endearingly stagy flourish that telegraphed to us he was about to crack a joke. 'It's never queer unless you're the one taking it!'

At this point I had to pinch myself. The other recruits in the room coughed and shifted their nervous bums about in their seats. Everybody forgot to laugh.

It's official, Steve: I'm not queer after all. And all the military men I've slept with are. Maybe, though, my size, aura etc., is to blame for the bottoming out I've witnessed.

The other potential recruits – about ten – in the room were a raggedy bunch. Most of them looked a bit overweight and were probably hoping the army would act as their free personal fitness trainer. Except for the guy next to me, with shaved head, gym-pumped body, and suspiciously orange skin, wearing a tight white Levi's T-shirt showing his pecs off to best effect. Despite his array of gay signifiers he turned out to be a very working-class, very straight boy. A bus driver, he'd been in the TA a few years previously (Parachute Regiment) and rejoined a few weeks ago. In the NAAFI bar upstairs supping cheap warm beer, he wouldn't stop talking at me – not so much chatting me up as chatting me to death.

It was partly my fault. I must have appeared to be listening to what he said and *interested* (of course, he wasn't to know that this was because, in a poignant reversal of the male–female misreading cliché, I was staring at his tits). He had a mate with him whom he buddied up with on the Selection Weekend: 'It's so much easier when you're a couple,' he told me, and I tried to believe him. His mate seemed like a nice bloke; fairly quiet, though – which no doubt will have helped chatty pecs decide that he was the right guy to 'marry'.

Which reminds me of the best joke the Sergeant came out with. Of course this one was unintentional – and particularly funny bearing in mind his earlier analysis of active and passive male sexuality. 'As you will probably know from reports h'about defence cuts h'etcetera,' he admitted sadly, 'the British h'Army is in *recline*...'

Hope your move to Seattle goes well. How's your novel coming along? Good luck with *The Masculine Marine* – can't wait to hear about your bookstore appearances/outrages.

Best,

Mark

68

Voyage to the Bottom

San Diego, September 5, 1996

Dear Mark,

Brain-stopping summer torpidity. An aching to aestivate. Mammals aren't allowed to, Alex says. Maybe if I stayed here I could guest-direct a Dirk Yates porn video called *San Diego Stupor*.

Tomorrow morning I receive advance copies of my Marine book. Waiting on this third child wouldn't be such a big deal, you'd think, but for weeks now I've been plagued by recurrent nightmares. In one, I open the book to find the illustrations section is a Chinese restaurant menu. In another, the cover features Alex, in drag, dancing with a female sailor; and a handwritten index referencing seaman Anthony: 'Voyage to the Bottom.' (?) But there's no big mystery behind my anxiety: *Barrack Buddies* came back with the cover the wrong colour, while *Sailors* had messed-up type, an improperly cropped front cover shot, and the wrong author pic altogether. My managing editor assures that no such surprises will greet me tomorrow. But I may still have to contend with how Alex chooses to react to seeing himself as a cover model. He's afraid that he's not good-looking enough. Indeed, David Lloyd told me that I am 'doing Alex a favour', and my publisher's advertising director

'Halloweener' or 'In-Betweener'? Alex's first time in drag, photographed with Max, using new Polaroid camera just received as gift from Andrew Cunanan

Alex in his dress blue uniform with baby Samantha

is said to have commented: 'wish Marine was more conventionally handsome.'

I could have had my pick of David's Marine models, some of whom look more like the boys from *XY* or the covers of the new *Advocate*-owned Alyson line. A literate Marine/porn aficionado I correspond with, Rolf Hardesty, even presented me with an unsolicited draft cover design he made himself using a blond, buff, hairless nude Marine, complete with an X on the spot where he thought a computer generated USMC tattoo should be added. Such an approach might in fact have been appropriate, though not in a way that most people would 'get'.

But I wonder: What will the book-browsing public see in those sharp black eyes of Alex's?

September 7, 1996

Well, on the finished product Alex's gaze isn't all that piercing. Disappointingly, the quality of the reproduction is such that he stares back from the dusky front cover as though through a thin film of Vaseline. But I suppose this may render him, and the book, more approachable. And the inside illustrations do include a severe, high-contrast copy of the same shot, capturing Alex in all his scowling (to me more seductive) glory.

Tucked inside was a yellowed, thumbtack-riddled Chinese takeaway menu. My managing editor, Bill Palmer, has turned out to be a true pal.

Alex told me he didn't want to see the book at all. I showed it to him anyway. He tried not to react, but he did say that the somewhat fuzzy reproduction makes his face *tabula rasa*. I think this pleased him very much. That I so rarely get excited or upset has always been the quality he most admires in me.

To celebrate, Alex and I drove up to Pendleton for another final visit. Yes, well, we both had need of $2.75 haircuts. The E-club was free of Marines and crushed Coleoptera. But I do have a new animal metaphor for you.

For a month or two I've been putting out food for a small black cat that comes up the steps to our second-storey door, usually late in the evening. One night, Alex noticed his cat Sammie hurtling her small voluptuous tortie lynx-point frame against the screen door. He thought it was the black cat she was attacking, but a closer look at the visitor revealed two white stripes down its back. Calmly Alex transferred Samantha to the next room. The next night the skunk returned, and for a month now I've been putting out food for it, too – much to the displeasure of my neighbours.

One evening I came up the stairs and surprised the polecat at table. Rather than retreat down the back stairs, it puffed up its tail and stamped its feet at me. To get back in my apartment I had to wait until it was done eating. Pussy-whipped again ... Alex jokes that by the time Oct. 1 comes around I'll have the skunk in the cab of the rental truck with us.

Of course I sometimes have occasion to think of Alex as a skunk. But our peculiar marriage has passed its three-year mark, and planning the move together has given us something new to talk about.

September 8, 1996

Thanks for sending your wonderful article 'Bum Rap'. No wonder you prefer Marines to sailors! I'm almost tempted to suggest that it may have been less than fair of you in 'Tijuana Brass' to reject sailors for their alleged geekiness. My dictionary defines geek as 'an odd or ridiculous person' or 'a carnival performer whose show consists of bizarre acts, such as biting the head off a live chicken.' Really you prefer Marines because, as we observed together in awe at the rodeo last summer, so many of them have such awesome asses, while so many (even straight) sailors are exactly like the gay 'arseless wonders' you deride ('Well of course,' one of my sailor interviewees explained, 'it's because they sit on them all day.'). Boatswain's mates and hull tech's excepted.

But I have to admit there are a lot of odd and ridiculous looking sailors hanging about San Diego. And I've seen more sailors than Marines who call to mind Ozzy Osbourne.

In another letter, one penned in some more favourable season and clime, I will have more to say about:

1) My favourite body part, and the implications of your analysis of David's theory about the size of Gore Vidal's penis when applied to the stereotypical skinny-guy-who-(unlike Ren)-doesn't-feel-the-need-for-muscles. I'm tempted to invest in an inflatable backpack-sized cushion to protect against this world's cruel surfaces, in particular tearoom toilet seats, which, after twenty minutes, exact an ever more terrible toll on my lower back.

For his part, Alex exhausted his melodrama allowance this summer when, in the company of my visiting ex-Navy ex-lover Troy, he stormed out of *Trainspotting*. Alex found the crib death scene a too-visceral reminder of his own druggie mom's neglect. Predictably I ran after him; predictably he snarled, 'I didn't ask you to care!' Troy, fresh from a community college course on Eastern Philosophy, offered that I am a fool for bothering at all about Alex's, his, or any creature's suffering. I liked Troy better when he was in the Navy and told me he couldn't imagine that anyone could actually just sit and read a book and not do anything else ... Throughout his stay, Troy and Alex had just a little too much fun comparing notes on my faults. Finally, when my old cruising buddy Phillip came over and spiritedly joined in, I tried to make the best of the situation: 'No, really, I'm curious: What's my very worst fault?'

Troy: 'See how controlling you are?'

2) Some remarks on subject v. object homoerotics. I'm surprised at your sergeant's comment, 'You're not queer unless you're the one taking it'. I'm doubtful that, in 1996, a US NCO would dare make such a declaration.

Have you read George Chauncey's *Gay New York*? I ignored it for a long time (he ignored a letter I wrote him), but really it's very good. He builds on his earlier essay 'Christian Brotherhood or Sexual Perversion?' which dealt with the 1919 witch-hunt in Newport, Rhode Island. The Navy recruited sailors to get blown by and fuck 'queers', 'fairies' and 'pogues', who were defined strictly by their 'passive' roles and effeminate behaviour. Fresh in port, sailors used to hunt out queens and pay them for sex. According to Chauncey, all that changed as middle-class men began to feel increasingly threatened by their more butch working-class counterparts:

72

The glorification of the prize-fighter and the working man bespoke the ambivalence of middle-class men about their own gender status, for it suggested that they, too, regarded such men as more manly than themselves – more physical, less civilized, less effeminate.'

The insistence on exclusive heterosexuality emerged in part ... in response to the crisis in middle-class masculinity precipitated by the manly comportment of working-class men and the subversion of manly ideals and sexualization of male social relations by the fairy ... Middle-class men increasingly conceived of their sexuality – their heterosexuality, or exclusive desire for women – as one of the hallmarks of a real man. It was as if they had decided that no matter how much their gender comportment might be challenged as unmanly, they were normal men because they were heterosexual.

Some of my 1990s interviewees do cite instances of straight men who excuse their sexual contacts with other men as your sergeant did, but always only as a last-ditch rationalization after the event. Alex's Marines made their concession that it wouldn't be 'gay' for a man to get sucked by a queer contingent on the queer getting bashed afterwards.

As for your wondering whether your experience with straight men wanting to get fucked has something to do with your size and build, well, I can only answer with my own anecdotes, but: every straight boy – and every Marine – I've bedded has intimated this same wish, and just about all of them were meatier than me. (Tonight I took the latest confession of Phillip, a 5-foot-4 civilian Filipino, who last night reluctantly obliged a straight assless sailor bottom he picked up when the two of us, as a farewell outing, hit Club Metro at 32nd Street Naval Station.) It may be, as Troy contends, that I habitually jockey for control. But usually I want to suck, not fuck, my straight-boy conquests. (I know that from your point of view this may seem a criminal waste.) There may be something to Captain Eric's contention that it is the straight boys who expect that we will want to fuck them.

3) Why, if I had to live through this San Diego summer again, I would probably be driven to murder David Lloyd.

I am envious of, and genuinely excited about, your enlistment in the Territorial Army. Of course I'm eager to hear more of your observations on the perversities of modern British military life. But I am hoping most of all that you will make a new friend or two.

I'm frankly impressed by your gall. Though I guess your photo doesn't appear on your books or accompanying your articles, and there is probably security in there being more Simpsons than Zeelands ... For my part, in my mid-twenties I fantasized about joining the Army – as a chaplain. In retrospect, I think the best US service branch for me would have been the geeky but to my mind still somehow romantic Navy. In between books, I sometimes dream at night of being among sailors in the hold of some ship.

Of course the hold is usually one giant locker-room, and the sailors are mostly in underwear (always baggy white Navy-issue, never Calvin's).

Sadly, goodbye to San Diego means goodbye to Marines, though wherever there are sailors, there are always at least a few jarheads. And it's a short ferry ride across Puget Sound to rugged, working-class Bremerton, where – who knows? – maybe I'll make a new friend or two myself.

Yours,

Steve

Do You Shave Your Chest?

London, 14 October 1996

Dear Steve,

I look forward to hearing your reasons why David Lloyd must die. Although I already have my own reasons. That this smelly old man spends his time photographing naked Marines who ask things like 'Do you want me to get hard for you?' and 'Shall I spread those cheeks or just clench them?' seems to me perfect cause to terminate his life with extreme prejudice.

Something I'm rather better equipped to do now than when I last wrote. Since my last letter I've spent a fortnight training with the Territorial Army in Northumberland on their summer camp. It was hell. In bed at 12. Up at 5 a.m. for PT with a sadist de Sade himself would have disowned and then miles of tabbing in full kit.

I loved it all, of course. Even the forty-year-old ex-regular corporal in our billet who snored like an artillery barrage. Just as you began to get accustomed to the unearthly noise and nod off in your bunk, surrendering to the fatigue of the long, *long* day, he'd begin shouting in his sleep. Then, in case you got used to that, he'd start sleepwalking and opening lockers and doors next to your bed, mumbling away. If this didn't keep you awake, he'd deploy his *coup de grâce*: go back to bed and start snoring like the end of the world again, this time getting so turned on by his own snoring that he'd start to *have sex in his sleep*: groaning and grunting and chuckling in an unmistakably obscene way.

Weirdly, nobody mentioned anything about it the day after; and it happened *every night*. Maybe it was another, oddly poignant example of *esprit de corps* (even though this corporal was unpopular – which may have been the cause of his nocturnal habits rather than the effect). Maybe it was just another example of 'boy, was I drunk last night'.

Not that it bothered me in the least. I was too busy being completely bowled over by the friendliness and kindness of the other squaddies: lending me expensive kit that I hadn't even asked for and *giving me food* (which, after his boots is a squaddie's most prized possession). Truly, it was heart-warming. They seemed particularly interested in my size. My nicknames were: 'Dolph' (Lundgren), 'Big Man', 'Bart' (Simpson) and 'Swede' (some meathead character in a Clint Eastwood US Marine movie called *Heartbreak Ridge*, apparently). I think that some of these nicknames might have had something to do with the fact that since I saw you in SD, I've gone back to a flat-top haircut. Something which provoked an odd, drunken encounter with one lad. Late one night after a few too many jars down the NAAFI (where I had been called upon to sing, a cappella, 'Suspicious Minds' standing on a chair), he kicked off by telling me, 'I know your secret...'

'You do?' I said, my palms beginning to moisten.

'Yeah. Don't worry, I won't tell anyone.'

'Oh, right. Cheers.' *Bet he wants a blow job now.*

'Yeah,' he added. 'Best that they don't know that you were in the US Marines – otherwise they'd take the piss out of you.'

When I tried to correct him, he interrupted me, saying, 'Look, I understand, Mark; if you told me about it you'd have to kill me.' As with the cacophonous corporal, sometimes it's best to let people's dreams alone even when they seem to involve you in an unconsensual way. After that there was a special bond of trust between us, based on our 'shared se-cret'. Meanwhile, the SF (which stands for 'Sustained Fire' i.e. machine-gun – not 'San Francisco') Platoon seemed very keen to have me: 'A big, good-looking guy like yourself is just what we're looking for,' the good-natured SF platoon sergeant told me.

To be honest, I think that the lads were even a little friend-lier towards me than towards most recruits – simply because I happened to look the part, when most of the lads didn't. Of course, most of them *were* the part, whereas I *wasn't*. But again, sometimes you have to recognize that what people invest in you is far more important than what you actually *are*. And do your best to live up to it. It's a question of good manners.

I didn't really find myself taking advantage of my position as a wolf – or skunk – in the hen-house. Partly this was because I was too tired and rushed off my feet even to sum-mon the blood for an erection, and partly because, even though I liked most of them a lot, *I didn't fancy any of them.*

OK, OK, a couple of ex-regulars in their early twenties were, it's true, very cute: Chris, dark-haired, blue-eyed, Irish, freckles, shy smile; Duncan, fair-haired, blue-eyed, Manx, shy smile and broken nose (a bit of a boxer). And it's also true that somehow it happened that one of them slept above me and the other in the bed beside me ... But I didn't find myself entertaining lewd thoughts about them. Honest. And besides, I wasn't the only one that had noticed how cute they were. Duncan's official nickname was 'Gorgeous'.

By the end of the week I was so over-exposed to men and so into the sublimated camaraderie stuff that I think I almost forgot how to be homo. One of the peculiar, and most de-eroticizing things I noticed about men during my time in Northumberland was that if it's the case that women who spend too long together end up menstruating in synch, men who spend too long together end up farting in synch – and not being able to tell their own from someone else's. I don't know, but this may also have something to do with the Army's habit of serving such colonic nutrients as cabbage, cauliflower, sprouts, baked beans and fried egg on one day. Perhaps there never was any such thing as bromide in the tea – perhaps the army's strategy was to put you off your buddy's bottom by feeding you food that would make it too stinky to bear thinking about.

The spectre of de-sublimation was invoked once or twice – but not, ironically, at my instigation. On one occasion, sleep-ing in the field (and having to get up every couple of hours for stag duty) I was getting into a sleeping-bag next to one especially friendly and helpful lad called Gibbsy (the same Gibbsy who had tried to recruit me for the GPMG Platoon on my first day). 'Now, no funny stuff, mind,' he said. 'I'm too tired.' I laughed and said that anyway I had a headache.

McDevitt, a diminutive Glaswegian corporal I'd first en-countered on the recruit selection weekend a few weeks pre-viously, was on camp. A plumber in civvie street, he was great NCO who was capable of being just as amusing as he was scary (and who especially liked to rib me). 'Big Man!'

this scrappy jock shouted across to me at breakfast one day when he spotted me. 'Yool be no doubt pleased to knoo I'll be teaching yoos peeps for Battle Drills this week.' Battle Drills turned out to include how to search dead bodies (i.e. people we'd killed taking a position). While the other stuff had been quite fun, and quite obviously *playing* at being soldiers, this stage of the proceedings was beginning to get a bit too real for me.

A literally fatal identification with the enemy had began to form in my mind on a wind- and rain-swept Northumberland hillside during a lesson on how to search dead bodies given by the irrepressible corporal, with me on my back in the role of the corpse:

'*The grenadier will have emptied a magazine into the fooker and bayoneted him a few times for good measure,*' he boomed above the wind, as the rain pelted on my upturned face, filling my eye-sockets with water. '*He's killed some of yoos mates and made yoos run up that fookin hill, so there won't be much left of him.*'

Then, without so much as a please or thank you, he grabbed my balls. Hard. I yelped and sat up, not knowing whether to laugh or punch his lights out.

'*Now,*' announced Corporal McDevitt to my assembled comrades who were pissing themselves laughing, '*it dinnae matter how big he is – he's only gonna keep quiet when yoos doo that if he's deed, a yoonuch or a pouf – in which case he'll quite like it!*' More laughter.

'Yoos dinnae think I'd doo that, did yoos, Big Man?' the little bastard said, turning to me, grinning. 'Gave yoos quite a surprise, dinnae?'

'That you did, Corp.' That you did.

*

Back in London, I've handed in my resignation. Though the Army doesn't know it, I originally joined after being commissioned to write an article. Of course, this was just a pretext. However, the magazine that commissioned the piece is making noises, and anyway I need my thirty pieces of silver. Three months down the line, I have to face up to my real status as homosocial tourist. Much as I admire this world and envy it (no doubt through the rose-tinted subjectivity of lack), I can't ever really be a permanent part of it. My aversion to learning how to kill was a symptom of that – this was after all the 'mission' or point which made all the rest possible.

But really, the camaraderie, sense of belonging and, yes, 'love' I experienced even amongst these weekend warriors was astounding. *Dumbfounding.*

*

Anti-Gay has been published here and has got up a few large, snotty noses. Have you received your copy yet?

I hope that *The Masculine Marine* launch is a hoot. I hope also that Seattle has proved to be all that you imagined it was. Of course, it can't be, but there's still hoping.

Regarding my 'audacity' in joining the Territorials – well, sadly, my infamy is restricted to the catamitical *demi-monde* (and, hand on my heart, I can't say that I met anyone during my time 'in' who I thought was 'gay' – *because of* rather than in spite of the flirting). The nearest I came to being 'outed' during my time in the Territorials was when I had my medical. The MO was listening to my chest with a stethoscope when she remarked: 'Do you shave your chest?'

'Err, yes,' I replied, adding rather too hastily: 'All the blokes at my gym do.'

'I see,' said the MO, unconvinced. 'Quite a few of the chaps I see go to the gym, and none of them shave their chests.'

'Ah, well,' I sputtered, 'it depends what gym you go to.'

'I suppose it does,' she replied dubiously. 'So why does anyone shave their chest?' she probed.

'Because it shows off muscle definition better?' I said, my voice rising uncertainly at the end, turning an answer into a dead-give-away question.

'Oh, *I see*,' she said, making that barely audible 'tut' noise that women make when despairing at the strange-but-charming antics of men, and I realized that I was in the clear.

Best,

Mark

PS I should mention that on the Selection Weekend I bud-
    died up with a stocky ex-Irish regular. Whenever I was
    thirsty, sweating after the log and stretcher runs, his
    water bottle appeared at my mouth. Whenever I was
    flagging beneath my Bergen, he offered me gentle en-
    couraging words. When I hesitated on the dizzyingly
    altitudinous assault course, he held out his steadying,
    square hand.

    His name? *Private Morrissey.*

Bonfire of the Vanity Partitions

Seattle, October 21, 1996

Dear Mark,

Two weeks after the most exhausting move of my life (three days and 1,300 miles – times two, the second time in the cab of a sluggish rental truck with two militantly unhappy felines, one of them with gingivitis breath) finds me feeling as though I've just awakened from a four-year sleep. The Pacific Northwest! How could it be anything less than what I hoped for? The window from Alex's and my one-bedroom apartment affords an inspiring view of ferry boats and white-caps on cold, choppy Elliott Bay ... even if you really need binoculars to see past the rather more conspicuous Seafirst Bank automatic teller machines directly adjacent. It's only a ten-minute climb to the beautifully landscaped Kinnear Park, from which you can gape in astonishment at the snowcapped majesty of the Olympic Mountains and Mount Rainier ... on those infrequent days when they are not hidden by black clouds. Alex zips along on the monorail to the (temp) job he found already his first week here ... though except for this anomalous World's Fair leftover, Seattle has only a rudimen-tary bus system, having consistently voted down commuter rail ballot initiatives. Polite Seattleites almost never jay-walk and seem to be forever apologizing for shortcomings that in San Diego would go unremarked. But it remains to be seen what they're like when, or if, you get to know them: Courtney Love told *Newsweek*: 'If you move to Seattle, be sure to bring your friends, otherwise you won't survive long en-ough to make any.'

Amazingly, my moody ex-Marine and I are still buddies, our friendship not unfrayed but less so, relatively, than the wallpaper in the Best Western motel in Roseburg, Oregon, subsequent to the attentions of our vandal undeclawed tortie lynx-point, Samantha, whom we smuggled in and, more an-xiously, out. Alex fumed it was the most white trash he'd felt since his escape from Wisconsin five years ago. (Great TV the night before: a documentary on Mount St Helens, and the best-ever *Ren and Stimpy* episode, the one with the Kodiak marmoset. 'What's Canada's greatest natural resource?' 'Dirt!')

Seattle has America's best beer. Beer is more expensive than in California, too. And to buy liquor you have to go to a Soviet-type state-run store that closes at 8 p.m. Come to think of it, just about everything is more expensive here than in San Diego. A lot more people smoke. Obesity is rampant. And traffic is hell – allegedly because of the influx of Californians, for whom the natives (or earlier transplants) reserve a contempt verging on xenophobia (we were quick to change our documents).

But: I didn't want to live in a GAP ad any more, right? And I am warming to the special charms of the region.

I already told you on the phone how our search for the fabled lumberjacks, stevedores and fishermen of Bellingham turned out: we found them and they were all lesbians. As for Bremerton, I went there alone on Friday.

The ride across the Sound was beautiful and cheap: two hours' round trip for $3.50. To get to Bremerton you can take either a car ferry or a passenger ferry. I ended up on one of the smaller boats. Upon boarding I made the mistake of seeking out the restroom, which turned out to be a tiny unisex closet. I felt like I was trapped inside a box  being violently shaken. Queasily I dashed through the hold packed with bored commuters topside to where a few smoking teenagers braved astonishingly severe winds prone on plastic benches wriggling like seals.

American sailor, early 1960s

Friday evening was probably the worst possible time to hunt for Naval Station Puget Sound sailors, most of whom must have hastened in the opposite direction. But in this sanitized, vanity-partition age (in which I discovered that the fabled Green Apple Adult Cinema of Bellingham has been converted into a chic Southwestern eatery, in the wake of a town ordinance outlawing video booth masturbation) it was a comfort to find the town's three sleazy arcades still in business.

If eerily empty.

I cast a suspicious eye on a neighbouring establishment advertising itself as a 'techno cyber café', but relaxed with a patronizing smile when I saw they had but one computer and a menu limited to microwaveable frozen hot dogs and pizzaburgers. As of late 1996 this rough little Navy port is still largely unyuppified: no $4 microbrews or soy milk lattes in sight. This pleased me, even if as a consumer I of course prefer craft beers and vegan espresso beverages.

It seemed too early to turn back, so I loitered where I could, stopping at the adjacent Humane Society Thrift Shop and buying a volume by Henry Miller I will probably never read . . . for thirteen cents.

Back in one of the arcades I was suddenly face to face with two handsome young men. My heart sank as their facial expressions betrayed *who they were*. Still, reluctant to concede defeat, and remembering the satisfyingly efficient attention I'd received four years previous on an excursion to the same town with my attention-deficient boyfriend Troy, I thought I might leave my door ajar and pretend to be trade. I mean, shouldn't I try to branch out?

Bad idea. I was disappointed at which of the two came barging in. But I was horrified when the fellow started to fully disrobe and mistakenly imagined I would enjoy his tongue in my ear. When, after seconds that felt like lifetimes, he at last caught on that I would not respond in kind, indeed could not respond at all, he wiggled back into his clothes and with a tragic, despondent air breathed: 'Was this . . . your first time?' 'Well . . .' I answered. Staring knowingly into my eyes he pleaded, 'Are you in the military?' 'Yeah,' I replied, out of charity. 'Which branch?' he demanded. 'I gotta go,' I muttered. This much at least honestly.

The winds had died down when I made the return trip, and the full moon on the water with the Seattle skyline before me looked like a postcard. This was the much larger auto ferry. A couple times I followed drunken sailors into the head . . . On my second or third call I encountered a post-grunge type who I thought might possibly – beneath his goatee and super-long sideburns – be handsome. He looked honestly scared, which charmed me; he darted surreptitious glances, and at last flashed his erection. But then I noticed that he wore a ball cap with a goddamned little rainbow squiggly thing. My resolution to never again attempt any kind of sex with a gay man was too fresh to violate. Besides, someone walked in and he panicked.

Disembarking I caught the eye of a sailor, one of those I had tried to ogle in the head but who – seemingly picking up on my intent – evaded me. Now he kept stealing glances back, to see if I was looking, and setting little traps for me (ducking into the ferry terminal McDonald's), to see if I would follow. I did, of course, but finally grew bored with the game. Like you, I need a little more invitation and encouragement.

I mean, there are times when I don't like myself. But not because I *like men*.

*

I was very glad to receive *Anti-Gay* yesterday. I'm anxious to hear all the gory details on the 'shitstorm' you've caused, and hope you stir up some trouble Stateside, too.

I read 'Gay Dream Believer' with excitement, and when Alex came home, I told him that I wanted to read it to him. I brought the book along with us, first, to an International District restaurant, where two men were seated at an adjacent table. *Anti-Gay* was lying face-up on ours. Before we finished eating, the two men lit cigarettes; we made grumbling noises. When they left, the waiter came up and, laughing, said, 'I think your book scared them.' I thought this was unnervingly funny, but Alex was just unnerved. When we stopped at Linda's (a non-gay bar, and the place where Kurt Cobain was last seen alive) for a pint of Moss Bay Ale, he squirmed when I started to read to him, and afterwards demanded that I turn the book face-down on the table. When I refused, he stormed out of the room.

Back at home, he offered the excuse that he was missing his friends in San Diego – the Aids-ravaged, meth-addicted, rainbow-flag-waving bar queens he said he wanted to move up here to escape.

Alex was nastier Wednesday night, the eve of my first-ever Pacific NW reading.

The week started off dismally. Monday, I rode back over to Bremerton – to cruise, of course, but also to try and get a decent haircut.

All the barber shops there are closed on Monday.

Bremerton has a spooky *Twin Peaks* quality about it: dark waters, looming firs, industrial bleakness, and a cheerful 50s normalcy. Returning to the adult book stores (rustic, dark, wood-panelled old theatres, with scary mountain man types behind the counters), I did see one agreeably rough-looking obvious sailor . . . leaving as I arrived.

On the ferry ride back to Seattle I followed four young Marines into the head. The least attractive of the group shot me a disgusted look and muttered something. As I had barely even glanced at him, and in fact saw nothing, I didn't think much of the incident. But just before docking in Seattle I happened to be standing at the trough again when the four returned. This time he loudly commented to his buddies, 'That guy there's a MEATGAZER.'

I exited the head and sought out the aft viewing deck. From there I could see the Marines circling around as if looking for somebody. I was almost as amused as worried (one Marine who doesn't like to be looked at?). This, by the way, was the first time, in all my years of meatgazing, that I have ever been so admonished.

Two days later, the night before my reading, I came down with a bad sore throat. Alex chose the same night, just after midnight, to lurch into his ugliest mood swing of this entire year. I demanded that we again talk it out, threatened that otherwise I wouldn't let him go to bed. With a wicked smile he intoned, 'You're the one who'll suffer. I can ruin your reading.'

But the next day he returned from work with a card and a little present. And the reading did not go badly. The good-sized crowd included the usual letches, as Alex calls them, but also as many active-duty military as in San Diego . . . representing every branch but the Marine Corps. The men (there was one woman present but, Faludi and Butler blurbs notwithstanding, she walked out soon after I started) were friendly, asked good questions afterwards, and a lot of them bought multiple books.

So, I love Seattle. The next day I found time to hit the tearoom at the University of Washington. After an unpromising start I met up with the most studly apparent-civilian (but who knows; there is a lot of ROTC there) piece of trade I have ever risked making a bad sore throat worse for. Eighteen or nineteen and the kind of face, body and frat-boy jock demeanour that would have David Lloyd whimpering. I was whimpering. I'd almost forgotten just how hard (everywhere I touched), and almost insanely horny a guy can be.

Afterwards, he patted me on the back.

Yours,

Steve

City of Lost Angels

London, 1 January 1997

Dear Steve,

Another 'holiday season' over. Bah, humbug.

This year I spent Xmas with my parents in York. At home with my Mum and Dad for Xmas at thirty-one. It really gives you a feeling of achievement, that does.

My mood wasn't improved by the persistent, insistent memory that the last couple of Xmases were spent in the sunny Canaries with Jason. I also can't help thinking that maybe there's some truth to the 'heterosexist' propaganda: that Xmas, in its stranded boredom, is when you find out what kind of life you're really living and what kind of attachments you really have.

Unlike most dysfunctionals, I can't even blame my parents for an unhappy holiday season. I, along with my brother (six years younger) and sister (three years older) were spoilt rotten – waited on hand and foot and force-fed protein, double cream and chocolate three times a day. Nor can I really blame York. In my travels, I haven't found many places as nice as this pretty town with its medieval walls, cobbled streets, gothic Minster and friendly farm boys. As 'Eboracum' it was the Northernmost outpost of the Roman empire. The first Christian emperor, Constantine, was proclaimed Emperor here by his Northern Legions. But then, I suppose all towns have something in their past to live down.

However, York isn't very far from a famous landmark left by a much cooler, and earlier, Emperor dude, Hadrian, who based himself in Eboracum for a while. It's a wall built from coast to coast about 100 miles north of the city to keep the Scots out (in those days they didn't shave and rarely washed). As you may know, apart from his wall Hadrian, a Hellenist and a successful general popular with the army, was famous for his open love-affair with a blond Greek boy called Antinous whose beauty was, as they say, legendary.

After the young man died prematurely (or perhaps just in time?) in a boating accident on the Nile, Hadrian proved his love and its virile victory over death in the traditional manner of the ancient world: he had Antinous declared a god and statues in his naked image erected all over the empire. Judging by those that survive, Hadrian had excellent taste, especially in the pert buttocks department. Hadrian's palate for posteriors must have been shared by others besides myself because pretty soon there was a fully-fledged Antinous cult going across the Roman empire with thousands offering sacrifices to those (literally) marble moons. Some historians argue that it was the prevalence of this cult which helped to 'shape' Roman Christianity's pronounced antipathy to homo-erotics: after all, their graven naked man wasn't as sexy as Antinous, even if it was kinkier. Thus, horny Hadrian starts a global botty cult, and killjoy Constantine puts an end to it (introducing compulsory castration for sodomites on the Roman National Health).

So, you see, York – where both emperors lived for a while – is the most historically significant place you could wish to grow up an arse-bandit. Even without taking into account the blond/red-haired, blue-eyed, fine-featured, large-handed genetic legacy of the Vikings – another bunch of martial men to base themselves here ('Yorvik' was the capital of Viking Britain).

After the Vikings were pushed back into the North Sea by the Anglo-Saxons, churchy people from Rome became very fond of flaunting themselves and their habits in these parts. It was the first Christian missionaries to Britain that founded my school, St Peter's, together with York Minister, in the seventh century, to ram their credos down the throats of the local lads. St Peter's provided the Holy Roman Emperor Charlemagne with a tutor by the name of Alcuin (who wrote love poems to a young man), and the Tower of London with a terrorist by the name of Guido Fawkes. Guy was a good Catholic boy who tried and failed in the seventeenth century to blow up the anti-Catholic Houses of Parliament and King Charles and whose capture, torture, hanging, drawing, quartering and burning (like a Hollywood movie, the State in those days had to kill the bad guys over and over again) is commemorated every year across the country by the ritual incineration of a 'Guy' effigy on a bonfire and the release of fireworks. It speaks volumes of the difference between us Brits and you, our North American 'cousins', that in the US fireworks are let off to commemorate the explosive struggle by the Colonies to rid themselves of a tyrannical ruler; while in Britain we let them off to commemorate the day that a proto-Republican's gunpowder *didn't* go off and he was hoisted by his giblets instead. (At St Peter's, even though it had long since turned Protestant, we were still not allowed to put a Guy on our bonfire on the fifth of November: it was considered 'bad form' to burn an old boy.)

Anyway, the most interesting thing about the Christian missionaries was that they were inspired to visit Britain in general and York in particular because the striking appearance of the slaves from this region caused great interest in Rome. The Pope was reputed to have demanded to know who these blond, blue-eyed men with fine features and large hands were. 'Anglos, sire,' came the response. 'Not anglos, but angels!' pronounced the pontiff. It's probably an apocryphal story, but I'm ready to believe it.

So, you see, there really is no excuse for being maudlin in York, even over Xmas. I blame my mood on my November trip to another City of Angels – albeit lost ones.

*

The best thing about LA is the view as you fly in. And leave. The city, so flat and geometric and endless, looks like a Martian settlement, which of course, it is. Or a vast mysterious circuit-board for some kind of super-dooper Nintendo game, especially at night when the lights twinkle and the thousands of moving car headlights on the freeways appear like those tacky electrical conduits out of *Buck Rogers* conveying obscure alien energy. Your heart races, you breathe a bit too fast as you consider that LA is one great big special effect full of weird and wonderful otherworldly possibilities.

And then you land.

Funnily enough, it's the sun that spoils it all. The sun which is the whole point of LA. It isn't earthquakes or subsidence that force architects to keep most buildings under two storeys high but the enormous weight of the *sunshine*, beating down on them from above. LA is a city of pastel-coloured straw-and-cement dough flattened out into the desert in the south and east and up to the edge of the sea in the west and the hills in the north by a sun that has rolled up its sleeves and spat in its hands.

I don't know what happened to me since 1990, when I spent six months in SoCal, and for the most part enjoyed the relentless sunshine and bleached culture. I suppose I've just got old. When you're twenty-five and from a country with too much history, too much society, too much culture, and too much mildew, SoCal's very blankness and sterility is exciting, *motivating.* The fact that you don't know what you want to do with your life becomes in this strange desert land a positive virtue. California's attraction isn't that you discover who you are so much as forget who you're supposed to be.

In SoCal most people's idea of what is 'British' is so meagre and cartoonish that you don't really have any expectations to live up or down to, beyond a 'really cool' accent. But going back there at thirty-one is very different. I can't afford to forget who I am any more; there isn't enough time left to remember again. The blankness and bleachedness no longer excites me, it just appals and terrifies me.

After a week in LA, interviewing what's left of Devo and a has-been actress for *Details,* I fled South three hours for small-town San Diego which, as you know, I used to profess a liking for in contrast to sprawling LA. Not any more. Although I *was* struck again by how uniquely beautiful San Diego can be. The Santa Ana was blowing and the air was as clear as a dry Martini. The city appeared even greener than I remembered it – especially that almost tropical drive along that palm-tree-bordered highway – the 163 I think – which takes you downtown through a verdant gorge.

But everywhere I sensed my own atrophy transmitted back. All the people I knew from when I lived here six years ago seemed to either be disappeared, on the run, ill or on loser-street. Possibilities hardened into realities.

Except Ray, the 'straight arrow' exception to the flotsam–jetsam drifters that pass through SD, with his nine-to-five job for the City Council and his own home. But his life has hardened into something else. He seems to have found a long-term boyfriend and retreated into domestic boredom. I tried to be happy for him, really did, but these new circumstances seemed to exclude *me* – and Ray is one of the funniest guys to be around I know. Mind, who could blame Ray for being fed up with me? I stayed with him for *three months* back in 1990, and have 'dropped in' several times since, including five days with a mumbling moody Glaswegian in tow last year (who slept in Ray's bed one night Ray was out of town because our double mattress in the spare room was 'too small').

That last time I was in SoCal I met, of course, your fine self and Alex. Your relationship continues to intrigue me. Clearly you both seek some kind of continuity in your affections and relationships, but have directed your libido outwards into the world and away from each other. On the one hand, this appears healthier than the retreat represented by the monogamous, self-sufficient gay couple; but on the other, it also seems like a very old-fashioned male habit of separating love and sex in Madonna/Whore fashion. To paraphrase Dirty Siggy: men desire what they do not love and love what they do not desire.

I wonder whether you provide Alex with unconditional love (i.e. maternal love), like the person that puts the saucer of milk out for the stray, slaggy tabby, and how much he is actually looking for conditional (i.e. paternal love), like the serious boy who joins the Marines. Like most of us, he's probably looking for both. And resenting you for not providing it when you don't and also when you do. I hope things set-tle down a bit for you in your new

USMC drill instructor and recruit, shopping

home. I think your move was a brave adventure. I salute you.

When I drove down to SD on Friday night, I made the inevitable detour through Oceanside and I immediately saw several jarheads to die for – after seeing not one attractive male the whole week I was in LA. But, after cruising in my car around the block near the pier halfheartedly a couple of times, instead of pulling over and stepping out to accost these young bucks, I stepped on the accelerator and fast-forwarded to San Diego. Why? Because they looked so young and fresh and clean and made me feel so ... *not*. I saw myself reflected in the Marine-boys' eyes as a predatory old queen. And flinched. But there was another reason I drove on, one even more depressing. As you know only too well, Steve, the really sad thing is that I don't just want to shag these boys, *I want to be their best buddy too.*

In SD I headed for the thin consolations of Hillcrest. In a sports-type bar, I caught a bloke with a high 'n' tight haircut staring at me admiringly as I recklessly downed two Buds one after the other without pause for breath. Feeling drunk already, I walked up to a young sailor from Georgia who was standing against a wall in his dress uniform. He claimed that he was a submariner and he'd been on Honor Guard duty for some officer retiring and had come straight over to the bars.

'Isn't it a bit of a risk?' I asked.

'Oh, I sup-pose so,' he agreed in his slow-running white-gravy accent. 'But I done it sev-er-al times be-fore and no-thing's come of it.'

'Except a lot of attention,' I said.

'Yeah, I sup-pose you could say that,' he admitted, grinning cheekily. His uniform certainly appeared convincing (decorated with submariner badges), and he certainly seemed to know how to wear it. As I'm sure you know infinitely better than me, Steve, you can usually spot a civilian queen dressed up in military gear a mile off – because only a civilian queen would wear military gear in a gay bar. All this is moot, however, since he suddenly announced to me: 'I've just been in-formed that Naval Intelligence are op-er-a-ting here so I have to leave.'

'Oh, *right*,' I said. 'Bye.' It wasn't the fact that he didn't fancy me that stopped us getting it on, you see, but the *United States Navy*. Another reason why wearing a uniform to a gay bar is good tactics.

The lad had barely been gone five minutes when the barman tapped me on the shoulder and shoved a beer into my hands – 'It's from the guy at the end of the bar,' he said, pointing to the maybe-jarhead I'd seen earlier, who lifted his bottle to me and winked slyly. I couldn't resist this gesture of gallantry and went over to thank him for the beer.

Brick – *great* name – claimed to be from Indiana and worked as a USMC recruiter in Chicago. He was in SD for the Veteran's Day holiday, he said. Again, I didn't really believe what he was telling me, but the Budweiser in me decided not to *disbelieve* it either. Besides, he had a Devil Dog tattoo, had 'the talk' down to a tee, had an extremely nice ass and asked me three times in hushed, slurring tones, '*Are you a top?*'

If Brick wasn't the real McCoy, who cared? (Well, I did, as you'll see.) So I went back with him to his hotel, which was a very swish one on Coronado Island. In fact, it was so swish that we had to be driven to his *villa* in a *golf cart*. He had a despot-sized bed, *en suite* bathroom with Olympic-sized jacuzzi. Hmmm, how much does a recruiter in the USMC make? Are they on some kind of *commission?* We did the dirty deed: he lay on his stomach grunting whilst I fucked his large but shapely, smooth butt. By this stage, I wasn't complaining about the holes in his story. Nor was he complaining, being the good Marine that he was or wanted me to think he was. Whatever I said, he barked: '*Sir, Yessir!*' Whatever I did, he barked: '*Sir, Thankyousir!*' In my drunken stupor I thought, 'This is so absurd – but I could get used to it...'

Come dawn, I woke up with a head that was too woozy to tell the difference between a hangover and regrets. He had to be at an early appointment in town and drove queasy me back to Hillcrest in his 'rental' car – a convertible Jaguar with car-phone. Driving across the orgasmic, concrete arch of Coronado Bridge, which seems to me to fly up and away from the island and the Naval Base like a freeze-framed ejaculation, my own bridge of suspended disbelief began groaning and collapsing. It was finally, irresistibly, dawning on me that I had spent the night with a drug dealer probably, a chartered accountant possibly, but most definitely *not* a Marine.

*

I was recently asked by a French magazine to come up with three New Year resolutions and wishes. My three wishes were: 'I) The English learn how to kiss, 2) the Germans forget how to kiss, and 3) the French learn how to floss.' My New Year resolutions: 'I intend to learn to I) criticize less, 2) love more. And 3) find a new job.'

Thanks for forwarding the US clippings of *Anti-Gay* reviews. I'm so upset that down-market International Male catalogue spin-off *Genre* didn't like it – dismissing *AG* as 'irresponsible' and 'leftist'. It makes a nice companion piece to the tautologous British reviewer for *City Life* who described me as 'a compassionless Margaret Thatcher'. The *Bay Area Reporter* I don't know very much about, except that one of its reviewers – someone I've never heard of by the name of Dan Harris – is straining a bit too hard to try and make a splash by hysterically attacking a book called *Anti-Gay* for not being, well, *gay* enough. Somebody should tell him that no one ever made a splash writing for such magazines – all they are capable of providing is a muted plopping sound promptly followed by a flushing noise.

I recently had an encounter at an *Attitude* party with the editor of one of the free gay bar rags here. That week it had greeted the publication of *AG* with the cover-line: '*Anti-Gay*: What's it all about?' An editorial on the first page frantically denounced the book and 'gay journos who are paid top dollar by the straight press to piss on gay men from a great height'. Inside was a 'How to spot an "anti-gay"' centre-spread which wittily tried to turn criticism of the gay identity into ... an identity. Clearly *Anti-Gay* had hit the mark, then.

Mr Gay Rag came rushing over, accompanied by his faithful Assistant, Igor, who kept muttering, 'Yeah, wot he said!' every time his boss opened his mouth. The first time he did was to ask fervently and quite seriously: '*What's the matter with liking Kylie Minogue, then???*'

'Ah well,' I explained, smiling thinly but broadly as you do automatically when talking to a complete idiot, 'If you read the book, I think you'll find it's asking: What's the matter with *not* liking Kylie Minogue?'

'Well,' he snorted, 'at least *I'm* not paid *top dollar* to *piss* on gay men from a *great height!*'

'If I wanted to be paid top dollar for pissing on gay men from a great height,' I replied evenly, 'I'd have an ad with a picture of my cock and my phone number underneath it in the back of your paper.'

He wouldn't take a hint, so I eventually had to tell him, 'Look, piss off, will you? *I'm not interested.*'

A huge gay disco here – Europe's largest, they say – called 'G.A.Y.' (standing for, I kid you not: 'Good As You') which has queues round the block of hairdressers and shopgirls itching to worship at the altar of Kylie has changed its posters so that they read 'Not *Anti-Gay*, but PROUD to be Gay!' You really know you've arrived when you influence the wording of disco-flyers.

It's just a shame that most of the punters can't read.

Best,

Mark

PS   I think you should call your novel *A Meatgazer's Diary*.

A Meatgazer's Christmas

Seattle, February 1, 1997

Dear Mark,

You couldn't know the chill I'd feel reading 'Xmas is when you find out what kind of life you're really living and what kind of attachments you really have' . . .

It's been five years since I spent Christmas with my parents. Actually, they no longer celebrate Christmas the way they used to anyway. Now, immediately after Thanksgiving my grandparents, in accordance with Michigan law, migrate to Florida. To accommodate them, my family observes a hybrid 'Thanks-mas.' This amuses me. At the Church of the Open Door, which I was forced to attend until I was seventeen (and still have nightmares of being forced to attend), there was always a lot of talk about Xmas 'taking the Christ out of Christmas'. (I'm eager to hear more about your family and life growing up in York. In a future letter I'll tell you a little about the town where I come from, a place with almost no history at all).

I have an uncle who lives in eastern Washington. He's twelve years older than me. Growing up I marvelled at his quick costume changes: college radical, soldier, fundamentalist preacher, alcoholic, nerdy junior high school band director; later, fat man poodle-owner, teacher's union arbitrator, cop, body-builder, reformed alcoholic, mid-life crisis wife-ditcher; now, soon to be half owner of hubby–wife bed and breakfast in Hawaii. He came up here in early December and took Alex and me out to an overpriced Northwest cuisine eatery (in the company of one of his co-workers, a young man from San Francisco who made scathing remarks about 'breeders'). Alex liked my uncle because of the fact that none of Alex's relatives are remotely middle-class. So he agreed to make the trek with me to eastern Washington for Christmas. I didn't really want to go, but my uncle was very insistent, and I do like him, and I was kind of curious to see my cousin Michelle. At my sister's wedding ten years ago she was a bubbly large-breasted teen cheerleader. More recently she's

96

written me bubbly letters in multicoloured girlish script with actual round dots on the 'i's. One was an 'I'm so scared you'll get Aids' letter. Perhaps my cranky response could have doubled as my contribution to *Anti-Gay* – I told her I wouldn't get Aids because so much of gay writing about Aids is boring and nauseating, and I wouldn't want to be tempted to contribute to it.

To get to eastern Washington you have to negotiate the Cascade mountains. Alex bought chains for his tires, and though the Christmas morning weather reports were ominous, we thought we could make it. Just as we were heading out the door, my uncle called, advising us against the trip. A good thing, too. BURIED THEN DROWNED, read the headline in the *Seattle Post-Intelligencer*. It was the heaviest snow in twenty years. There's no telling where we would have been stranded, or for how long. It was bad enough just being stuck in this ever-shrinking apartment with virtually everything in the neighbourhood shut down; cars, buses, even a cop car abandoned on the street outside. In the park up the street a homeless Vietnam Vet was buried alive when the hillside gave way. (Today I noticed a little American flag someone stuck in the mud there.) But through it all one valiant espresso stand remained open round the clock until the crisis had passed. (I should explain that in Seattle espresso drinks are not a trendy gay or yuppie thing, but as common as rolled tacos in San Diego. There are espresso stands in bait-and-tackle shops, grubby auto repair places, and in the parking lots of the bleakest industrial landscapes. Espresso is believed to stave off suicide stemming from SAD [Seasonal Affective Disorder].)

Christmas morning the storm had not yet hit. Since Alex and I were geared for a trip, I suggested we drive up to the Olympic Mountains. On each of the last three Christmases we drove to Mount Laguna in eastern San Diego county, where there was always enough slush at least on the ground to remind us of our happy childhoods in

Zeeland 'Bardot-ing' Alex, a.k.a. 'Baby Seal', Christmas Day

Wisconsin and Michigan. (Or, in Alex's case, not always so happy childhood. One Christmas morning his mom, having blown her savings on alcohol and drugs, informed the tykes that Santa was dead.)

On the cross-sound ferry I could not resist multiple extended forays to the super-trough in the men's' room. A Navy guy came in and, even though there was no one else there, stood pretty close by me. I wonder if he didn't want to impress me. Certainly he didn't feel a need to call me a meatgazer as though that were a bad thing, and when he left I couldn't help but think: Wouldn't it be nice to have someone (or -thing: I could get the jump on gay novelist Robert Rodi and call my book *Size Queen*) like that in my apartment instead of this moody, extortionist pus plug of a person (who could impress me if he wanted to. It wasn't me who instituted our whore/Madonna split). But of course I betrayed no hint of what I was thinking to Alex, and as we approached Mount Olympus – the white peaks resembling some cheesy old Yes album cover about to absorb us – everything seemed normal enough. Abruptly Alex announced that he was turning the car around. Of course I calmly demanded a reason (we had driven this far, this was our tradition, what was wrong with him?). He had no reason. Finally he explained that he resented my comment a day or so previous that he had done nothing the last two months but play Super-Nintendo. Alex's TV is next to the kitchen door. He said he knew I visited the kitchen more often than necessary purposely to disrupt his game. In fact, he was so sick of my presence that he couldn't stand being in the same car with me, or eating Christmas dinner with me – 'couldn't bear the thought that I exist'. He announced that he was moving out when the lease expires in March. Naturally I ordered him to drive to the mountain anyway, and he did, but by the time we got there I too had given up.

If I seem a little bored recounting this ... A cowbird's gotta do what a cowbird's gotta do. Perhaps the saddest thing is that the incident lacked any of the rich Tennessee Williams flavour of Alex's earlier work. (For example, the time he discovered that his car had been broken into while parked in front of my apartment. Missing were his green

suede jacket and car vacuum cleaner. He quite naturally concluded it must have been me who drove the screwdriver into
his trunk, and without explanation appeared at my door and
started gathering his belongings.) My main concern was that
Alex should grant me custody of his cat Samantha, which he
did (as we're still living together at the moment, the immediate difference is that now I get to pay all the cat bills). My
main annoyance was that my dinner on Christmas consisted
of a box of Wheat Thins. And the most depressing consideration now is that I soon will have to pay double rent.

By last week things had improved enough that we watched
two videos together. Inspired by your article on Jim Carrey,
he rented *Ace Ventura: Pet Detective*. Because he likes sci-fi
and has been listening to my old Bowie CDs (a welcome
change from the fag-bar music), I rented *The Man Who Fell
to Earth*. He pointed out a resemblance between Bowie's body
and mine (from someone else, somewhere else this could be
a compliment), and offered that were I to remove my contact
lenses and expose alien cat eyes it would come as a relief,
since he already knows I'm not human.

Which, do you suppose, contributes more to my writer's
stagefright: years of shame over meatgazing (you told me
before you thought it was good I could still feel shame –
when I was embarrassed over taping the Marines at the Area
51 enlisted club) or choosing to love someone who does such
a good job of making me feel undesirable?

I know it must sound like I'm looking for sympathy. Or
more abuse. But really I'm not even feeling sorry for myself.
Well, not that much. It's all so predictable. But if this
Christmas is the sum of my life ... One thing that does
disturb me is the echo of my last year with Troy, whose habit
it was to drive us to some spot of breathtaking natural splen-
dour only to refuse to leave the car once we got there; he
preferred to just sit and listen to hip-hop CDs, alone. (Oddly,
Troy and I split up at about the same point after our move
from California to a one-bedroom apartment in Washington.
Please tell me that I'm attracted to similarly damaged boys,
and not that I somehow make them this way.)

When Alex and I returned in silence to the apartment, the
blizzard had begun. I locked myself in my room and went to

work on my novel. His nasty behaviour had its benefits: I spent the ensuing stormy days escaping deeper and deeper into my writing, back to a happy time of walls and wilful isolation.

Over the last couple years I seem to have developed a fear of bridges. Walking over the canyon under First Avenue in San Diego, or, less often, on that same bridge in Balboa Park high over US 163 that so entranced you, I sometimes enjoyed pesky little panic attacks. This isn't exactly a fear of heights, for I found I could walk the paths on the cliff of Point Loma without anxiety. The trigger seems to be a lack of solid ground on both sides. Anyway, after the snow gave way to rain (*Blade Runner*, by the way, was not really filmed in a future-world LA, but in Seattle, where half of LA looks bound) I took a solitary walk to Ballard. This is a blue-collar part of town, formerly predominantly Scandinavian-American, which skirts the canal that connects saltwater Puget Sound to freshwater Lake Washington. Lots of Alaska fishing boats (and bowling alleys). There's a very long bridge over the canal there, with a drawbridge in the middle. I made it half-way over when I started to feel panicky. Looking over my shoulder, I decided that turning back would only make things worse. Just as I cleared the drawbridge the sirens went off and the lights started flashing. It was here that I came upon the idea of a prologue for *Diary of a Meatgazer*.

I've already written you about sex with my best friend from high school, GI Brent, in a cold hotel room where he only communicated by written notes. (How funny that I've gleaned my tiny smidgen of notice from the world by making tapes of military boys talking about sex.) That happened just after Christmas. Walking along the bridge in Ballard reminded me how every Christmas in the immediate post-Brent years I used to ride the Army train to West Berlin to wallow in isolation and gloom, listening on my Walkman to Nico and side two of 'Heroes' and 'Low', flirting with the MPs and taking pictures of the guards on the other side, but avoiding any spoken human contact. I made Christmas into my personal holiday of Brent. I think this is where *Meatgazer* has to start.

Do you think anyone will get the humour?

Now that Alex and I can hardly stand being in the same room with each other, it's hard for me to remember the intense sexual excitement he once inspired in me. Early on in our relationship he developed a boil on his thick meaty inner thigh. Alex invited me to examine the infection. It was a near dime-sized hole filled with a viscous amber 'plug', as he called it, that separated from the walls of the hole as he fingered it. And finger it he did, constantly, playing with and worrying it, doing his damnedest to make it fouler than it already was.

Today, I mailed an early draft of the first half of my book and an outline of the rest to someone whose opinion I'm interested in but not that interested. I think you should probably be one of the last to see it. That is, when most of it's written. Because if you didn't like it, I'd have a hard time finishing it. 'And what else have I got besides that smell?' – a John Cale line from his Ren-like diatribe on 'Leaving It Up To You'.

*

I relished reading *Anti-Gay*, and I thrilled to the Anti-Gay experience via the huge sheaf of angry reviews you sent me. Gosh. I am proud to know you, Mr Simpson. God save the queen and the fascist regime (in my best William S. Burroughs impersonation).

In my last letter I promised more detailed comments. This may have been a mistake, as too much time has passed for me to convey my immediate impressions. If it's my least favourite of your three books, it's only because it's the slimmest. I'll also embarrass you by objecting that the rest of the book is not as good as the preface and first article. I enjoyed all the other pieces, especially John Weir's (the second one), and Paul Burston's (if I wrote in *Barrack Buddies* about one GI whose only information about homosexuality came from the 'virulently homophobic' *Cruising,* it was sour grapes because that soldier was so freaked out by the movie that all he could talk about was how he couldn't have sex with another guy [me] without thinking about getting stabbed. Or so he claimed. A perfect match for Alex's 'steak-knife'?). But the other essayists don't match your wit and adrenaline. Still, taken together all the pieces in *Anti-Gay* work effectively as a sharp slap in the face, or I guess great gob of spit on the

Stonewall Inn lawn. As the slapped and spat-upon have not been shy in admitting.

On these shores, the *Bay Area Reporter* did not choose to review *The Masculine Marine*. I'm lucky to have such low expectations. Most people are lazy, ignorant, stupid and weak. Ultimately, though you're quicker at vitriol (and much better at it. I don't tell you that your pieces are the best in *Anti-Gay* to flatter you but because it's my blunt biased opinion; still, it occurs to me I should try to stay on your good side. I picture Miss Gay Rag subsequent to you hanging up as resembling a pumpkin about three weeks after Halloween), I wonder if I'm not at heart more of a misanthrope. The refrain of the single I put out with my industrial band back in Grand Rapids, Michigan, was 'People are dirt!' Something they taught me at the Church of the Open Door.

*

So why didn't I stay in San Diego, then? I wish you had a better time in the States, but I can only concur with everything you said about California. Edmund White was right when he wrote, 'The polite friendliness of Californians is an ambiguous quality. Within the first ten minutes a visitor is showered with affection and familiarity, but that may be as close as one is ever likely to get.'

As I remember it, the moment on the ride back from Camp Pendleton when I began to grate on your nerves was when I started in on how much I hated 'Vauxhall And I'. And I did hate it, so much that I somehow managed to persuade the used CD store where I bought it as an illegal promo to give me my money back. Later that summer I was visiting Troy in Colorado when I heard 'Why Don't You Find Out For Yourself' on the radio. Through this song the album, track by track, wormed its way into my heart. Now, after 'Viva Hate', it's my favourite. (The Mexican Valium I bought last summer may have helped. 'Vauxhall and I' is the most Valium album I know of. Is Morrissey an insomniac? I am, have been since I was five. At Bart's insistence, I tried the gentle, natural 'wonder drug' melatonin. It gave me blood-curdling nightmares. He responded, 'You need to learn how to take control of your nightmares.' Obviously he's been in California too long.) Practically the last track to win me over was 'The Lazy Sunbathers'. But in the softly drumming Seattle rain it's just so perfect to imagine the bodies on Black's Beach (San Diego's gay beach):

> *The sun burns through, to the planet's core*
> *it isn't enough, they want more*

I guess I'll be back down there myself in another month to collect stories for my next book: *Uniformed Trade: The Corruption Sets In.*

*

Of course this is a sad letter. Not only is Alex leaving me, he's intent on finding a room in Capitol Hill, the gay ghetto, so that he 'won't have to feel guilty about driving home drunk'. It's a defeat all around. Since beginning this letter I did go through a couple of days of rage. But Alex and I will still be friends. No. Alex and I will still be something resembling a family.

Alex asked me to tell you that even though *Anti-Gay* provoked one of his psychotic episodes he still likes you.

Speaking of age, I think you exaggerate yours. It's true that we're both too old to bond with young military guys on their level. But there are a lot of guys who, like Alex, are looking for somewhat older men to cling to and torment. Or should we just stick to lemurs?

Yours,

Steve

The Gestures of the Dead

London, 2 March 1997

Dear Steve,

I was sorry to hear that you've split up with Alex.

Well, I think you're supposed to say something like that in these situations. It's not that I didn't like Alex, or that I didn't think that you were suited to one another (whatever that might mean); it's just that whenever a friend ends a relationship with someone the custom seems to be for condolences. I'm not entirely sure why that should be – after all, if the relationship isn't working then, theoretically, the decision to break up is good news, something to be congratulated and encouraged, a new beginning, etc. But then, actually to say such a thing would be to cast yourself in the light of someone who never thought you should have been seeing 'X' in the first place and suggest you are rubbing your hands with glee now that your Cassandra-like prophecies are being realized. All things considered, 'I'm sorry' is the much more diplomatic response. So, once again, I'm sorry.

If nothing else, the preceding paragraph illustrates the ineptitude of intellectual and analytical responses to actual life and loss, and why no one in their right mind would want me as a friend, even at long distance. But of course that doesn't stop me. For example, this 'pus-plug' thing is quite a Case History in the making. First, there is the obvious implication of the discovery of a 'hole' in your (ex)boyfriend's 'meaty thigh'. Alex's fondness for 'fingering' it, doing his damnedest to 'make it fouler than it already was', reveals the full enormity of his masculine betrayal. Then there is the irony that, like me, you tend to choose almost literally 'wounded soldiers' as partners. The 'pus-plug' is part of the 'package' – and their showing us their pus-plug is probably the very heart of our relationships; the measure of their intimacy/dependency. It's all part of the masculine/feminine, tough/soft, sweet/sour dichotomy that enmeshes us. Also the phallic/vaginal one. For perhaps the 'pus plug' is also the penis? When the 'pus-plug' is squeezed does it not ejaculate?

Is not semen yellow-white-coloured and smelly? Is it not, when separated from the vagina, a fluid connoting decay rather than fruition? Or is perhaps the image more easily resolved as one of the penis literally 'plugging' the vagina in an attempt to prevent all its 'foul' contents rushing out?

In the end, boys like Alex may be fucked up, but we are too for loving them. In case that thought doesn't rally your spirits, then think that at least that you rescued him from San Diego. I don't know much about Seattle, but I'm fairly certain that, if for no other reason than it's north rather than south, it can't be as gay as San Diego. You say that his move into the gay ghetto in Seattle represents your failure. But, after all, where else can a single young man like Alex exist who isn't a professional outsider like you and me, who isn't even going out with a professional outsider like you and me any more, and who isn't in the Marines any more? More to the point, where else can he get the attention he and all other inverts crave? (Which reminds me of that marvellous moment in *Independence Day* when the aliens arrive and Harvey Fierstein gets into a panic – he rushes over to the telephone and *calls his mother*. The conversation goes something like: 'Mom? *Mom!* The aliens are getting more attention than me in this movie! *What do I do?*' Though, I don't suppose Alex can easily call his mother.)

*

I recently went to give a talk to an Oxbridge 'LesBiGay Society'. I'm not sure why I agreed. OK, that's a lie. I had an idea in the back of my head that it might be fun to bask in the adulation of bright-eyed, bushy-tailed young things. Of course, it didn't quite work out like that.

I read the intro of *Anti-Gay* again. When I finished, there was a long prickly silence. After I asked if anyone wanted to ask a question or comment, there was an even longer prickly silence. Finally, I said: 'Surely *someone* disagrees with me?'

And of course, someone did. A skinny Asian bloke in John Lennon glasses in the front row who'd been staring at me intently while I was reading, as if examining me for horns, piped up: 'Yes, *I* do,' and proceeded to rattle out a list of my offences as if he were the chief prosecutor at a Maoist show trial – adopting of course the jargon of Queer Theory, the

Maoism of the 90s. I can't remember the exact nature of my crimes, but they were heinous and legion – so heinous and legion that he could barely catch his breath listing them and reminding me how 'ashamed' I should be. After a while I decided that even a prickly silence was better than *this* and interrupted him.

'That's really *very interesting*,' I said flatly. 'Does anyone else have any *questions*?' Mr Curried Theory flounced out of the room.

When the meeting adjourned, a nice, shy lad came up and thanked me for the book, explaining: 'For a long time I felt like there was something wrong with me because I didn't like gay discos or have many gay friends – now I know I just wanted to be an individual.' Yes, I thought to myself, but will the nice idea that you're an 'individual' keep you warm at night?

By the way, someone's making a TV programme about the book over here (for the arty, low-audience channel) and they kept asking me to tell them what the 'next step' was. It's like in *The Life of Brian* where Brian, sick of being followed around by a crowd beseeching him to show them The Way, shouts: 'Why don't you just fuck off!'

'Yes, Lord,' the crowd says, 'But *how* shall we fuck off?'

They also kept going on about an 'anti-gay movement'. Now, as you know, I dissociated myself from the idea that the book might represent a new 'movement' in the introduction. But a number of people have insisted on writing about 'the anti-gay movement' anyway; they need it to be a bandwagon so that they can clamber on it. So I talked instead pointedly of an 'anti-gay moment'.

'When was that?' asked the TV woman quickly.

'Why,' I said, 'when *my book* was published, of course.'

*

In my last letter I explained that I spurned the delights of Oceanside because the Marines all looked so young. What can I have been thinking of? Most of my recent 'conquests' have been in their early twenties – including an engaged scaffolder who had 'never done this kind of thing before'. He asked if I minded the fact that he was inexperienced: 'No, no that's OK,' I answered, trying to sound patient and indulgent instead of excited and desperate.

There's a thin bleeding line between vicariousness and vampirism. I remember that in one of your letters you jokingly chastised me for suggesting that you, like me, valued military trade for their integrity and wholesomeness, when in fact you like to 'corrupt' them. I'm sure this is true; after all, we all kill the thing we love, or rim it a little, but I think it is also true that what we eroticize is the 'normalcy' of these boys. By having sex with them, we hope to import some of their everydayness and imagined ease with life and living into our own sadly deprived/depraved existences – as homosexuals who are writers, we are doubly Undead. We act all hurt and surprised when they betray us and turn out to be not so 'normal' after all, and almost as weird and dysfunctional as ourselves.

*

Gay Times has published another attack on *Anti-Gay*. The third in as many months. As Glenn Belverio put it, 'are they gonna change their title to *Anti-Anti-Gay Times*? The only problems I can envisage would be typographical.' Here's the funniest part:

> ...while the 'anti-gays' enjoy their fleeting moment of glory with the heterosexual establishment, how long will it be before they loose [*sic*] this precarious status and end up mocked and reviled by those they tried so hard to please?

I don't know about you, but I'm terrified of 'loosing' my imperialist running-dog privileges as a lackey of the 'heterosexual establishment'. How could I live without my Buck House Garden Party invites, my free Fortnum & Mason's hampers and, of course, the naked lesbian slaves I keep in the basement of my mansion for household chores and the occasional cannibal binge?

*

Was Alex's Mum perhaps a reader of Nietzsche? This might give a philosophical justification for her announcement 'Santa is dead'. I suspect, however, that your Tennessee Williams reference is probably closer to the mark. In case it isn't already blindingly obvious, I'm a bit of a TW devotee. I read all his plays in one go when I was about eighteen in a few days of melodramatic bingeing, and I don't think I've ever fully recovered. I love the poetry of his dialogue. And his embrace of sadness. OK, perhaps it's a tad self-destructive, and the empty bourbon bottles soon fill up your kitchen sink, but it is a lot less embarrassing than being, oh, Larry Kramer...

My friend Simon is also a fan of TW (when he isn't understudying for Dorian Gray) and is living proof that privilege can sometimes be almost as harrowing as the kind of deprivation Alex endured. Simon is an aristocratic queen of indeterminate age, from a nineteenth-century Scottish entrepreneurial family who bought their way into the English aristocracy and then found themselves completely, gloriously enervated by its decadent blood. Simon himself, who looks like a matured Rank matinée idol – sort of Dirk Bogarde crossed with Edward Fox – was bequeathed great genes, a few neuroses, but no money. The family fortune was largely squandered – Simon's uncle, Stephen, a sometime lover of the painter Rex Whistler and the war poet Siegfried Sassoon, famously went to bed at thirty and never got up again. He lived on a diet of ice-cream and decreed that all the mirrors in the house be removed. How many queens do you know who would love to do this but don't have the resolve (or the staff)?

Simon's TW qualities are rich and largely beyond his control – which is the way it should be (and being an English aristocrat is, alas, the nearest one gets in this country to being Southern). Apparently his mother, a society beauty, was a huge TW fan, particularly, as her own beauty dimmed, of his Blanche du Bois character. As a homosexual, a struggling writer, and an impecunious blue-blood he is a walking three-act play with a tragic motif. Fortunately, he isn't himself tragic and manages to be ironic about his heritage and laugh a little at himself.

Simon always has an anecdote to tell about his delightfully batty family that will make light of his fate: such as his Malapropizing aunt who, talking about the architecture of a church she was taken with, described it as being 'castrated with flying buttocks'. Or the way his regal grandmother, who was quite probably the vainest woman in England, used to lie on a sofa all day with her feet raised on cushions so that the blood would circulate around her face, maintaining her much noted bloom. Or how Uncle Stephen, when he was about five, had a habit of cocking his ears and listening to the blooms; asked by his mother what the flowers were saying, he'd reply: '"Stephen, Stephen, Stephen".'

The young toddler would also wait at the gate in the afternoon for the army trucks on their way to Salisbury Plain to pass his house; as they rattled past he would turn round, his back to them, and slowly lower his short trousers.

Or how, a little older and a lot wiser, he stole cigarettes from his parents to bribe squaddies into giving him the kind of attention he'd tried to semaphore his interest in with his short trousers a few years earlier.

*

It's a crime of global proportions that your book hasn't attracted more attention. I still think, though, that you should try to get yourself on a TV talk show. Middle America really needs to hear about America's finest taking it up the ass.

Perhaps you should tell them the anecdote included somewhere in the twenty-page fan letter you received and thoughtfully copied for me, the one about Robert Mapplethorpe's lover losing his erection when he realized that the Marine he was fucking wasn't born when Kennedy was shot and ordering him to sing the Marine's Hymn whilst he got tubed to make him fully hard again. Sometimes deviancy really has to be worked at.

*

I have also received a similar kind of 'fan-mail'. In the form of plagiarism. Given the fact that the plagiarism is so obvious and so frequent, that I was sent a pre-pub copy of the book, that it's titled *Call Me* and tells the story of a nightmare journey into the world of gay 'lonely hearts' columns by a serial killer, *literary stalking* might be a better description. As an example, here's me on bingo:

> Somewhere in Britain there's a paint factory, opened circa 1948, producing colours exclusively for bingo halls and municipal leisure facilities. Sad colours that think they're gay ... Those unhealthy reds, those sighing

blues, those suspicious creams and that eerie salmon pink ... A good proportion of that factory's sorry output has ended up on the walls of this Top Rank bingo hall in London's Camden Town. [*It's a Queer World*, p.39]

Here's *Call Me* on York Hall baths (a sauna in Bethnal Green popular with gay and straight-but-curious men):

Somewhere in the UK there's a paint factory, opened circa 1953, producing colours exclusively for prisons, bingo halls and municipal leisure facilities. Dull greens, sighing blues, insipid creams and greys. A good proportion of that factory's sorry output has ended up on the walls of York Hall in Bethnal Green. [*Call Me*, p.151]

I wrote about York Hall Baths in an *Attitude* column that didn't make it into *It's a Queer World*. Cue the scary danger music.

The author is a photographer called P. P. Hartnett (a made-up name, I hope). The novel isn't bad. It isn't terribly good either, but it's quite a clever, photographic/plagiaristic way of writing a novel when you're not actually a novelist. He apparently reprints verbatim the letters that he received in reply to his personal ads placed in gay papers and recounts the stories they tell him. I shall try to get you a copy of the book; after all, in some senses it's close to what you've done with your military interviews. Except he doesn't appear to have asked his interviewees' permission, nor has much real interest in any of them save for how he can exploit them – and I believe that you *are* a novelist, and probably a very good one, if you only give yourself a chance.

*

I have recently been rediscovering Jean Genet. His pessimism about the human condition in general and fags in particular is positively heartwarming. His letter to Sartre in 1952 about pederasty, reprinted in Edmund White's *Genet*, is utterly bleak and, I think, utterly fascinating. Perhaps this says more about me and Genet than pederasty, but I reproduce parts of it here for your edification/mortification:

... from childhood on, a trauma throws the soul into confusion. I think it happens like this: after a certain shock,

I refuse to live. But incapable of thinking about my death in clear, rational terms, I look at it symbolically by refusing to continue the world. Instinct then leads me toward my own sex. My pleasure will be *endless*. I will not embody the principle of continuity. It is a sulky attitude. Slowly instinct leads me toward masculine attributes. Slowly my psyche will propose to me funereal themes. Actually, first I know I'm capable of not continuing this world in which I live, then I continue, indefinitely, the gestures of the dead...

Well, I know *that* feeling. Jean also has some illuminating if characteristically depressing thoughts on the subject of straight/military trade:

As for the appearance, at certain moments, of pederasty in the life of a normal man, it's provoked by the sudden (or slow) collapse of the life force. A fatigue, a fear to live: a sudden refusal of the responsibility to live...

Marines and soldiers are, in a sense, already dead. When they join the Corps, they are giving up on life, literally signing it away. What is Boot Camp if not a form of suicide? Maybe one of the things that draws fags and jarheads together – apart from their fear of women, their love of drag queens and their fetish for short hair – is the fact that they both inhabit a 'dead zone'. When you forswear suburban heterosexuality, the religion of the Western world, you cease to exist as a fully-fledged member of the human race.

Even Andrea Sullivan, Catholic evangelist of suburban *homosexuality*, writing in the *Independent on Sunday* on Aids (the 'gestures of the dead' made into a virus) recently quoted Mark Heprin's 'A Soldier of the Great War' as an example of 'what almost every gay man ... has also learned: "The war was still in him, and it would be in him for a long time to come, for soldiers who have been blooded are soldiers for ever. They never fit in ... that they will never allow themselves to heal completely is their way of expressing their love for friends who have perished."' If Genet is right, the suggested bond between soldiers and homos may be even more apt than Andrea and GMFA realize.

III

However, it gets worse. There is for Genet a kind of murder in the possession of a young man by an older man:

> . . . it's the possession of an object (the beloved) who will have no other fate than the fat of the lover. The beloved becomes the object ordained to 'represent' *death* (the lover) in life. That's why I want him to be handsome. He has the *visible* attributes when I will be dead. I commission him to live in my stead, my heir apparent. The beloved doesn't love me, he 'reproduces' me. But in this way I sterilize him, I cut him off from his own destiny.

The 's/mothering' impulse that I suspect most military chasers suffer from could easily be interpreted as a desire to have the Other 'reproduce' us – regardless of whether they have their own ideas about how to live their life (which we hope, being soldiers, they don't). It's difficult to work out which is worse – the 'vampirism' I talked about before, or Genet's 'bodysnatching'.

I think all military chasers exhibit a mixture of both. On the one hand, Steve, you save your boys from the 'dead zone' of the military, interest them in books, send them to college and teach them table manners. On the other, you do get them to reproduce your own vegetarian values. I, for my part, being far too lazy to reproduce even by 'commissioning someone to live in my stead' only went as far as trying to interest Jason in The Smiths and Mexican food (I was only 50 per cent successful – guess which 50 per cent). Sometimes I wonder if Jason didn't up and leave because I wasn't more successful at getting him to reproduce me. Or at least more interested in trying.

Meanwhile, I wonder if Alex announced that he 'couldn't even stand the thought that you exist' because he felt 'sterilized' by you, cut off from his own destiny as a psycho Marine? Or was it just because he had no one else to torment?

Perhaps I should mention that Genet was going through a bad patch in his life when he wrote his Queen is Dead letter: he had writer's block, was unlucky in love, and was very depressed. Which sounds like a regular kind of day to me.

Best,

Mark

PS Please stay away from bridges and high bar stools. In my own transatlantic, mediated, blocked, intellectual, Platonic, Anglo way I love you very much. And guys can love other guys you know, without there being anything, like, y'know, filthy and faggy in it.

The Unclean Fraternity of the Smiling Alligators

Seattle, March 25, 1997

Dear Mark,

Thanks for saying you're sorry about the split with Alex, though I'm afraid my hard luck Christmas story didn't leave you much choice.

Four weeks ago, in execution of the first truly unilateral big decision he ever made, Alex dissolved our household. I moved to a small apartment in the same building; he sought out a one-bedroom in Capitol Hill within staggering distance of The Cuff. Alex is the only residential tenant in a building housing a violin maker and a year-round Christmas shop. His kitchen's on the ground floor; a narrow staircase leads up two flights to the three-quarter bath and bedroom, which affords a stunning view of Puget Sound, the Space Needle, the city skyline and the Olympic Mountains. He even has access to a customized fuck platform on the roof (though he had better watch out that one of his Cuff tricks doesn't tumble through the skylight into Santa's workshop). When I inspected his place, I told him it was too bad about the view, it being bad luck: 'Everyone knows that pregnant women who look at the Olympics suffer miscarriages.' But really I didn't need to be mean. After only a few nights he confided that he finds the company of the elves unnerving. Also, neither the oven nor the heater work. And he even managed to tell me that the move was a mistake and that he missed me – if not as much as Samantha, the only creature he is comfortable admitting to ever having loved.

But no one misses anyone as much as our geriatric Siamese cat, Max, misses Alex. Or at least his late night entrances with a greasy paper bag of Burger King food.

Alex and I had been best buddies for more than a year, and he'd already been staying with me for a month or two, but it wasn't until the night before we moved into our first apartment together that we met Max. We'd been out celebrating at an Italian restaurant and I had too much Chianti, apparently. Pulling into the Bank of America in Hillcrest to use the ATM

Alex said, 'There's that cat they're offering the reward for.' I focused my eyes on a handsome Siamese, meatloafing on the pavement. I staggered out of the car to accost it. The cat started, oddly, as if not seeing me until I was only inches away, but then rubbed its glands affectionately against my legs. I noticed that a substantial patch of fur was missing from its back. Even under the sickly light of the street lamp, I could see that the bald spot was black with hopping tiny dots. So of course I did what anyone else would have done – spirited away the unprotesting flea-ridden feline (someone's pet?) and installed it on the carpeted floors of my new home. Upon which he promptly pissed ... But then of course in my Navy book I had already dubbed this apartment complex, to which I was returning only because it was cheap and Alex had no job, *Casa de Las Pulgas*. House-o'-fleas.

The vet informed me that the as yet unrenamed stray was a declawed neutered male at least ten years old, conservatively estimated, who required $300 in dental work.

Well, so did I, I reasoned, and I was getting by well enough without it. But eventually I did come up with the money (for the cat, not for me), and trundled him off for oral surgery, only to be told that advanced periodontitis was not his biggest trouble. Lab tests showed that Max had 15 per cent of his kidneys left; probably he wouldn't live six months.

I named him Max because I thought he'd already been through too much to adapt to a less generic moniker. For the most part he was an unobtrusive personality. But the fur grew back, he never again missed his litter box, and once in a while he'd surprise us. Like the time (to my horror, and Alex's hysterical laughter) he began autofellating. Or the incident with the mouse.

One bright San Diego morning I was just about to put some bread in the toaster when a rodent jumped out. It scuttled right by Max, who, sunning himself on a rug on the kitchen floor, didn't appear even to see it. I turned the toaster upside-down in the sink and with the crumbs a few turds fell out.

The next morning, resigned to going without any toast, I noticed on the living-room floor a small clump that I supposed to be a hairball.

It was a dead mouse. A wet dead mouse. Max has very few teeth; apparently, he gummed the mouse to death.

But for the most part Max eschewed activity. In fact, the reason Alex adopted Samantha was because he was irritated that Max wouldn't play with a $6 cat toy he bought. A lot of the time Max looked like he was already dead.

One scorching night last summer Alex stumbled in from The Hole with a bag of fast food. I was still awake and sat with him in the kitchen. We heard a crash and went to investigate. The electric fan had fallen from the window. Returning to the kitchen, we saw that Max had leapt onto the table and hauled down a Burger King Whopper. Hearing Alex's shocked 'Max!' he looked up and in a couple of quick mammoth near-toothless gulps managed to ingest the entire *bun*.

Fast forward. Against all odds, and despite a gradual but steady weight loss, Max seemed to survive the move to Seattle. But apparently, like Alex and Me, he didn't. Since Alex's departure he's grown ever more spectral and has started yowling horribly in the night, every night, whenever the room temperature dips below 80 degrees. (The radiators in this building are always either very hot or very cold.) As I confided in my last letter, I am a light sleeper and this 'studio apartment' is what you in Britain I believe would call a bed-sit. It actually has something that until now I only knew from old movies: a Murphy bed – the kind that folds down from a swivelling closet door. I've tried shutting Max, and Samantha, in the spacious 'walk-in' closet (there's a small window, and a $100 'cat tree'), but it's colder in there and the cries only become amplified.

This isn't my only noise complaint. At midnight the first night here I was exhausted from the move, depressed from the split, and ready for sleep. The tenant below me was teaching himself electric guitar. The man across the hall was playing some (still) unidentified Asian percussive instrument. The tenant above me was broadcasting the radio, LOUD. Even through the ceiling I could recognize it as National Public Radio. When at 2:00 a.m. I dragged my body upstairs to knock at her door, I discovered she was gone for the weekend; the middle-brow chatter was intended to discourage would-be burglars.

On the night/morning I decided that Max would have to be euthanized I was still painfully awake at 7:00 a.m. and as a last resort reached for the Xanax.

*

I've been reading Genet too. *The Thief's Journal.* And so I was comforted to stumble on:

> Those whom one of their number called the Carolinas paraded to the site of a demolished street urinal ... It was near the harbour and the barracks, and its sheet iron had been corroded by the hot urine of thousands of soldiers. When its ultimate death was certified, the Carolinas – not all, but a formally chosen delegation – in shawls, mantillas, silk dresses and fitted jackets, went to the site to place a bunch of red roses tied together with a crêpe veil ... The faggots were perhaps thirty in number, at eight a.m., at sunrise. I saw them going by. I accompanied them from a distance. I knew that my place was in their midst, not because I was one of them, but because their shrill voices, their cries, their extravagant gestures seemed to me to have no other aim than to try to pierce the shell of the world's contempt ... When they reached the harbour, they turned right, toward the barracks, and upon the rusty, stinking sheet iron of the *pissoir* that lay battered on the heap of dead scrap iron they placed the flowers.

This passage was new to me. I think my piss-trough remark grew out of a Burroughs quote I can't even remember exactly, something about wanting to have his body dumped under a boys' school privy. (The lemur reference that closed my last letter was also a reference to the crazy old coot of Lawrence, Kansas. In a recent interview with *The New York Times* he called humans a 'bad species', and articulated a preference for the company of cats – and lemurs, a certain species of which he wants to seek out on Madagascar before he dies.)

Eerily enough, your comments on Genet also return us to our first letter exchange. I asked your opinion on Bersani's *Homos*, which concludes with his endorsement of a gay outlaw 'anti-communitarianism'.

Mock it though he may have, in his letter to Sartre Genet

testifies to his unquestioned faith in natural masculinity. I can see the appeal this might have in our twisted sheep-cloning age. But I strongly doubt that most yuppie heterosexuals equate manliness with fathering children any more.

In this country, at least, the traditional family is fucked up.

Though exceptions, there are gay couples with kids, and 'breeder' couples with no kids. I'm not a little like a mom/dad to Alex and Troy, and Troy is a very present step-dad to his divorced fag-hag's three kids, even as his lover of three years is a strong father to his own son and still lives with his wife. (Troy fills the role of the traditional macho Mexican's mistress, or boyfriend-bottom.)

Despite the fuckedupness of my relationships with Troy and Alex, I don't think it's an exaggeration to say that the end result has been a strong familial bond. I say familial because it's different from love between even the best long-term friends in that there's a certain dogged loyalty rooted as much in duty as in shared interests or consistent affection. (Were they, God forbid, to ever get sick, of course I'd 'be there' for them – and – violent shudder – maybe I would even write about the experience. On further consideration I realize I was being a little disingenuous when I called gay writing about Aids 'boring and nauseating'. Obviously some of it is, but probably what really bugs me about Aids is that it's been done. Where's the creative niche for me? Also, it irritates me that Aids has completely devalued the currency of gay suicide. When one queer writer [an Englishman, Mark Finch] jumped off the Golden Gate in 1993, all the papers wrote about was the puzzling fact that he seemed to have been HIV negative.)

But – I don't want to switch on the light when you're lying on the floor listening to '(I'm) The End of the Family Line' (or for that matter 'There's A Place In Hell For Me And My Friends'). As you know, I love these dark moods myself. Genet's pessimism is exhilarating. If somehow a little too Catholic for me to fully identify with . . .

Some of the literally blackest days I can remember were in Germany at the peak of the early 80s cruise missile hysteria when I worked in that on-base sporting goods store housed in a remodelled abattoir. Through the barred windows I'd stare out at MPs rolling mirrors under cars to check for bombs. When the Germans did their monthly test of the air raid sirens, Armed Forces Network radio always made a point to play especially upbeat music. I used to ache to be at the turntable and put on something like, say, Throbbing Gristle's 'Heathen Earth', or, if forced to select among AFN's limited standards, at least the Doors' 'Rider on the Storm', if not 'The End' (*Apocalypse Now* version, or better still Nico's cover from 'June 1, 1974').

So maybe I can redeem my gay feelgood outburst by reciting my favourite passage from *The Thief's Journal*:

> The atmosphere from the planet Uranus appears to be so heavy that the ferns there are creepers; the animals drag along, crushed by the weight of the gases. I want to mingle with these humiliated creatures which are always on their bellies. If metempsychosis should grant me a new dwelling place, I choose that forlorn planet; I inhabit it with the convicts of my race. Amidst hideous reptiles, I pursue an eternal, miserable death in a darkness where the leaves will be black, the waters of the marshes thick and cold. Sleep will be denied me. On the contrary, I recognize, with increasing lucidity, the unclean fraternity of the smiling alligators.

Now why does this remind of my new adult bookstore hangout, Taboo Video?

I think there was a typo in your last Genet quote, but it fitted with the tearing-down-the-mirrors-at-thirty idea. (I loved the Stephen Tennant anecdote, and was jealous of the flowers' whisperings.) You typed that pederastic love is 'the possession of an object (the beloved) who will have no other fate than the fat of the lover'.

*

One thing that really does depress me is my fear that our anti-gay projects are doomed to remain marginal curiosities. I'm glad and of course not a little envious that your book made the huge splash it has. I take cheer in the fact that it can't help but make a lot of gays stop and think. But the whole thing kind of reminds me of my habit of watching Holocaust documentaries in Germany. They always came on after eleven, when the only people likely to watch them were nervous, sensitive, guilty insomniacs who were unlikely to come away with anything they didn't already know or feel. The response of most of my gay bar friends to any sort of queer theory provocation is easy to caricature, but the response of my liberal straight yuppie friends is too sad to mention.

Part of me would love to be on Oprah. But I expect that in response to a question from the audience I would inevitably at least imply a contradiction between official prohibitions of 'homosexuality' and, say, official training procedures that include rows of naked Marine recruits shaving each other. And I know that the fall-out would not lead to a more open-minded view of 'homosexuality', but, if anything, an end to recruits shaving each other naked. And anyway, though I almost never even turn on the TV (which is stupid snobbery, because I missed that hazing footage on *Dateline*, though I've seen some private tapes), I'm told that in the wake of public, media and Congressional pressure daytime TV has 'cleaned up its act'. Donahue has retired. An hour devoted to the many rich anecdotes I could share about the alleged Marine preference for anal receptivity would have been much more airable two years ago. Now, Oprah prefers to host Toni Morrison.

*

That's what novelist Matthew Stadler told me at the first party I attended in Seattle. Relations with Alex had thawed so much that I invited him to accompany me. (The split has restored a genuine if unstated joy in seeing each other again. Though we did have one tiff last weekend, after emerging from *Lost Highway*. The sky was violent, street lights were flickering, traffic was bad and Alex started screaming that he wanted to PUT A CROWBAR THROUGH SOMEBODY'S HEAD. At the next stoplight I wordlessly left the car and walked home.) It was held at the home of D. Travers Scott, a smart and very ambitious twentysomething Texas sex writer and Marc Almond cultist who has just sold his first novel to St Martin's. I also met Matt Sycamore, an extraordinarily other-worldly short story writer and male prostitute with hair of many colours. Both have read the work of my best writer friend and had good things to say about *Male Impersonators*, though Sycamore did zero in on page six of your intro to *Anti-Gay* where instead of Ohio it says 'Gap-less town in Cleveland', when Cleveland is a gross million-plus rustbelt metropolitan area long notorious for pollution so poisonous that in the early 70s its river caught fire.

Not in attendance at the party was the town's biggest-name homo, Dan Savage, who writes a nationally syndicated sex-advice column called 'Savage Love' and hosts a late-night local radio show called 'Savage Live'. The night I listened he fielded a call from a man who masturbates wrapping his dick in hot pizza. Savage boasted of his new condo (book deal with Dutton) and appearance in drag at a party honouring Washington governor Mike Lowry, with whom he casually joked about fisting.

*

Where's that glorious Jean Genet dragging-about-the-surface-of-Uranus abjection when you need it? Certainly not in the pages of *Wonder Bread and Ecstasy*, the best-selling Joey Stefano bio. I have to say I was disappointed. The author, Charles Isherwood, clearly took pains not to write a tacky, sensational celebrity bio. Which is too bad, because ultimately the book is neither serious nor sleazy enough to satisfy. The limited analysis is of the most timorous gay feelgood pop psychology (Richard Isay) sort. And though he quotes Jeff Stryker saying that 'she snorts the paint off the walls, she does so much coke', Isherwood tells us that no matter how many drugs s/he may snort, or inject into porn star veins, Chi Chi LaRue is a real trooper who always shows up for a shoot on time.

Isherwood takes a half-hearted stab at Susan Faludi's theme in the Jeff Stryker section of 'The Money Shot': Stefano suffered because nobody wanted to know the 'real' him behind the box cover image. (Unlucky for Stefano, because he was a bottom, there was no market for latex moulds of his dick.) And he does a commendable job of exposing the hypocrisy, and toll on Stefano, of gay men who greedily consume porn while spewing contempt on its makers.

But, you know, of course it's not really their fault. And Stefano's drug problems weren't his fault. It's as though

Isherwood feels ashamed of delivering the dirt and so has to force it all into some awkward uplifting pro-gay message:

> Stefano certainly didn't grow up in a family, or a social milieu, that held sophisticated views on the subject. 'Back where I come from,' he told an interviewer in 1990, 'gay life is not very popular, it's not accepted ... I had problems with drugs and drinking, and I was in a program for two years.' It's clear from his yoking the two phenomena together that one influenced the other: his drug problem was in some ways a reaction to the pain he'd felt growing up gay in a world that sneered at it.

But at the funeral we learn that Stefano's suburban Philadelphia family and friends – heretofore presented as simple, wholesome straight people far removed from the sleazy world of porn – delighted in the quality street drugs he shared with them when he came home on visits.

*

As part of saying goodbye to Max I spent some extra time holding and hugging him and feeding him disgustingly unhealthy people food. He came back to life a little, and I cancelled the appointment. A little love is all it takes to prolong anyone's suffering.

Love,

Steve

Strangers in the Night

London, 18 April 1997

Dear Steve,

I don't like cats.

I used to. Or at least, I used to like *one* cat. When I was about nine, I, along with my sister Gill, decided we really, really, really, please Mum, please, please Dad, we'll be ever so good and won't want anything for Christmas or birthdays ever again, wanted a pet.

I actually wanted a dog, but my parents, whom I suspect didn't really want a pet of any kind, decided that the best compromise solution to their sprog's whining was to get a cat. After all, cats are in theory a low-maintenance pet – if you forget to feed them, they catch a bird or two or go next door and rub themselves up against someone else's leg for a saucer of milk. This tarty trait of self-sufficiency probably clinched the matter, since when I was five and Gill was eight, we were allowed to keep a couple of guinea-pigs, but I think that after the novelty of having something captive to love wore off, along with the excitement of watching a large stuffed sock with whiskers nibble on lettuce, we first forgot to change their straw and then we forgot to feed them. I suspect this may have been the reason why one day we discovered they were dead, probably when rummaging around in the garage where they were kept looking for something else more interesting. (Of course, my culpability didn't stop me feeling sorry for myself, and I remember crying my heart out on the stairs – so my parents could hear me – feeling very unhappy but also very grown-up and sophisticated, seeing as I had experienced my first real encounter with death and loss.)

We ended up with a slightly runty ginger tom cat who we christened 'Caesar'. I can't recall whether it was actually my idea, although the fact that I was studying Latin at school and was obsessed with the historical TV series *I Claudius* (which, because it was *cultured*, was by far the dirtiest thing on telly in the 70s) would suggest that the blame for this ridiculously middle-class aspirational name was mine. Calling out his name in my squeaky just-breaking voice must have entertained the neighbours no end. Interestingly, there's now an up-market cat food called 'Caesar'. Obviously I was ahead of my time again.

Caesar was a Manx. I don't know whether you have Manxes in the States, but over here they're cats without tails, just a stubby little bob an inch or two long where they should have one of those long swishy things they use to keep their balance and draw attention to themselves. It goes without saying that in a household where we had to take our shoes off at the door and the mention of the word 'sex' on telly would instantly provoke a deathly hush, Caesar was spayed just as soon as possible – lending a special poignancy to his mutilated tail which still tried to wave itself about, as if it weren't missing ten inches.

But I loved that cat. I loved it so much I almost brought those long since rotted guinea-pigs back to life. I fed it, stroked it, and even forced it to sleep on my bed. Since I was forbidden to do this by my house-proud mother, who exiled Caesar to the back garden in the night and the utility area of the house during the day, spending the night together involved a certain romantic ritual whereby I'd retire to my room and call out from my window the Roman emperor's name into the night, until he'd scrabble up the drainpipe and into my bedroom, purring loudly.

That I did all this with an extreme allergy to cats, which makes me sneeze, wheeze, weep and brings my skin up in hives, tells you something about how lonely I was and probably explains my adult need to suffer for the things I love.

Later my attachment to Caesar waned as I was kept company by schoolmates staying the weekend, who slept purring in a camp bed next to mine. For a while Caesar refused to accept my betrayal and used to walk up and down the window-sill outside my bedroom meowing mournfully and rubbing his neck against the glass so his fur flattened against it. I just drew the curtain.

I now hate all cats. I just see them as smelly bags of allergic reactions and fleas. But they all love me. Without exception, every single cat I come into contact with wants to rub their glands against me and sit on my lap. Of course, my disinterest, if not actual repulsion, just makes them even keener. And whenever a cat comes on to me, I find myself instinctively mentally undressing them, shaving them of their hair, and making fun of their ridiculous and disgusting naked cat bodies.

Do you still like me? Can you still have me as a friend, knowing this about me?

I am now seriously considering getting a dog. But I wonder if I only want a dog because they chase cats?

*

> No job.
> No money.
> No self-esteem.
> No confidence.
> All I have is my looks and body,
> and that's not working any more,
> I feel washed up.
> Drug problem.
> Hate life.
> HIV positive!
>
> Joey Stefano

I've just finished reading (eerily enough, this section on Joey was written before receiving your letter) *Wonder Bread and Ecstasy: The Life and Death of Joey Stefano* by Charles Isherwood. Have you come across it? It's difficult to avoid it here if you visit the gay section of bookshops, as it seems to be usually taking up a whole shelf, cover facing outwards.

And it *is* a very *nice* cover: the delectable Joey with no clothes on, his knees drawn up, looking into the lens sideways-on with that sultry, sulky look of his and those feral–angelic, heavy-lidded green eyes. The cover makes a memorable tombstone. The delectable *deceased* Joey – how much more desirable, unattainable and *fuckable* is a dead porn star? There's the ultimate bottom for you. That *Wonder Bread* looks like one of the wank books that dominate the gay sections of bookshops is, I suppose, entirely appropriate. Death and beauty look very similar when you squint at them with your right hand clenched.

That list of despair I quoted is something Joey wrote after

one of his (eventually successful) suicide attempts. One of the various rich lays that decided to try and 'save' him asked Joey to write out a list of reasons why he was unhappy, so that 'we can talk about them and try to solve them'. It's excruciatingly frank. Joey was just twenty-six, but as a porn star/hustler living in West Hollywood, everything was that little bit more intense, that little bit more accelerated for Joey – everything to do with being gay, that is. It's clear, however, from the account given here, that he suffered from that 'sulkiness' that Genet identified long before he arrived in West Hollywood.

I have to confess I always found Joey fascinating. I wrote about him in *Male Impersonators* in the porn chapter in my analysis of 'More of a Man'; that's the Out and Proud gay porn video made in 1990 in which Joey plays a closeted Dodgers fan who learns to love himself and his vocation – sitting on very large penises – through his friendship with DQ Chi-Chi LaRue and being tattooed by 'Humungous' Rick Donovan. Oh, and being rogered by Michael Henson inside a tent on a float at the Gay Pride Parade. If I remember rightly, the vid ends with Joey being fucked on a table by the entire clientele of a gay bar in a ritual of initiation into the gay community. Perhaps the film was cleverer than I realized.

In some ways Joey was your prototypical Marine-before-boot-camp: unrequited love for Daddy, no education, no prospects, from the Midwest, drug habit, a desire to be looked at, a need to belong, a hole in his soul – and also in his ass. Considering how many Marines end up in gay porn, perhaps you could say he took the short route. Although his suicide could be interpreted as just more of the same abdication that characterized his final year or so, I think that it might also have contained within it some decisiveness, some *character* lacking from the rest of his life. To quote Morrissey on hearing the news of Kurt Cobain's shotgun fellatio: 'I respect his decision.' Perhaps the gay community should strike a medal – the 'Joey': For Valour in the Face of ... Nothingness. It could be fashioned in the shape of a bottle of poppers.

In the end, I think that boys like Joey are not a particularly 'gay' problem – they merely exemplify in anatomical fashion, sleep-walking America's desire to inhale, inject, import, impale itself on desire and the Big Other in the hope that it will wake them up and *tell them who they are,* or at least who they are *supposed* to be. The title of Isherwood's book, *Wonder Bread and Ecstasy,* was apparently inspired by Joey's diet – although his drug of choice was not ecstasy but the dissociative and psychosis-inducing 'Special K' or Ketamine. All-American nutrition.

(By the way, did I tell you that the English porn star Aiden Shaw loved *Anti-Gay*? In an interview in NY *Time Out* he said, 'This is the best thing to happen in years ... Thank God someone did this! We've created this big pink *thing* and it's killing us!' To which my response is: 'Well, take it out of your mouth!')

In the same bookshop where I found *Wonder Bread* I came across some other fabulous gay books, mostly of the self-help variety (rather than self-abuse). For example, the Rod and Bob Jackson Paris coffee table volume about their wonderful life together, including 'family' portraits of them with their parakeets and spaniels. In view of their recent split, I wonder if Warner will be issuing an addendum slip for this book: 'Correction: Bob and Rob now hate one another and try to steal each other's trade whenever they run into one another at the bath-house.'*

Or Michaelangelo Signorile's – *Outing Yourself.* A work which is beyond satire. Well, almost – one of my predictions for 1997 in the New Year edition of *Attitude* was: 'Following the success of his book *Outing Yourself* Signorile publishes a book called *Outing Your Internal Organs.* Says the blurb for the book: "It's time to learn to love your squishy bits! It's time to stop *hiding* your liver and spleen! It's time to bring them *out of the dark* and *into the light*!" At a bookstore reading Signorile is rushed to hospital having disembowelled himself.'

Or, how about How To Make the World a Better Place For Lesbians and Gays. Apparently this involves publishing books with dipsy underlined titles that fill the whole of the front cover and featuring chapters with names like: 'Acknowledging Your Own Homophobia'. Funnily enough, I don't need

---

* This is meant satirically and not to imply that Rod and Bob really hate one another, steal one another's trade, or visit bath-houses.

to buy a book to tell me how to do this.

Ah, well, I'm just jealous because I know that all of these books will outsell *Anti-Gay* several times over. Regarding your remark about wondering whether our anti-gay experiments are doomed to remaining gay curiosities: well, *of course*. After all, this anti-gay thing *is* rather eccentric and self-indulgent, isn't it? For me personally the book was supposed to be a burning of bridges, a cauterizing moment – but it looks like it's almost becoming a new lifestyle...

The current issue of France's main gay glossy *Têtu* has devoted the cover and no less than eight pages to the book (the cover has a sea of rainbow flags on some Pride parade superimposed with '*Anti-Gay* – A few things you're not going to want to hear...'). They interviewed me and translated 'Gay Dream Believer'. *

An 'anti' *Anti-Gay* column they commissioned to inject a bit of balance, started off admitting I was right, what's more I'm *drôle*, but then attacked my 'extreme snobbery' and the abuse of my 'privileged position'. Fair comment. It went on to say that 'Simpson would have been the first to throw something at the Stonewall Riots, the first on Fire Island, the first at The Saint Disco...' It finished by declaring, bizarrely, that 'in ten years all masculine homosexuals will be like Mark Simpson'.

Now, isn't that a terrifying prospect?

*

What a weekend. On Friday evening I went to see Carrey in *Liar, Liar* and alarmed my accompanying friends by being insanely animated by Carrey's electric performance (not up to *The Cable Guy*, this being basically a family schmaltz vehicle, but still phenomenal). After a few drinks with them I went 'walking after midnight' in Hampstead Heath, a local park famous for its wildlife. I often go for strolls there – it acts as an alternative of sorts to the gay scene (even though most of the clientele are merely the decanted dregs from the bars at closing time).

As I walked into the cruising area down the windy path lined by silent, single men, my thoughts turned inadvertently

* *Têtu*'s editor at the time, Pascal Loubet, was ousted shortly after this issue appeared.

and momentarily to Jason. Coincidentally or not, at that precise moment I saw somebody scuttling away who, in the dark, looked like ... Jason. I was rooted to the spot with a mixture of shock and embarrassment. To see *him* here; to be *seen* here ... Should I be shocked, angry, ashamed, *happy*? When I finally went to investigate, to find out whether the shadowy figure was indeed Jason, he'd vanished. A little later I came across someone lurking under a tree who, from a distance, looked like him. I went back to the path.

I haven't seen Jason for about nine months. Not since that last weekend when I evicted him. I'm ashamed to admit that I continued for some time to send him the occasional post-card or CD, as if nothing had happened. No response (and no returned CDs). I have, however, spoken to him once since the split. On Xmas Eve I called his mum's telephone number, figuring he'd be there. The phone rang twice and he answered. As you might imagine, the conversation was some-what one-sided. Wading into waist-high freezing mud, I tried to justify the call by saying, 'Well, I can tell you aren't very keen to talk to me, but I wanted to call because the year's nearly out – I haven't heard from you, and I want to know where things stand.' *Where things stand.* How *pathetic*. It was obvious that there wasn't a single beam, brick, stick, stone or even mote of dust left standing of the House of Jason and Mark.

'It's a bad time,' he replied. All ice.

'Oh,' I said. 'I see,' my heart locked in an elevator to which the cable has just been cut.

Unprompted, he promised to call me back. He asked for my number and wrote it down.

He didn't call.

On the Heath, having satisfied myself that I *hadn't* seen Jase, I went back to the path and stood there with the other lemurs, waiting for, well, whatever it is you wait for in those places. After about ten minutes I saw him. Walking towards me down the path. The moment he saw me he ran into the bushes again.

It's funny how, although it was a moonless night, I saw Jason as clearly as if the sun were shining, as if we were on the beach on holiday in the Canaries, or walking together across the (non-cruisy) part of the Heath as we used to do on a Sunday afternoon in the days when he would drive hundreds of miles to see me every weekend without fail. A thousand years ago.

Of course, I ran after him. I could see that he didn't want to speak to me, or even acknowledge that I was there. I sort of sensed that it wasn't going to be the dreamt-of reunion. But, on the other hand, I couldn't live with the thought of going home having seen him and pretending that I hadn't. Eventually, despite his frantic attempts to get away, I caught up with him (my night battle-skills were better than his). He seemed to be pretending to ask some startled middle-aged punter the time (perhaps in the hope that if there was a witness I would be less inclined to kick his fucking head in).

'Hullo, Jase', I said neutrally, as I approached him from behind his left shoulder. At this he half turned his body towards me, waved his hands in front of him, as if I was a particularly insistent hawker or beggar – which of course I was – while averting his head away from me over his right shoulder. I was too pitiable, too dishevelled, too *horrific* to even look at. 'I don't want to talk to you!' he spluttered. 'I don't want to talk to you! *Leave me alone!*'

It was like Macbeth encountering Banquo's ghost. No it wasn't. It was more like Don Murray in *Advise and Consent* when he's spotted in a twilight fag bar by his former male lover from his army days – before he decided to go straight and become a senator; 'Why didn't you return my calls?' whines the jilted john trying to catch his arm; '*Getaway from me!*' shouts Don, running out of the bar and shoving his ski-panted ex into a large puddle.

But these comparisons didn't occur to me at the time of course. Instead I stood rooted to the spot for a moment, stunned by the freezing white fog pouring into my head from somewhere (the usual meteorological effect of warm water meeting cold water). Then I was angry. I ran after him. Catching up with him on the path, I shouted at his back, '*So you don't want to talk to me, eh? Well,* I FUCKING WELL WANT TO TALK TO YOU!' (It felt like righteous anger, though I suspect it may have been a little too late to get in touch with my needs).

Jason whirled around and tried to walk past me, repeating his stop-haunting-me routine: 'No, no, *no*! I don't want to talk to you!' Adding, almost as an afterthought – '*Here*.' And then he ran off again into the night.

'Here' was less than a mile away from where I live.

I didn't follow him this time. I actually felt sorry for him. Poor guy; he'd just gone up there for some casual, meaningless, *anonymous* sex, probably after driving three hours on the motorway from his base to stay with friends in London (or maybe his new *boyfriend*?). And he ran into *me*. What a downer. Still, I can't help but wonder why he didn't leave straightaway when he saw me the first time, as I would have done if I'd been in his shitty shoes.

Even in the dark I thought I could see the queens silently smirking where they stood along the side of the path. They must have thought it was show-time. But this bad cabaret act didn't care for his lines or the venue and so I left. And as far as I know, Jason remained to find some person/s in the dark with whom he had no unfinished business. Someone – anyone – who wasn't me.

He was right. It *was* the wrong place to end an already expired relationship – just as it was the wrong place to start one, which we did over three years ago on a crisp January Sunday late afternoon when I thought I was just having a bit of 'casual', 'no-strings' fun. (Ironically he wasn't even my first choice; I tried several times to lose him, but he wouldn't leave me alone, walking determinedly after me like an over-friendly stray.)

Weirdly, even in the dark, I could see he was wearing the same sweat-shirt as me – he bought me mine as an Xmas present and liked it so much he got one for himself. As we stood so close yet so far I felt like pleading – 'Don't you *see*? We were *meant for one another*! Look, we even *dress badly in the same way*!'

But some people just don't want to hear the way it is, do they, Steve?

*

Thanks for forwarding the cuttings about the hazing scandals in the US Army.

I found myself agreeing with the letter from the former

Army captain defending the hazing of military boys (and not just because I was thinking of Jason): 'Moms and Dads of America, the service isn't for everyone. We train people to kill other people. It's nasty, dirty, hellish business, and we can't childproof it and make it look pretty all the time.' The 'blood wings' ceremony in which newly qualified Marine parachutists were 'impaled', to quote one alarmist report, with their badges by other Marines smacks of a tribal initiation ceremony. Mutilation and pain are always going to be sought-after experiences by young men because they tell them they're alive and that they belong – it's contact, 'penetration' that they're looking for. I suspect that if you take away this kind of thing, you just get more of the kind of drugs that killed Joey.

ARMY RULE CHANGE TO END BAN ON GAYS says the front page of *The Times* today, 24/3/97 (clipping enc.). Of course, it's about money – and Britain not being an island any more. The Ministry of Defence was recently forced by the European Court to pay out a load of dosh to women it sacked because they became pregnant. Their lawyers are now telling them that the bloody Euros can't be relied upon to understand the MoD's attitude towards homos, and this is likely to cost them a great deal more money than even the women with buns in the oven they booted out. In fact, it seems unlikely that the ban will actually be lifted, at least not for some time yet. But this is the first time the MoD has even countenanced changing its policy – which, we are told, the 'top brass' are very much attached to.*

I can reveal that the reason homosexuality is such a problem for the top brass is our *class system*. The British Armed Forces are the last redoubt of class privilege – almost all the ranks are working-class in background, and most of the officers are public- (or grammar-) school educated. The officers' mess is basically a gentlemen's club – usually for those who weren't bright enough to go to Oxbridge and/or the City. And one of the interesting effects of the British class system has been to make much of the history of homosexuality in this

---

* It was finally lifted in January 2000 after a ruling by the European Court of Human Rights that the ban represented an invasion of lesbian and gay recruits' human rights.

country, at least up until the 50s, the history of upper-class nobs knobbing, or more usually being knobbed by, the lower orders; the English gentleman has never been able to resist a bit of rough (and nor has the bit of rough been able to resist a bit of nob – either for their guineas or for the exotic *difference* that class bestowed upon them; sex with a toff was not queer because it was business and because a toff wasn't another lad).

The last great homosexual scandal which precipitated the Wolfenden Report into the policing of homosexuality (and prostitution) which led to private, consenting, twosome, over-twenty-one homosexuality being decriminalized in 1967 was the Lord Montagu scandal of the 1950s, in which Monty and some of his poof pals were convicted of gross indecency by the evidence of two young airmen who had turned 'Queen's evidence'. The prosecution made a meal of the fact that these were gentlemen of high rank who had consorted with and exploited these low-born boys. Significantly, the law reform of 1967 exempted the Armed Forces and the Merchant Navy. (Twenty-one, which remained the age of consent for male homosex until it was reduced to eighteen a few years ago, was chosen because at that time National Service was still in operation and covered the years eighteen to twenty-one. Monty's saucy RAF boys were National Servicemen.)

I think the Ministry of Defence top brass know the appeal of the ranks very well and are terrified that if the ban were lifted their officers would not be able to resist the temptations of all those fit young lads with their direct manner, trusting natures, and apparent lack of middle-class neurosis. Or I could just be projecting again.

Regarding Wolfenden, according to *Heterosexual Dictatorship: Male Homosexuality in Post-war Britain* by Patrick Higgins, which I've just finished, most of the experts addressing the Wolfenden Committee thought that 'The pervert is not a homosexual, but a heterosexual who engages in homosexual acts,' or that 'the pervert is simply a filthy-minded heterosexual'. Which sounds to me like a good argument for sex with heterosexual men.

And, if you think about it, all this anxiety about non-homosexual men being tempted into perversion makes sense

– frumpy 50s heterosexuality must have made the invert's bumhole look like Ali Baba's Cave: forbidden, naughty, and free of familial, marital and national obligations (i.e. free). It's why the report was also concerned with prostitution – any alternative orifices to suburban sanctified state-registered vaginas had to be sealed up or at least have a heavy veil drawn over them. And in fact that's what the Wolfenden Reform tried to do – it decriminalized homosex in private between two men over twenty-one, that's to say the kind of homosex that was ungovernable in the first place and criminalizing it made it devastatingly public through scandals like the one that engulfed poor Monty.

Higgins includes an account from Montgomery Hyde's much older history of British homosexuality, *The Other Love*, which I thought you'd appreciate:

> When trains arrived from the port with sailors on leave, the stations of the main London terminuses (Paddington, Victoria and Liverpool Street) offered some possibilities.
>
> On arrival of the train there would be scores of young sailors tumbling out of the train, all it seemed in violent need of a good piss. They ran helter-skelter in to the large lavatory on the platform, and pulling down the flap of their trousers, pissed for all they were worth … If they happened to note some eager looker [meatgazer?], they would exclaim: 'He's a beauty isn't he? Like him up your bum, chum?' This sally would be followed by gales of laughter from the other pissing fellows. If the pubs were still open, one at once said: 'Come along for another one, Jack, before the boozers shut.' And, once safely behind a pint at the bar, as often as not one succeeded in dragging him back to one's room [where one would interview him for one's next book].

*

I travelled to Brighton the other day with my friend David, a.k.a. The Divine David, a performance artist so anti-gay he makes me look like Michaelangelo Signorile. I met David in 1984 in a King's Cross 'alternative' pub called The Bell.

The Bell was full of young people like myself and David who had run away from the provinces or suburbia to be at the post-New Wave post-New Romantic cutting edge of things, on the dole. This was where I met many of my current circle of closest friends (I haven't been out since the 80s), including Nick, an academic ex-rock star, ex-associate of Malcolm McLaren, – and my closest confidant this side of the Atlantic. One of the things that attracted me to Nick was that in a display of true sartorial terrorism he used to wear a *blazer* to this den of drunken supplementary benefit anarchists and struck up conversations about Continental philosophers; 'So,' he'd shout above the din of Blondie's 'Sunday Girl' on the hefty PA, 'What do you think of Heidegger's archetypes of the Beautiful Soul and the Hard of Heart? Do you think it's possible for them to ever be fully reconciled and integrated in one person, as he recommends?' In his own sweet way, Nick is just as scary as The Divine David.

David had been through the mill. From Blackpool, his father in the Merchant Navy, his mother an amateur dramatist (The Kitchen-Sink Technique), he'd taken his route out of madness by becoming a cabaret performer specializing in Shirley Bassey impersonation at working men's clubs at the age of sixteen. And long therapy sessions with Dr Smirnoff and consultations with Mr Speed.

David decided he wanted me as a friend, and I had no choice in the matter. 'We *are* going to live together one day, Mark,' he would announce, matter-of-factly. 'There's no point fighting it. You'll want for nothing, of course. You'll have your own bank account. You'll even have you're own room. *But I'll have the key.* There'll be electric fences and machine-gun towers around the perimeter of the compound – for your own safety, *naturally.* And when we're having dinner – ALONE – the phone might ring. A butler will scurry in and whisper in my ear, "*It's 'is sister!*" And I will whisper back, covering my mouth with my hand so as not to spoil your enjoyment of your Pavlova: "*Tell 'er 'e's not 'ere!*"'

Shortly after I met him, David developed chronic hepatitis and returned up North, sending me compilation tapes of tracks by the B-52s and Mark and the Mambas, interspersed with snippets of him impersonating John Hurt impersonating Quentin Crisp (Crisp Senior [*Exasperated and disgusted*]: Do you intend to spend the rest of your life admiring yourself in the mirror!? Crisp Junior [*Casually*]: 'If I poss-sibly caaan.') and pictures of himself in make-up and lounge-act ear-rings with a motorcycle jacket over his shoulder, pointing at the camera, legs apart *à la* Marc Bolan with 'Leather Rat loves ya!' emblazoned across the bottom of the photo in silver nail varnish.

Now he's returned to London, liver regenerated – well, at least those bits absolutely necessary to sustain life – reincarnated as The Divine David. Thanks to his appearances at Duckie, a pop/rock performance art club run by two pals of mine, Simon and Amy, which attracts those people who used to go to The Bell ten years ago who have survived Aids, house music, and having to get a job. David has become a big hit here.

Which I'm very glad about, for many reasons. Flattered as I was, the years when I felt like I was his only audience often produced unnerving moments. Once, visiting him in Manchester, he performed Hawkwind's 'Silver Machine' to me in his tiny bedroom. I had nightmares for weeks afterwards.

On the train to Brighton David was talking, as he does, about suicide, and why he's never paid a bill in his life, when a very cute laddie in his early twenties got on at Crawley and sat behind us on the other side of the aisle. Now, mind you, this boy wasn't merely cute. This boy was offensively beautiful. He sported an absurdly, impossibly fetching little broken nose, so uncalculating in its perfect crooked beauty. This was the sort of boy that makes you think: 'Well, I'm sorry, really I am, but looking like *that* you just don't have any right to live because you won't live with *me*.'

At least, that's what David and I found ourselves thinking.

This vision of frustration sat on the aisle seat with his almost-but-not-quite-as-pretty-because-I-want-to-be-the-centre-of-attention blonde girlfriend of about the same age on his right. Almost immediately, without even having the decency to wait until the train pulled out of the station, they began snogging and groping. Nonchalantly glancing over my shoulder, pretending I had a nervous tic or a perfectly natural curiosity as to what was happening in that part of the world every fifteen seconds, I could masochistically remind myself of their happiness. David, sitting in front of me, only had to move his eyes fractionally to his left to take in the scene. Which he did, frequently.

'Girls don't really *appreciate* lads like that,' I sighed bitterly, and only slightly ironically.

'No, you're right,' agreed David. '*They* wouldn't get him to sit on their face so they can stick their tongues up his arse and swivel them around for hours, would they?'

The train rattled on, through the bright sunshine and thickening heat of the year's first truly warm day. Trees and bushes sprouting bright, hopeful blossoms and fresh, tender new leaves eager to absorb another Summer's energy flashed past the window. As if in tune with the rising sap of the countryside around us, the pawing, groping and chewing on tongues behind us gathered a furious pace that would have put Stravinsky to shame.

'I don't believe this is an accident,' said David, his eyes flicking over my shoulder again. 'I believe this was ordained to remind us of our hopelessness.'

By now the heavy petting behind us had become so heavy that it would collapse the top shelf of W.H. Smith. It became apparent that these innocent, carefree young lovers were a little *exhibitionistic*. Their sex-show was not so much taunting as philanthropic. 'An act of generosity', as David put it.

'I told you it wasn't accidental,' said The Divine One, as the display behind me reached some kind of climax. 'It's a sign.'

Suddenly the train shuddered to a halt, and the guard announced that the undergrowth and brush alongside a stretch of the track ahead of us had unaccountably burst into flames. It took several engines and scores of men more than an hour to extinguish the mini inferno.

The brush fire took a while too.

Love,

Mark

PS Hope 'Max' and whatever else he symbolizes is still alive.

PPS OK, OK I give up. You win the Jean Genet self-loathing quotation competition.

Killer Queen

Dear Mark,

If gay studies books are like record albums then it's time for me to die in a plane crash. Or open up a bar.

Back when I cared about such things (your grumbling about age is contagious, especially as I'm five years older than you and have another birthday bearing down on me one week from today. When's yours?) I observed that rock bands are almost never worth listening to after the third album. Most, of course, don't merit even one single, but I'm talking about the good bands. By the fourth album at the very latest rock performers are no longer tormented teenagers with strange and dangerous notions but public figures (even 'minor' or 'cult' ones) who find they have nothing else to write about but their new position in life as public figures. To spare the world their militantly annoying irrelevance, I had the idea that all such persons should either die or open a bar in their home towns where a couple of nights a week they could trot out their old standards. Anyone who really feels a need to see, say, New Order, should have to go and buy drugs from them in their Manchester hacienda (or whatever). Iggy Pop belongs in Ypsilanti. Neil Young in northern Ontario.

But of course there are serious musicians who only get better as the years go by. And there's even the occasional rock star who doesn't turn into a silly old fool 'with mascara and a Fender guitar who thinks he can arouse us' (why hasn't Morrissey included that particular B-side on any of his recent compilations?).

Having milked the interviews-with-military-men for all it's worth short of self-parody (though, not, apparently so much as to preclude inspiring a rip-off imitation: see below) I find myself now authoring a book about the audience for my first three books. Worse, for a while I was afraid that all I would have to write about in this letter would be my new acquaintance with other writers.

But then I had my little adventure with Navy Davy.

I loved the story of your train ride with The Divine David. I, too, have just experienced public sex with a straight couple, even if in my story the girl was on paper.

Dave is a thirty-eight-year-old Navy officer who introduced himself to me at my first reading here last fall. I gave him my e-mail address and he started forwarding me postings from the Servicemembers' Legal Defence Network, a gay military advocacy group that he is involved with that made headlines here a few months back with a report showing that discharges for homosexuality have dramatically increased under Clinton's 'Don't Ask, Don't Tell' policy. (Proportionally, the Air Force is the branch with the highest discharge rate, followed by the Navy. The Army, and especially the Marine Corps, have had far fewer.) Eventually we got together for coffee.

Dave's tall, genial, articulate, not unhandsome, but a little desperate. His web page is one big lonely hearts ad, and he's offered his friends a $700 cash bounty for information leading to the capture of a husband. He never had sex with a man until he was thirty. He underwent his gay conversion only four years ago. He's at Naval Station Puget Sound in Bremerton. In one of my e-mail messages I told him about my disappointing visits to his city. I wished it was more like Brest in Fassbinder's *Querelle*, all giant phalluses and drunken swaggering Brad Davises. He confirmed that the town is always pretty dead, and added that, *to get his hair cut*, he drives down to Fort Lewis, the large Army post one hour south of here. He mentioned that he had heard there were some cruisy spots on base. Two weeks ago he invited me to accompany him there. I accepted, thinking it might be fun to get haircuts and maybe ogle some soldiers in a fast food restaurant.

It was my first visit to an Army post since I left Germany. Due to heightened security accompanying the two-year anniversary of the Oklahoma City bombing and current Timothy McVeigh trial, there was a long line of civilians waiting to sign on. But since I was with Dave, the gate guard just waved us through. Our first stop was a PX mini-mall. Dave marched me into the men's room and motioned for me to investigate the stalls. I complied, and was impressed to see lots of very detailed graffiti, and a sizeable, well-worn glory hole. The middle stall was occupied. I looked through and saw what appeared to be a teenage dependant frantically stroking his small penis. He wasn't what I was there for. Plus which my tour guide, whom I'd taken to be a prim, good middle-class gay, was waiting outside. Our next stop was the nearby on-base Greyhound station, which Dave explained serves as the 'holding area' when the mini-mall tearoom gets too busy. Finally we ended up at the food court in the main PX, where the gleaming new men's room stalls are of black graffiti-resistant tiles. Dave asked me whether the graffiti I'd seen at the mini-mall tearoom was recent. I told him that one of the messages I'd read was dated that very day, though advertised a late evening meeting. 'We can stay here until then if you want,' he offered, very earnestly.

Do I need to tell you that this man is now my friend?

Dave ate some food, and I studied the Army boys around me. I was struck with the popularity of a new hairstyle: a sort of modified Marine Corps cut, not as 'tight' on the sides but shorn higher, leaving just a little ovular 'pussy patch' on top resembling a beanie.

I said that maybe it was time we checked the mini-mall again.

This time, a peek through the hole revealed . . . something that wasn't for me. I came back out, sighing, but Dave was having none of it. 'You're giving up much too easily. You just need to stay in there and wait for that guy to leave. Otherwise you might lose your place in line.' He assured me that he didn't mind waiting. He'd brought several gay studies books.

After another half hour the undesirable cruiser left. Per Dave's instructions I moved into the 'alpha stall'. Within minutes a soldier in camouflage came into the adjoining stall and tapped his boot. I saw just enough of his face that when he stuck his flaccid dick through the hole I didn't hesitate. He quickly got hard. I heard, but didn't think anything of, the sound of rustling paper. When the bathroom door squeaked he hastily repositioned his boots. It was then that I saw what he was reading: a pussy magazine. I could see the pages clearly – not a penis on any of them. At first I suspected this might just be a prop, but when the interloper left

I could hear the soldier excitedly flipping the pages, trying to find just the right image. Then there was another interruption, and another and another: busy queens, it became apparent. Another half hour went by. Finally he passed me a note:

I LOVE HOW YOU SUCK MY COCK –
CAN WE GO TO THE BUS STATION BATHROOM?

I wrote back that I was new around there, and on foot.

I'VE GOT MY CAR – GO OUT FRONT DOOR.

And he drew an intricate little map of how to find the bus station. I exited first. Dave was positioned in the food court with his eye glued to the door. To his irritation, the GI used the moment to slip out the back door. Dave pointed the way to the bus station and again urged me to take my time.

A pair of boots awaited me. I locked myself in the neighbouring space and waited for the guy to again instigate things. When he didn't, I tapped my foot, and was just about to kneel down and stick my head under when the door opened and another GI came in. The boots I'd been advancing on belonged to the wrong guy.

As soon as we were alone again, the soldier did 'the limbo', sliding his knees and dick under the partition. He had smooth olive skin with just a little dark body hair, untrimmed pubes, non-Calvin white underwear and about 6½ to 7 inches, conservatively measured. Intermittently he thrust his hips like he was fucking my face, all the time still flipping through his magazine. At first I pushed my knee against his thigh, but he drew his leg back as though he didn't want to be touched anywhere else. But both of us eventually forgot this barrier, and I guess I got my 'revenge', because when he came (reluctantly, I spat), I was just too lost in the moment to notice that I'd targeted his leg.

I left my stall first, and was washing my hands when a (civilian or off-duty military) man came in with his small son. Right under their noses I hastily scrawled a note on a square of paper towel, and tossed it under his door.

CALL ME WHEN YOU'RE IN SEATTLE. I HAVE A VCR.

Naturally I wanted a better look at him. From a corner of the bus station coffee shop I observed that he was tall, pretty built, with head shaved almost bald, twenty-four or twenty-five, a handsome face but that silly Army Hitler moustache.

Dave was eager to hear all the details. At first he was appalled to learn that I had played bitch to a straight soldier, but I didn't have too much trouble convincing him that I was not unhappy. He said that he was relieved: he'd been so afraid that I wouldn't get anything.

On the ride home the conversation turned to his sexual experiences with women. There were two, both in the Philippines. He was there in the aftermath of the big volcanic eruption a few years back, helping evacuate the Americans. His ship was blanketed by the still-raining ash. Among the first buildings the Filipinos hastily put back up was, of course, the brothel. Anxious to do his part for the local economy, the captain of Dave's ship generously saw to it that each of his men got laid, and himself insisted on buying Dave a woman. Dave rose to the occasion but irritated the captain by declining to share all the juicy details.

I was touched that Dave wanted to bond with me like this. But I was disappointed to learn that my experience with the soldier is not at all unusual. When I called my old sailor buddy Anthony in San Diego and told him this story, he said, 'Oh. Well, that's ... not uncommon.' He confessed that on the naval station in Yokusuka, Japan, he blew more than one pussy-rag clutching sailor at the Exchange, but had been too embarrassed to tell me. Now that I think about it, he did send me a photo of the base glory hole after it was boarded up.

*

You write that you are squeamish about cottaging. Tearoom sex is a relatively recent pursuit for me, though I have been an avid men's room voyeur since I was ten or eleven. (You did say that, like Genet's Sublieutenant Seblon in *Querelle*, you love reading bathroom graffiti. Another favourite Simpson quote is that you know you're in hell when there is none. There are few places more lonely than a dead tearoom.

Two days ago Dave and I returned for a second visit to Fort Lewis. Nothing. I was reminded that after too long an uneventful visit, say, more than two hours, a men's room turns into a kind of sensory deprivation chamber, with one sense remaining and growing ever sharper. I should have known it was going to be a slow day when I noticed an abandoned newspaper on the floor of the stall. It was a publication called *Senior Scene*.) And I've never really been much for glory holes. To me, a disembodied penis suddenly poking through a wall is usually more unnerving and comical than erotic. I would prefer to kneel before a man that I can see in full – or stand before a kneeling man that can look up at me. But I love the *promise* of a glory hole.

Seattle City Councilmember and mayoral candidate Jane Noland is fascinated by glory holes, too. As the very first move of her campaign, she's sponsoring a special city ordinance to outlaw them. According to the April 27 issue of the alternative weekly *The Stranger*, Noland's special interest originated when a neighbourhood organization busybody invited her to tour a north Seattle business called the Love Boutique.

> The store-front seemed innocuous enough, but inside, down a dark hallway divided into booths where customers pump quarters into coin slots and channel-surf from one bad porn flick to another, the councilmember and the neighbourhood activist found a dank and pungent den of sin – jism on the walls, used condoms on the floors, green mould on the vinyl chairs, strange holes cut into thin walls separating the booths.

And I haven't even been there yet.

> Informed of the function of these 'glory holes', Noland was appalled – something had to be done. Seattle vice cops informed Noland that dozens of arrests had been made at the Love Boutique, but they were difficult to prosecute because the law only addressed the issue of more than one person in a booth at a time – putting certain body parts through glory holes was not technically illegal. Vice requested a new law, one that would affect all the video booths in the city ... The resulting ordinance ... would make the penetration of glory holes a crime. It would also require that the arcades rearrange their booths so they all face toward a closely monitored public space. Finally, the half doors [sawed-off, unlock-

able] that allow customers to enjoy 'semi-privacy' (while also allowing workers to monitor how many feet are inside the booth) would be removed.

A porno panopticon, anyone?

The Love Boutique is in a part of town far removed from Seattle's gay neighbourhoods, and its glory holes are reputed to cater to the married and 'closeted'. As a straight chaser, my selfish interest in the preservation of such venues is obvious. Their demise eliminates one of the very few places where straight men can have sex with other men without having to surrender to what you call the dictates of late-twentieth-century sex pedantry. Bars, bathhouses and sex clubs are GAY. Personal ads require sexual identification in print (the worst kind, I'm sure you'll agree). And I don't suppose that, except for the police, non-gay men have many handy excuses for wandering public spaces like Hampstead Heath at night.

But I like tearooms even better than video arcades. They're free. And they can totally fuck with the lines between gay and straight, private and public, sexual and non-sexual. Men are also freer to have sex with men who don't fit their standard 'type' in such places. I still want to write a big Marjorie Garber-type book on toilet sex, with lots of bad puns about fluidity.

*

My preference for tearoom and arcade trade is probably not unrelated to my own porn star ineligibility. As a result of something that happened to me a long time ago I have a scar on my chest. This makes me uncomfortable about removing my shirt in front of even one other person, let alone a camera. (As recently as two years ago I went to a San Diego gay bar with a cute young sailor and his young lover. Both men imagined themselves very hot, and could not conceal their annoyance when some strange woman came running up to me and begged me to model for her 'boudoir photography' – I had that 'pseudo-European' look that was in just then, she said. I tried to sell her on Alex, but she made a terrible face when I said he was Jewish/Native American.) I've never once gone to a bathhouse. Friends always tried to assure me: 'You can wear a towel.' But that wasn't the part of my body I wanted to hide. In tearooms and video arcades I can proudly display my best assets: my face and my penis. The only role I could have played in porn is stunt dick.

Actually, during a period in my twenties when I first got my hands on a camcorder and obviously had way too much time on my hands, I videotaped myself masturbating from every conceivable angle. When Kyle, the southern-boy soldier you said you liked best in *Barrack Buddies*, asked me to copy some porn for him, I used the insert edit function (on my Army engineering office boss's camera) to dub my own penis over some nameless porn star's in the come shot. I guess I wanted to leave him a souvenir. Kyle never noticed, but a quick-witted Liberian queen he showed the tape to did. As both men were central to the gay Frankfurt scene, you can imagine what ensued. For months afterwards, I'd meet gay soldiers in the club who could only stutter and blush. Later I found out that Kyle regularly screened the video at parties, delighting in pointing out the penis that belonged to 'that book writin' bitch'.

*

How funny that we were reading *Wonder Bread and Ecstasy* at the same time. And how interesting that our reactions were in some ways so similar, and in others so different. You loved Joey Stefano. I saw some of his videos but don't even remember him.

Flawless bodies are nice, but not all that fascinating to me. Inappropriate body hair, moles, pockmarks, zits, absent pecs or even a gut aren't necessarily obstacles to my arousal. I suppose this could have something to do with my image of my body as flawed, though awareness of their own physical shortcomings doesn't seem to keep many gay men I know from holding to the most exacting standards. I think it's probably more that my turn-ons are (as ex-porn star Scott O'Hara recently wrote in his comments on my novel-in-progress) hopelessly abstract. What excites me about the boys in *Good Morning Marines* are certain of their body movements, certain looks in their eyes. Vague hints of qualities that I associate with my own ideas about that Middle West mystique.

But it does pain me a little that you were seduced by the

Alyson copywriters into believing that Joey Stefano is from the Midwest – 'the heartland', as the dust-jacket copy has it. Really he's from greater Philadelphia, an East Coast urban hell far more nightmarish than any part of Los Angeles you may have seen during your US sojourn.

I lived in Philadelphia for a little over a year in 1984–1985. It's a period I delete from my official biography. David Lynch (who hails from Washington state) credits Philadelphia as the inspiration for the ugliest elements in *Blue Velvet*, *Eraserhead*, *Twin Peaks*, etc. I was mugged there. I witnessed a woman slashed on the subway. I saw a housing project where people threw refrigerators and German shepherds out of windows and stabbed old women with scissors for $4 in stairwells that were pitch black and covered with ice because the lights and elevators didn't work, because the contractors were as crooked as the rest of the city. To evict some squatters, the city dropped a bomb from a helicopter, incinerating 60 houses. I have actual transcripts of arrest records of the more than 100 cops and judges indicted on corruption charges during my stay (my roommate was a law student who worked in the city jail). Did you ever see *Witness* with Harrison Ford? The cop cars used in that film were bugged by the FBI and later used to uncover a Philadelphia Police crime syndicate. And there's a scene in the film uncannily similar to the ride I took with the police there after my mugging in which they pulled some black kid out of a video game arcade, slammed his face against the squad car window and demanded, 'This is the guy, right?'

Sorry to lose my composure. (I'm learning that people are suspicious and uncomfortable when I actually react to something.) But Joey Stefano did not come from the Midwest.

I'm struck by the irony of you, the Oxford-educated Englishman, enthralled by Hollywood movies, and me, the Midwestern state university drop-out preferring my films subtitled. But it worries me a little that your time in the US was spent mostly in Southern California, a place that processes images of, but hardly represents the rest of this country. Maybe Channel 4 would pay for you and me to rent a car and tour, Tennessee Williams' 'Two On A Party'-like, the bars and glory holes of the American Middle West and South? I think you'd be both exhilarated and disappointed. But I guarantee your picture would change.

*

Jack Hart and Alyson Publications seek hot true stories about gay military sex

> Ten-hut! Jack Hart, the editor of *My First Time* and *The Day We Met*, is seeking submissions for an anthology from Alyson Publications of true-life gay sexual experiences involving members of the military. If you've scored with a soldier, sailor, Marine, or paratrooper (of if you yourself are – or were at one time – a man in uniform), I'd like to hear your story. Military encounters can occur in the barracks during basic training, in the trenches during time of war, or on the home front (a pick-up at a bar or tearoom, for example). Send your sexiest true stuff, men! ... Dialogue – reconstructed to the best of the author's ability – is strongly encouraged.

Paratroopers, of course, are members of the Army, not a separate branch of the US Armed Forces. I'm tempted to write Jack Hart: 'Just because I slighted the Air Force doesn't mean you have to do that, too.'

One of my new writer friends in Seattle is Matt Bernstein Sycamore. He's twenty-three, seductively sweet and strange, and a true star. A few years back he did his first porn video in San Francisco. He wasn't quite prepared for all that he was put through. A leather hood was placed over his head. He was dragged along the ground. He was gang-'raped'. He told me that he quickly went into a kind of shock, and just tried to remove himself mentally from the proceedings. But when a dish of dog food was shoved under his face, he screamed 'Blue!' – the emergency code-word to indicate that his participation was no longer consensual. Filming stopped, the lights were shut off, the hood was removed. Matt explained that he's vegan.

A month back *Culture of Desire* author Frank Browning was in town. He's writing a book about apples. We were supposed to get together Saturday night, but he ended up calling me a day early and inviting me to dine with him and syndicated *Stranger* sex advice columnist Dan Savage. At last I got to meet Seattle's most famous gay.

By the time I got to Café Septième, Browning and Savage were both pretty sloshed. Holding court in the restaurant where he once worked as a waiter, Savage (who is thirty-two and quite pretty) intermittently molested the waiters, made a mess out of the handful of extra butter tabs he demanded, and amused himself scorching napkins on the tealights. When at one point he flatly declared, 'Gays are stupid,' I thought it was the right moment to produce a copy of *Anti-Gay*. Savage made sounds of delight, but put the book down when he came to the dust-jacket mention of Bruce LaBruce. 'I've seen *Hustler White*. Talk about mediocre.' So I pressed that book into the hands of Frank Browning, and gave Savage a copy of *The Masculine Marine*.

Frank wanted to go to The Cuff, where he was supposed to rendezvous with a trick from a previous visit to Seattle. The guy wasn't there, but Alex was. Frank, who must be about 50 but looks great, quickly succeeded in picking up someone half his age. As they tongued down, I asked Alex if he could drive me home. He cheerfully assented, but once outside flew into a rage. Why, he wouldn't say. At his apartment, he started violently kicking the little picket fence to the Christmas house. Of course I should have left, but I didn't want to let him off that easily. I forced him to talk, but all he could say was that he didn't care about me, didn't care about anything, that I should give up on him once and for all and adopt some other 'project'.

Over dinner I'd told Browning and Savage about the 'two-headed rabbit' incident – the time at the sex club in LA when Alex and I accidentally started having sex through a glory hole. When I realized it was him, I didn't stop. When he saw it was me, Alex went crazy. He accused me of carefully planning the deception; betraying him just as his abuser had, etc. For two years he put the episode to best advantage to avoid intimacy and generally villainize me. Savage wasn't hesitant about offering his assessment: 'The guy's a fucking asshole. Get over him!' This from a man praised by the *New York Times* the following Monday ('"Dear Abby" Doesn't Live Here Any More') as the hottest of a new breed of advice columnists, and it didn't even cost me a 32-cent stamp.

*

At the peak of the 'screwdriver incident' I referred to in my last letter, Alex sought advice from my rival for his affections, a man named Andrew Cunanan. Andrew replied that he didn't know me well enough to judge whether I would break into Alex's car trunk to steal a car vacuum cleaner and suede jacket, but offered to kill me anyway, if Alex liked. Later, when Alex confided to Andrew that his suspicions were a paranoid delusion, Andrew laughed and, quoting a John Waters movie, said, 'Baby, you're fucked up in the head.'

During the same period, I used to visit the tearoom of the bowling alley at 32nd Street Naval Station. Three times I had sex with a beautiful Navy lieutenant who liked me to stick my pinkie into his meatus. We never spoke, but eventually I matched the little Mighty Mouse tattoo on the lieutenant's tanned, hairless thigh with Jeff Trail, one of Alex and Andrew's circle of club friends.

Flashy, high-spirited and very free with his cash, the twentysomething Andrew had a crush on Alex. He regularly invited him to dine at the toney California Cuisine on University Avenue in Hillcrest. It seems sadly humorous to-night to recall conversations I had during that time with my friend Lieutenant Tim from *Sailors*, in which I voiced reservations about Andrew's character. My qualms did not, however, prevent me from accepting drinks from Andrew on the few occasions I saw him in the clubs, nor free 'trial samples' of Xanax. Andrew sold prescription drugs. He showed Alex the pistol he carried and boasted of his connections to the 'lavender mafia'. Most of his money, however, came from rich sugar-daddies.

Tonight Andrew Phillip Cunanan is the number-one featured criminal on the prime-time TV show *America's Most Wanted*. The Navy lieutenant with the Mighty Mouse tattoo was bludgeoned to death with a claw hammer. Chicago architect David Madson, with whom Alex also once dined, was found in some reeds beside a lake in Minnesota, shot in the back of the head. The seventy-two-year-old Chicago millionaire Lee Miglin was discovered in his luxury Gold Coast townhouse wrapped in plastic; he'd been tortured, stabbed, and had his throat sliced with a bow saw. At this writing Andrew's still on the lam. Last night he murdered a grounds-keeper at a Civil War cemetery outside Philadelphia.

Informed that his one-time good friend was a serial killer, Alex merely said that he was glad he left San Diego. But after a few minutes' reflection he recalled his last trip to the beach with Andrew. My aspiring marine biologist Marine ex liked to poke about in the tide pools, admiring his beloved marine invertebrates. Andrew wanted to feed a crab to a sea ane-mone. The crustacean he set his sights on eluded him, scut-tling into the crevice of a rock. Andrew attacked it with his car keys, stabbing it then prying out mashed pieces to stuff into the anemone.

Of course, it's too easy to attach an exaggerated signifi-cance to such memories now.

Enclosed is the first photo taken on the Polaroid camera Andrew gave to Alex: the psycho Marine and the killer queen. As photographed by the murdered lieutenant.

Alex with 'gay spree killer' Andrew Cunanan

The press reports that many of Andrew's closest friends are fleeing San Diego. I'm headed there – to interview military predators and turn thirty-seven.

Love,

Steve

Unnature Will Find a Way

London, 23 June 1997

Dear Steve,

Just before receiving your last letter I went to see *Jurassic Park II: The Lost World*. It turned out to be another strange case of synchronicity.

You seem puzzled that I should see so many Hollywood blockbusters. There are many reasons why I enjoy watching them, but perhaps the most important is that I like to see how Big Money goes about seducing Little People. It's why I also like advertising. There's a very definite pornographic angle to it – what is pornography if it isn't watching big assets trying to force their way into little receptacles, or, for that matter, feeding pieces of freshly mashed crab to a sea anemone?

But it's also sociologically (and therefore respectably) interesting to see what Hollywood thinks people's fantasies, hopes, dreams and nightmares might consist of. The best part of *JPII* – and now the most resonant – was when a T-Rex is brought back to *San Diego* and runs riot, Godzilla-like, smashing up petrol stations and fast-food joints and devouring the local residents. At one point it trashes a video store that looks suspiciously like Blockbuster in Hillcrest – tanned men with shiny faces in T-shirts run hither and thither screaming.

Come to think of it, Andrew does have very large teeth in those pictures.

'Only humans kill when they're not hungry', one of the characters tells us (obviously she's never seen what a well-fed dog can do to a field of sheep, or a well-fed, toothless cat can do to a mouse...); dinosaurs, you see, should be respected and allowed to go about their business of killing people because they're Natural and it's what they were born to do. 'Nature,' Mr Goldblum tells us, 'will find a way.'

According to the press cuttings you sent me, Andrew was not a hungry cat, nor even a sadistic one – just some queen who wasn't at ease with his sexuality: 'he murdered to try and kill that part of himself he wasn't happy with'. So Andrew was just *misunderstood*. He was *resisting* his Nature. Really, I sympathize with him. You go through all that trouble of murdering your friends, cracking their skulls with claw hammers, cutting their throats with bow saws, torturing them, wrapping them in plastic, and still the press won't accept that you kill not because you're full of 'self-loathing' but *because you enjoy it.*

Even when it's written all over your face. I looked at that snap of Andrew with Alex which you enclosed before I read the letter and immediately thought: 'Who is that mad scary bitch?' (But then, people say the same about me.)

Andrew's very monstrousness and madness is what makes him familiar to me. Is he really so different from any of us? Especially those of us who use other people to act out our fantasies (which means pretty much everyone)? It's darkly amusing to think that the Grim Reaper, who has been stalking these letters for some time now, even if only in the abstract, has finally made an appearance – as a Hillcrest Amex queen living in a world of her own making and some gullible older fag's paying.

Be careful, Steve. If gay studies are like murder novels, then you'd better watch out for the final plot twist in which the hunter becomes the hunted, the analyser becomes the analysed, the deducer the deducted. Wasn't it Genet who said that every time he knelt before his trick, he felt he was kneeling before his executioner?

*

Some people get fed-up waiting and decide to become their own executioner. I went to see *JPII* with my pre-op tranny friend Michelle who is impatiently looking forward to The Chop. While waiting for scalpel salvation, she collects dinosaur models and *Star Wars* memorabilia, and records any TV programme featuring major surgery. She is particularly interested in plastic surgery which goes horribly wrong. Three years ago she was a tattooed body-builder on steroids called Mitch who worked as a very popular male stripper called Stud-U-Like, but one day decided to jack it all in and take female hormones instead. Many queens now refuse to talk to Michelle, full of resentment because she killed off the very

Mitch, a.k.a. Stud-U-Like

Michelle shows us her tits

fuckable Mitch and replaced him with someone with *soft* tits and *long* hair. She, for her part, after many exhausting years fruitlessly trying to embody the gay ideal, has a very low opinion of gays now that she hopes to cross the sexual Rubicon very soon (she likes to startle people in the street by shouting 'GAY!' in an accusatory way out of my car window at unsuspecting men that don't come up to her high standards of masculinity).

She is already very convincing and attractive, with long blonde hair, perky tits and a very pretty face. Michelle is a great mimic – my very own transsexual Jim Carrey is a schizoid jukebox of pop cultural camp, throwing inspired and frankly scary impersonations of David Sylvian, Darth Vader and Barbara Streisand into conversations about the weather. Not surprisingly, her man-made femininity is a medley of several pop classics: part Jessica Rabbit, part Madonna, part Marilyn (the 80s gender-bender rather than the Monroe imposter), and a lot of Sally from *Third Rock From the Sun*.

To me her attractiveness is only enhanced by her impulse to slightly sabotage her demure ensemble by shouting out 'HEL-LOW!' in a frighteningly deep voice or 'RAPE ME!' in a high pitched screech whenever she sees a man she fancies (about every three minutes). Or her habit of standing in the lingerie department of Marks & Spencer throwing underwear around and yelling: 'SEX!' and 'I NEED A COCK IN MY MOUTH!' at the top of her iron lungs.

But it is her sharp-edged executioner's approach to sexuality that I most admire. Before *JPII* began (which, of course, she loved for its special effects: she is, after all, a special effect herself) Michelle was talking loudly about somebody I suspect she doesn't like very much. 'He's got *two* hits against him,' she said acidly. 'He's *gay* and has HIV. I've only got one – I've got a *penis*.'

*

Talking of penises, I recently attended the Mr Gay UK Contest in Birmingham to write a satirical piece for *The Face* magazine. Of course, it was a mistake to agree to the commission, since an event featuring lots of buffed, orange men in designer underwear being asked what their ambition is on-stage is beyond satire.

One particularly buffed, particularly orange man in particularly complicated underwear was asked by the compere: 'What's was the most embarrassing thing that ever happened to you?' Instead of replying, 'This competition,' Mr NW Town recounted a rehearsed story: 'I came out of this club, *right*, and got into this taxi, *right*, and said "Jenson Street, mate", an 'e said "Fuck off, I'm not a friggin' taxi!" I was dead embarrassed!' No one laughed.

Availing myself of the free 'VIP' bar a bit too freely, I spotted a fit twenty-something lad. I asked him if he could tell me if there were any contestants in the room.

'Just look for the fookin' freaks, mate!' he laughed. 'Anyone really unattractive wearing silly pants – that'll be a contestant.' Strangely, I felt an instant bond with this lad. He introduced himself as Mike and invited me to join him and a quiet small lad standing next to him I'd completely failed to notice called Alex, his *boyfriend*.

Mike was twenty-two, and from Lancashire. He said he was a professional rugby player who played for England several times when he was a teenager. I mentioned that some of the contestants I'd spoken to already seemed to be itching to get into one another's designer pants. Two in particular had the hots for one another – hilariously, they had both confided to me, 'I've got a boyfriend, but . . .'

'The gay scene just doesn't respect relationships,' said Mike, gripping Alex's knee for emphasis. 'Commitment means nothing. It's all about sex.'

'And,' I added, not realizing – I swear – what I was saying, 'those couples you do meet on the gay scene are usually looking for a threesome scenario.'

We had a few drinks together and then went on walkabout. By the dance floor Alex disappeared to the toilet, and Mike immediately turned to me: 'Are yer coming back wi' us tonight, then?'

I nearly spilt my pint of lager down my shirt. 'What?'

'Are yer coming back wi' me and Alex? *For sex.*'

I took a deep breath and slurred, 'Eryesokaywhynot?'

'Great,' said Mike. 'Now, could yer do us a favour?'

'Anything, Mike. Anything.'

'Could yer ask me boyfriend for us? I'm sure 'e's up for it. But it would be best if yer asked 'im yerself like.'

'Er, right...' I agreed, trying to pretend to myself that this made sense. Poor Alex. I walked over to him and casually destroyed his innocence: 'Er, Mike asked me to ask you if it'd be OK if I, er, came back with you two to the hotel tonight.' He looked shell-shocked.

'*What did you say?*'

I repeated myself, even more ineptly and brutally than the first time.

'*Mike said that to you?*' he exclaimed, appalled.

'Er, yes...' I said, realizing that things were now not going too swimmingly. Alex rushed over to Mike, who was standing sheepishly about a metre away pretending to be extremely interested in the pillar next to him. Words were exchanged. Heated words. I decided to split. I mumbled a comically inappropriate 'Sorry' at them and ratted out.

Half an hour later I ran into Mike again. 'Alex's gone back to the hotel,' he said. I apologized again. 'Don't worry about it,' he said. 'It was bound to 'appen sooner or later. It's just lucky it 'appened with someone so nice.' I think that was my cue to stick my tongue down his throat, but I hesitated. I felt it would be wrong. I felt it was really unfair to Alex.

So I grabbed Mike and shoved my tongue down his throat. Then he took me by the hand and led me into the bowels of the club – along tunnels and down stairs that he'd clearly negotiated many times before to a dark, dusty service corridor with a humming ice machine and a flickering fluorescent tube. Before I could say, 'But my hotel's only five minutes away,' Mike had taken my trousers down, sucked my dick, put a condom on it, turned round and, displaying the kind of balance and co-ordination only a pro rugby player could, crouched forwards and aimed it right up his smooth, round, hard and rather talented arse.

He was a fantastic fuck – even if it was another classic pushy controlling bottom scenario: 'Use me! Do what you want with me!' he demanded. 'Not that! *This*! Not there! *Here!*'

Afterwards, he disappeared into the night to tell his morti-fied boyfriend some unconvincing lies and left me swaying by the dance-floor listening to Gina G (*'Oo, ahh, just a little bit more/You know what I'm looking for!'*) and wondering if any of this had really happened. And why I'd given him my phone number. Was it in the hope that I might find myself in Alex's shoes in six months' time?

On the way back to my hotel in the early hours I allowed myself to be accosted in the street by Mr NW Town – the one who told the embarrassing taxi joke. To be honest, his hu-mungous stupidity was something of a turn-on. Of course, some more meaningless sex was *not* what I needed. But it's what I got. 'I like being watched,' he said, back in my hotel room, sucking on the end of my cock while playing with himself. 'Watch me,' he commanded.

I had a sudden urge to look anywhere else but down. He solved the problem by moving himself and my dick to a posi-tion where he could watch himself in the dressing-table mir-ror, with one of those beaver magazine 'Aren't I naughty?' expressions on his face. He seemed quite happy. But there's always something else, some missing ingredient, the pre-sence of which will make the scenario even hotter...

'Play with my left tit *very gently* I've only just had it pierced do you like *threesomes* do you know anyone else we should have picked someone else up off the street I like being watched w*atch me.*'

What's the most embarrassing thing that ever happened to you? I had sex with a Mr Gay UK contestant who didn't even make runner-up.

*

Mike didn't call, of course, but there is a coda to this story. As my flatmate David lives in the North, where there are only three gay people and they meet in one another's front room every Thursday evening, I asked him about this lad. Initially he said he didn't know anyone called Mike fitting that description, but he later remembered that one of his friends who had been at the Gay UK Contest that night told him he'd met someone the next morning in the hotel breakfast room who said that they'd just split up with their boyfriend the night before. He couldn't be sure, but he thought that something was mentioned about rugby. After some encouragements and threats from me, he phoned his mate. The loud laughter I could hear through two doors confirmed, before David brought me the news himself, that it was indeed Mike.

Apparently they met over the sausage hotplate and went upstairs to shag before they reached the grapefruit juice.

You see, Steve, the gay scene just doesn't respect commitment.

*

I enclose a cutting of a piece from the May issue of *Details* called, 'Her fate was SEALED'. It's about another murder in San Diego, this time of a young girl by two Navy Seal 'swim buddies', Dustin Turner and Billy Joe Brown – two good-looking, blond and brunette all-American boys who turned out to be killers in their free time as well as when on duty when they picked up Jennifer Evans, a nice college girl out for an evening with her friends.

It would appear that the author is not unaware of the homoerotic story-line here. The piece dwells lingeringly on the culture of group sex among Navy Seals (well, it did appear in the Sex issue) and how Turner and Brown would frequently pick up a young woman and fuck her together. It's clear that the Seals in general and these two in particular often used women merely as an insulation against the incest of homosexuality, an acceptable Other receptacle for their penises to share and ejaculate into without becoming Same.

It's sadly familiar that Brown and Turner make much of how they were like 'brothers'. Few expressions reveal the inability of our language to express male love more than this cliché. After all, how many brothers *really* love one another? How many brothers want to spend any time with one another, let alone all their time – work *and* play – as Dusty and Billy did? How many *married couples* want to do that?

Of course, the phrase is used as much for what it positively represents – love – as what it negatively disavows – homo love.

All the same, I think that the kind of love between men that Turner and Brown exemplified – leaving aside for the moment that they are now revealed as cold-blooded murderers – is extremely rare amongst homos. Perhaps because sublimation makes for greater passion, and perhaps because, to go back to Vidal's haunting aphorism, a friend in bed is an enemy in the making. Sex is a kind of war, and therefore it must be directed towards women, who are 'targeted', hunted and then ambushed, as Turner and Brown did many times at bars and clubs around SD. Once they've served their purpose, mopping up the two lovers' semen like a Kleenex, they are thrown back into the night, taking the shame and the violence of the act with them, leaving these two All-American boys pure and unstained in their love and virility. Such men have a fierce ambivalence towards women – needing them yet resenting them; resenting them for needing them, resenting them for being born of them, resenting them for *existing*. Sometimes that ambivalence can be murder.

Each now claims the other did it and that they covered up for them because they were, like, y'know, Swim Buddies.

TURNER: If I met him in the civilian world ... we would probably just have been acquaintances ... It's different from the relationship with my best friend growing up in High School because of the training Brown and I went through together. That brought us extremely close. Even though Brown did something incredibly stupid, I had to look out for him ...

BROWN: I've never felt that much dedication to anyone or anything before. If one of us was having a problem, the other one didn't criticize. We clicked so well.

Their 'love' is now broadcast to the world to get themselves off the hook at the other's expense. According to the interview, some of their acquaintances wondered if they were lovers in the carnal sense. Turner flatly denies that there were any 'homosexual tendencies' between him and Brown. The reporter follows this denial with the observation, 'Brown apparently loved his swim buddy so much that he even considered raising his son with him. He and Turner were moving in together, and Brown thought the two men could make their house a home. Brown said that if he could get custody of his son, they "would be good role models for Billy Jr.".'

It's rather interesting, isn't it, that I've just spent a couple of pages rationalizing and explaining Dusty and Billy's murder in terms of repressed homosexuality after having dismissed this explanation of Andrew's killing spree in one line. But I suppose in my defence I can say that (apart from the fact that I didn't fancy Andrew) Andrew's homosexuality was not repressed: as an openly gay man its *expression* defined his life and also the shape of his psychosis which ended the lives of other gay men; whereas Dusty and Billy's *repressed* homosexuality defined theirs – this is not to say that their homoness was the most important thing about them, the thing which 'explained' them: rather that its *repression* did. (And of course it's their repression that interests me.)

*

A few weeks ago Stéphane, the 'cub' reporter on *Têtu* who interviewed me about *Anti-Gay*, was visiting London – with his mother. Stéphane, who is in his mid-twenties (and very cute, but not my type: he's literate), was understandably very embarrassed that he was travelling with his mama.

I rescued him from engulfment and the stuffy hotel he was staying at and took him for a drive. Since it was already after 11.30 p.m., pub closing time, and since neither of us really had the stomach – or the drugs – for a club, I took him to Russell Square, a cruising area in the centre of town. We sat on a park bench chatting as shadowy, silent men circled around us.

Stéphane told me that a lot of gays in Paris were abandoning the gay scene for hanging around dirty bookshops hoping to find 'straight' men to connect with. Of course, what Stéphane really meant was that *he's* been hanging around a lot of dirty bookshops lately. Apparently the 'post-Aids' gay scene there, like here, has gone more and more explicitly sexual, with lots of sex clubs opening where you can fuck and suck without having to dance, buy drinks, or talk about the latest fashions, but this hasn't stemmed the defections to the 'heterosexual' red-light district.

'I think that gays are no longer finding other gays so desiring,' Stéphane explained. 'I think that they are less interested in all that and want something more, 'ow you say? *Ordinaire.*'

On his return to Paris, Stéphane faxed me a letter which mentioned that he ran into some gay activists. Apparently they were horrified by the interview I gave in *Têtu*. An argument ensued which, Stéphane said, 'ended with the same and non-original: "But, what about this poor young guy trapped in his 'omophobic provincial town blah blah blah". As you see, Mark, 'ere too the activists 'ate you, which is not the case with most of the average gays I talked to.'

Naturally, this 'poor young guy trapped in his homophobic provincial town' is really the activist who hasn't grown up or left home in his head.

Which brings me to the clipping you kindly sent me of the review of *Anti-Gay* in *The Harvard Gay & Lesbian Review* by Michael Schwartz, which contains the outrageous slur: 'Mark Simpson . . . comes across as unaccountably smug.'

What does he mean by 'unaccountably'? I'm younger than him, smarter than him, a better writer than him and – since he's a queer academic – almost certainly better looking. My smugness is *entirely* accountable. Schwartz reminds me of an English academic reviewing *Anti-Gay* in *Gay Times* who denounced the 'metropolitan world-weariness' of the contributors and how out of touch this was with the lives of 'ordinary' gays. I sent him a letter that said, 'Talk of metropolitan world-weariness only makes sense if you believe that the point of urban living is the edification of the peasantry.'

Thank you for alerting me to the *New York Observer* review of Daniel Harris's book *The Rise & Fall of Gay Culture*. Of course, this can't be the same Daniel Harris that reviewed *Anti-Gay* in the *Bay Area Reporter* last year? No one would be so foolish as to put their own name to a review hysterically dismissing a book which has just made their own old news a year before it was published, would they? Or if they were, they'd have to declare an interest, wouldn't they? I wrote to the *New York Observer* that 'I get the impression Mr Harris is something of a nostalgic rad-fag who hankers after the days when he imagines homosexuality was a mixture of tinkly cocktail laughter and frightening the horses (something which, judging by his jacket blurb photo, he has a natural propensity for)'.

They didn't publish it. No one seems to publish my letters. Are they too nasty or something?

*

I recently ran into Jean Baudrillard. Literally. I was at the Institute for Contemporary Arts (a place where lots of unemployable graduates mooch around in black all day) where he was due to give a talk when I walked straight into a short fat ugly man who looked like a French farmer in glasses wearing an expensive brown jacket and grey cord trousers. I apologized, but he serenely refused to even acknowledge that I existed – just like the Gulf War. Then I recognized the features of the world's leading theoretician of postmodernism and hyperreality.

The talk itself was hilarious. I can't remember what it was billed as being about. No one else did; they'd come to see Jean. He talked or rather read for about forty-five minutes in appalling English about nothing in particular, the only words I could make out were 'modernism' and 'postmodernism', repeated over and over, with the occasional 'simulacra' thrown in. Since it was warm and dark in the auditorium, I promptly fell asleep to the sounds of the poststructuralist lullaby and, so I'm told, snored very loudly. Five minutes before Jean finished I woke up.

A snooty woman on the other side of Nick, my friend and escort for the evening, was giving me death-ray stares, but I pretended not to notice. Then the questions came from the floor, courtesy of a mike held by an oleaginous creepy bald ICA flunky who looked like Homer Simpson's boss but behaved like his p.a. and who introduced Jean with much hand-wringing and over-the-top obsequiousness and loudly professed thanks to Mr Baudrillard for gracing his humble establishment with his august presence, etc. He also very proudly announced that questions would be taken 'from the audience here with a *cordless mike*, from the audience watching Mr Baudrillard via *close circuit TV* in the other hall and via *e-mail* from the *Internet*, where this talk is being transmitted *live around the world!'*

Another flunky sat on stage next to Jean, eyes self-effacingly lowered, allegedly to help with translation. Every minute or so, in the middle of a sentence that no one could hear anyway, Jean would struggle with a particular English word or phrase he needed and would lean back and over to the right to whisper the French towards the translator, who would snap to attention, eyes still lowered, then eagerly whisper something back in Jean's ear, at which the great man would then shake his head dismissively, lean forward, and go on struggling nobly by himself.

After the sixth or seventh time that he had done this and the translator was beginning to look as if he might strangle himself with the mike lead, I couldn't help but laugh out loud. It was such a hammy reminder that no one else, especially not a *translator*, could possibly supply the words Jean wanted. Nick chuckled along with me, not being able to resist the Pythonesque quality of it all, like the scene in *The Life of Brian* where the Roman consul has a comical speech impediment which makes him a laughing stock ('I ought to thwow those outwageous wevolutionawy wapscallions to the wions!'), but has anyone who corrects him executed.

By the end, the woman to Nick's right had crucifixion in her eyes.

The funny thing is, I really rate Baudrillard's work. It's just Baudrillard that is such a disappointment. But then, maybe that's the postmodern way he wants it.

*

Alas, I can't match your Navy Davy experience, but I did recently meet a Crazy Stevie from Exeter on Hampstead Heath in the early evening, a young lad of twenty-one.

Afterwards, we got chatting and I invited him back to my place for some tea. He told me he was staying in London with a married man that he used to shag in Exeter, which he visited on business quite regularly. The shagging stopped the day his wife turned up on his mum and dad's doorstep demanding to see him. She'd found a photo of him in her husband's wallet. 'But we're best of friends now,' he said. 'And she's always happy for me to come and stay with them in London.'

'Really?' I said. 'Do you still bonk her husband?'

'Oh, no,' said Steve, hurriedly. 'I don't fancy him any more. But he still tries it on. He still carries that photo of me around in his wallet.'

We talked a bit about London and how busy it was compared to Exeter. He told me he didn't like London much. 'It's a bit worrying sometimes,' he said. 'I mean, people keep coming up to you an' asking you for things. Sometimes they won't leave you alone.'

I'd noticed that Steve was a bit smelly. I put it down to the fact that it was a hot day. At my place I drew him a bath and lent him a shirt. And then, just as I was beginning to wonder how to get him out of the flat (I hate sharing a bed with strangers) he announced that he had to be going now and disappeared into the night.

But not before I'd given him my telephone number – a strange thing to do perhaps with a casual pick-up that you didn't really fancy that much.

Of course, precisely because I didn't really fancy him that much, he called me. Two days later, on a Sunday evening when I was preparing for an early night with a cold and a hangover. 'Hello, Maark? It's Steve,' said a small voice, which apart from the West Country accent barely sounded like the confident lad I'd met on Friday. He whispered into the phone like someone afraid of being overhead by himself: '*Can you come an' get me?*'

'Where are you?'

'I'm at Marylebone Station, in the Guard's Office.'

'What are you doing there?'

'I've been followed around all day by eight men. I'm really scared.'

'*You've been followed around by eight men?* Why?'

'I don't know. They just started following me around Leicester Square this morning an' they haven't stopped. They're waiting outside now. Can you come and get me, Maark?'

'Well, yes ... I suppose so. Er, don't worry,' I added, realizing that I sounded very reluctant, 'I'll be there soon.' At this point I asked to speak to the Guard – I could hear men's voices in the background. To be honest, I wondered if this was some kind of set-up. There was something very fishy about it. I asked Steve to put the Guard on the line, who told me in a businesslike fashion: 'Yes, that's correct. The young lad is being followed by a group of men, and I strongly suggest you come and collect him as soon as possible.'

'Have the police been informed?' I asked.

'No, the police have not been informed – *for obvious reasons.*'

'*Obvious reasons?*' Now I really was worried.

On the way to Marylebone it suddenly dawned, through my catarrh and thumping headache, that Steve was probably a bit doolally. '*It's a bit worrying sometimes. People keep coming up to you an' asking you for things. Sometimes they won't leave you alone.*'

At the station I saw Steve, perched on the edge of a bench like a small, frightened bird. I knew the truth instantly. He looked like he'd been sleeping rough since I last saw him, all grimy and scruffy. His eyes were bugging and twitching. When they locked on me, they bugged and twitched some more and he stood up gingerly, like someone expecting to be smacked over the head and told to sit down again.

I tried to calm him down and said that the best thing would be for him to go back to Exeter. Escorting him out of the station, I asked him where these strange men were. He pointed out a man in his mid-twenties who was seated on the same bench as Steve had been, with his sports bag, innocently enjoying a hot-dog. 'He's one,' he hissed. 'An' he's another,' he said, gesturing to a middle-aged man in a tweed jacket using a payphone.

I took him to Kentish Town to collect his bag from the couple he said he was staying with. On the way, various other members of the conspiracy against him were identified standing on platforms or reading newspapers on tube trains. But once we arrived in Kentish Town, he couldn't remember the number of the house. When I suggested walking down the street until we found it, he decided he couldn't go down the street 'because, you see that van parked there, it's full of *them.*'

I put it to Steve that he was actually homeless and that there was no flat. He frantically denied it. 'No, no, it's true. I was staying here. I just can't go there now because *they* are here.'

'Well, let's call the flat and leave a message for your friends.'

'I can't.'

'Why not?'

'Because the number's in my bag...'

'Which is at their place.'

'Yeah.'

I suggested he call his mum to let her know that he was going to be coming back tonight and arrange to be met at the station. We found a callbox and he dialled a number and got no reply. 'She's probably still at work,' he said, putting the phone down.

'Oh, right. And your dad?'

'He's still at work as well.'

It was 6.30 p.m. on a Sunday.

'You do have family in Exeter, don't you Steve? Coz there's not much point me putting you on a train to Exeter if there's no one for you there, is there?'

'Yesyesyes, I've got family there.'

'I've got to ask this: Have you been taking any drugs?'

'Nonono. I've not been taking any drugs.'

I didn't have the heart to ask if there were any drugs that he was *needed to* take but had forgotten to.

At Paddington I asked him if he wanted to try his mum again before he got on the train, which was leaving in ten minutes. I turned to look for a phone, spotted one, turned back, and Steve was already about fifty yards away from me, loping towards the gents, head half-turned towards me in a form of sheepish apology. Since I met him at Marylebone two hours previously, he hadn't moved more than twelve inches away from me, so this new development did suggest that our relationship might be entering its final phase.

I didn't run after him.

Instead I went over to the payphone and called a shelter for young homeless people for advice. When I told them that Steve was a little fruity, they practically hung up on me, declaring that they *wouldn't have anything to do with mentally ill people*, that *no shelter would*, and that *the police would have to deal with it.* I looked for Steve in the toilets: no sign. I wandered about the concourse for about twenty minutes looking for him. Still no sign. To be brutally honest, I was a bit relieved. Steve wasn't my problem any more, and a ticket to Exeter would have cost me over £50.

A week later I got a message on my ansafone. 'Maark. [Pause] This is Steve. [Pause] I'm coming up to London at the end of the month. [Long pause] *Miss you.*'

*

I received a sad letter from Jason about ten days after the midnight 'reunion' I mentioned in my last letter. It contained an apology and my keys.

I'd asked him to return them via a polite message sent on his text pager. Something that I had posted to him a few weeks after the last terrible weekend we'd spent together, in the laughable hope that sending messages to him at premium rate charges with no knowledge whether he'd received them or not might somehow solve our communication problems. Sad to say, the fact that he'd got rid of his mobile phone, and with it our only opportunity for verbal intimacy, both of us being emotional cowards, had probably hastened the break-up. Naturally, he kept the pager (so useful for discreetly conducting a promiscuous homosexual lifestyle), but didn't answer any of my messages. Except the one about returning my keys.

His letter was quite touching really – if you're a soft touch like me, that is. And I couldn't help treasuring the War Movie convenient poignancy of the line: 'I've been posted abroad for three months. By the time you receive this, I'll be on my way to the Far East...'

Love,

Mark

Uncle Monkey Is Dead

Seattle, July 28, 1997

Dear Mark,

My drug dealer and love-triangle rival became the most talked-about man in America[*] and all I got was this lousy computer.

July 21, 1997

I'm writing you from aboard a sweltering Northwest DC-10 stalled on the runway in Minneapolis. I'm on my way back to Seattle from Grand Rapids, Michigan. (There is another, smaller Grand Rapids in Minnesota.) The battery light on my battered, semi-functional laptop is blinking.

My essay on Andrew will be the cover story in the next issue of *The Stranger*. It hits the stands the day after tomorrow. As this alternative free weekly is not widely distributed outside of Seattle, it seems unlikely that Andrew will see it. Still, the FBI says he could be anywhere. The mainstream media may quote from it. I have to reckon with the possibility that Andrew will learn of my unflattering revelations and move me up on the list he is said to be keeping. I admit that I'm a little nervous. But this didn't stop me from titling my first draft, 'Come Get Me, Andrew'.

In a way it would be a relief.

Andrew's Grim Reaper, as you put it, has made me take stock.

I was a gospel singer for a while. I've been most everything. I've been in the armed services, both land and sea, at home and abroad. Been married, been an undertaker, been with the railroads, ploughed Mother Earth, been in a tornado, seen a man burnt alive once. I've even seen a woman flogged.

No, wait. I haven't done any of those things. Neither, probably, has Andrew. Those are the accomplishments of 'The Misfit', the serial killer in Flannery O'Conner's short story 'A

---

[*] On 15 July 1997 Cunanan shot and killed Gianni Versace on the steps of the fashion designer's Miami Beach mansion.

Good Man is Hard to Find'. How funny that my first published feature story should be about Andrew. I've never read
any true crime stuff, or *American Psycho* – not even Dennis
Cooper. But for some obscure reason when I rediscovered
the O'Conner story three years ago, I felt a need to read it
aloud to Alex at Christmas. He loved the story, too, and lines
from it became part of our running routines. When we
adopted Samantha, we talked about naming her 'Pity Sing',
after the cat in the story.

In my essay, I fantasize that Andrew will grant me an
exclusive interview, my last and best-remembered. At its
close, in a slightly desperate stab at humour, I'd quote
Flannery's grandmother: 'You don't look a bit like you have
common blood. I know you come from nice people!' As my
body falls limp to the floor, Samantha would rub affectionately against Andrew's leg.

At least the market value of my letters to you would
increase.

28 July 1997

I didn't want to go to Michigan. It would be too hot there. I
told my mother I'd been having a hard enough time getting
to sleep as it was.

'I have some extra Xanax,' she cheerfully offered.

I didn't have the heart to tell her that she, my father and I
all became acquainted with this anti-anxiety medication directly through Andrew.

In your letter from last Christmas you wrote about York. I
promised/threatened that I would eventually write you about
my home town. That, however, must now wait until the
swamping distraction of a certain superfamous killer queen
has abated.

Descending to the bucolic flat landscape that skirts the
Grand Rapids 'international' airport, my seatmate – a talka-
tive family man and recreational boat owner of about my age
returning from a business trip to North Dakota – pointed to a
row of cars parked even with the runway. These belonged to
families who had taken their kids to the airport to watch
planes land. Needless to say, the sight prompted a smile from

me – patronizing, yet reflecting a genuine sense of comfort, even relief.

My own family used to do this.

Five minutes after leaving the airport I received my first shock. I mentioned to my parents that I had given their number to some friends.

'Will we be getting a phone call from Andrew in Miami?' my father asked.

My father and I have always had a hard time talking about anything. My homosexuality has never before been directly acknowledged. Andrew made my father want to talk about it.

*

Lieutenant Tim reports that Andrew had the opposite effect on his father. At the request of the family of Jeff Trail, Andrew's alleged first victim, Tim went on the Fox TV show *America's Most Wanted* to talk about what a great guy Jeff was. He'd given his parents' number as an alternate contact. *America's Most Wanted* called the family home to leave a message. Tim's father called him up in a rage: 'You're using this tragedy to get your face on TV! That's the most contemptible thing I've ever heard of!' Tim told him to calm down, that's not the way it was. His father screamed: 'Fuck you fuck you fuck you!' and hung up. Tim said his father never used language like that with him before.

Did you ever see *Annie Hall*? Tim is Jewish and from New York. I can't help but picture his family resembling Woody Allen's, living under the Coney Island roller coaster. Mine is not that far removed from Diane Keaton's, Midwestern so-normal-it's-scary / repressed.

My father owns a small business. On the ride from the airport he told me about one of his more colourful new customers, Charlie, a morbidly obese, foul-mouthed middle-aged homosexual who owns a liquor store in a predominately African-American part of Grand Rapids. To my astonishment, Dad proposed taking me to meet this man. He'd told Charlie ('and his ... lover', my father articulated) that he had a gay son. If he didn't bring me by, he'd never hear the end of it.

The next day my father and I drove to the liquor store. Charlie looked exactly like Large Marge from *Pee-Wee's Big Adventure*. It was a very odd experience exchanging banter

with this queenly ruin, his handsome, much younger companion, and my father, who, as is his way, was for the most part
content to quietly smile and nod. Like everyone else I en-
countered on this trip, Charlie was anxious to hear all about
Andrew. I showed him the Polaroid of Andrew and Alex,
and, without asking his permission, spontaneously snapped
his picture on Andrew's camera. The camera jammed; permanently, it appeared. None of us knew quite what to say
after that.

Leaving, the younger man asked me about my books. I
promised to send a flyer.

On the ride home with my father, I told him that if Charlie
did see my books he would find much to give my father a
hard time about. My father said, 'Oh, I used to read those
kinds of books.' I blanched, terrified to hear what he would
say next. 'You know. *Penthouse*, things like that.' I breathed,
and protested that, though some people see it otherwise,
really my books aren't pornographic.

'I don't really know what gay people do,' he said.

I was glad to leave it like that.

*

Shortly after my father dropped me off at my hotel (I couldn't
stay at my parents' house. It's not air conditioned) Brent
picked me up. Yes, *the* Brent, the guy I followed to Germany.
He's back living in Grand Rapids. We had our first true face-
to-face conversation since 1984.

Brent's hair is greying, and his clothes are inadvertently
80s retro. But he's obviously been working out, and at thirty-
seven has retained his boyish good looks. I'd forgotten how
big he is – a good five inches taller than me. A month or so
back he remarried, for the third time. His wife is pregnant.

We went to a Mexican restaurant. Brent, too, couldn't hear
enough about Andrew. He urged me to exploit this potential
ticket out of obscurity for all it's worth. At length he asked
what else was I doing to make a living. I brought him up to
date on my books, and showed him the profile on my work
that appeared in *The Stranger*, which begins with the inevitable recital of my obsessive pursuit of my best friend from
high school who joined the Army. I told him that people love
this story, and that I had learned how to exploit it as the core

of my personal myth. He nodded, but made no comment.

After a few beers, however, Brent shocked me. He revealed that he likes to cruise the lesbian chat rooms on AOL. That a straight guy would thrill to images of female–female sex is, of course, hardly news. But he told me that in an attempt to entice sex stories out of women, he sometimes gives an account of the time I pressured him into having sex with me.

Brent added that he has experimented with the gay male chat rooms. Those, however, bored him. 'Every guy on there says he has a twelve-inch dick. It's so explicit. It just seemed so fake. There's no . . . build-up.'

*

All my old jock-druggie buddies and idols from high school turned out for Brent's wedding, he reported. To a man, they all have huge bellies. Brent informed me that all of them know I'm gay. His younger brother took it upon himself to tell everyone. Brent said that he's heard a few joking asides at my expense, but nothing really derogatory.

I have one brother and one sister. When my brother married, his wife went to great pains to display her generous tolerance for the special people God made gay. I sent her my first book. When I asked her about it, her lips turned white, and she was unable to speak.

When my sister married, everyone thought that her husband was one person who could never be told about me. Rex cuts steel in a factory. His father was a boxer in the Army. One day my sister thought she saw her husband about to pick up a letter of mine to her. She screamed, 'Don't touch that!' He looked at her. She sat him down and explained. He frowned and said, 'That doesn't bother me. I just have so many questions for him.'

My brother-in-law was a star football player and bodybuilder in high school, and even after ten years of marriage he meets the gay 'body fascist' standard.

Prior to this trip, my sister told me that Rex wanted to take me out drinking with a buddy of his from the factory, a man who had been in the Army in Germany. She complained that they didn't want her to come along. Would I mind? 'Um. Maybe you and I could have a nice quiet dinner alone, and then later I could go out with them.'

Sadly, it didn't come to pass. Army Buddy's wife didn't want him going out that night, and my brother-in-law granted my sister's wish to spend the evening alone with me.

Rex has yet to put his questions to me.

It turned out that my sister had a few revelations of her own. Army Buddy, it turns out, is hot for her.

This only frustrated me more. My sister and I look a lot alike.

*

Owing to a severe thunderstorm, my flight out of Grand Rapids was delayed by an hour. I sat with my parents in the tiny airport's coffee house. As lightning flashed, my father filled us in on the latest Andrew news from CNN and the radio. I read aloud from the humorous *New York Times* report on all the false sitings. 'One report brought a chuckle even to the police. The caller swore that he had seen Mr Cunanan in a field of okra in Arkansas.' (One of Alex's co-workers insisted that Andrew could be seen in the new Ikea catalogue. Tending a field of lingusberries?) Before I finally left, I half-jokingly extracted a promise from Mom and Dad that if both Alex and I were killed, they would adopt Samantha.

*

More than a week before I went to Michigan, I finished my essay and e-mailed it to *The Stranger*'s book review editor, Matthew Stadler, author of the novels *Landscape: Memory* and *The Sex Offender*. He's in New York state teaching a summer writing course, but promised to read it and get back to me within four days. He didn't. I e-mailed him again. He apologized for the delay but said he needed another four days. Again, no word. Finally, I called him up. He promised to read it the next night. The next morning Versace was killed. Stadler read my essay.

He liked it, but wanted me to cut some parts and expand others. He suggested that I should further explore the relationship between the monstrous and the everyday. Unsure how to explain that I have a hard time distinguishing between the two, I questioned whether there was time. And indeed I'd hardly got off the phone with him when Emily, his editor, called and told me she wanted to rush the piece into print just as it was, as their cover story.

I decided not to demand more money. We already had an agreement; I respect some of the paper's writers; they'd just done a very nice write-up on my books (enclosed); and I hope to work for them again. I wrote the piece at the invitation of Stadler, a writer I admire. Plus which I retained full copyright, and could resell it as I liked.

Also on G-V day Frank Browning called. I'd e-mailed him my essay the night before. He had two questions. Did Alex and I want to be interviewed on National Public Radio? I told him no. A book on Andrew could be lucrative – very lucrative. Was I thinking of doing one? I pointed out that I have no training as an investigative journalist, am a slow writer, and would have a hard time competing with bloodthirsty pros. On the other hand, I did have an inside track, and through writing my essay had come to feel a certain investment in the story. Within five minutes we agreed to explore the marketability of a collaboration. Browning has worked as an investigative journalist, and his first book was called *The American Way of Crime* (co-authored with John Gerassi, who wrote *Boys of Boise*). As I was headed to Michigan the next morning, I left it to him to draft the proposal.

When Alex got off work we headed to *The Stranger* offices. They needed a high-resolution scan of his photo. Emily had just left on vacation. After dealing with the art department, I was taken to Dan Savage. 'I'll be editing your piece. Everyone gets edited, even me. We're all grown-ups here, right?' 'Um, sure. But Emily and I have an agreement that certain things can't be cut.' 'Oh. I sure wish people would let me in on these agreements. What things?' I told him that the sting-ray opening and anemone closing had to stay, but that I was open to suggestions about everything in between. He promised to e-mail me the edited version the next day.

I was sitting with my parents in their living-room when I downloaded the Savage edit. He did an excellent job tightening the piece, but made one mistake. I e-mailed him back: 'Please restore the short paragraph about the Tupperware party to immediately follow the *Pulp Fiction* anecdote. The two have to be coupled. The comic banality of Andrew competing for a melon-baller belongs beside the image of him thrilling to the image of the exploding head, which otherwise takes on an exaggerated significance.' He wrote back that he saw my point, commented 'fab piece', and kindly offered to pass it on to his contact at the *Village Voice*. Throughout this experience, Savage was eminently decent, thoughtful and professional – very different from the bad-boy image he projected when I met him last Spring at Café Septième.

Back in Seattle, I called the *Voice*. The editor told me that my piece was 'fucking great', which was nice to hear, but that they couldn't use it. They'd sent out their own people the day Versace was killed.

Browning said I shouldn't worry – there would almost certainly be other takers once the piece appeared in print. Also, he cautioned me against giving away too much more of the book. His agent thought the proposal would fetch $150,000, minimum, and maybe a lot more. Harper & Row was interested. A news story even went out over the wire that Browning was about to sign for a book with a collaborator 'who for security reasons cannot as yet be named'.

On July 23, the day *The Stranger* was to appear (it comes out just before midnight), it occurred to me that it was probably time to think about reselling Alex's photo. None of my writer contacts could tell me how to go about it. Browning didn't know either, but gave me the number of a gay photojournalist at the *New York Times*. He'd call him first just to be sure it was OK. A minute later my phone rang. 'Don't call him.' Browning relayed the *Times* man's advice: if I didn't want to go directly to the scandal sheets, I should contact any of the big photo agencies in New York. 'He says, "They're all sharks," but you should start with the biggest agency and ask them how much they can give you.' He gave me the name of the chief.

I was surprised that anyone even answered. It was almost seven New York time. I was given some assistant. 'I have an exclusive photo of Andrew Cunanan.' I was transferred to the chief. 'How big is the image? What is Cunanan doing in the photo? How sharp is it?' I explained that I wasn't in any great hurry, that I was just calling to find out how much it might be worth. 'If it's a really good photo, we can give you an advance of $5,000. But of course I have to see it first.' I e-mailed him a jpeg. When I called back I detected a certain awe in the assistant's and chief's voices. 'How much do you want?' As you know, I'm normally pretty lousy at business. 'Well, I'm thinking that people have to be really tired just now of seeing the same photos of Andrew over and over. *People* called Andrew "the most wanted man in the world". And I think this has to be the creepiest photo of Andrew so far.' The chief agreed that it was creepy. 'So I think we need $10,000.' A pause. 'That's a big chunk of money. It's late in New York. I'm not a magazine publisher, I'm an agent. [Brief pause.] Let me call you back.' Almost an hour went by. I called back. 'I was just about to call you. The most I can offer you tonight is $7,500.' Brightly: 'OK.' A courier was sent to retrieve the photo, a contract was faxed back and forth. Still unresolved was the question of whether Alex's face could be published in the photo.

By this time, Alex had arrived at my door directly from his job. In shirt and tie he actually paced the floor, something I've never seen him do before. (Normally he just tears small patches of hair from his arms, legs and head.) When I'd called him at work and told him the agency paid 50%, he scoffed, 'That won't be much.' When I told him the advance I'd obtained, he was dumbstruck. Within minutes, however, he was quibbling over the split.

I agreed to give him two-thirds. After all, it was his photo. And he had signed over to me all media rights to his Andrew stories. I would scavenge my ghoulish windfall from the book.

After much deliberation, it was stipulated that the photo of Alex and Andrew could be published full-frame in Europe, but in the US the photo would be 'cropped or altered in such a way that the individual next to Cunanan will not be recognized'. Thus were Alex's grandmothers in rural Wisconsin spared potential heart attacks.

But of course we knew that Andrew would probably be able to place the photo – from his Nautica jacket, his haircut, the distinctive Polaroid grain, not to mention the ZEELAND credit. That's why Alex was pacing. What would it be like to wake up every day knowing that Andrew had registered Alex's betrayal and my insolence?

My response was to spend my $2,500 even before I got it.

Alex drove me to CompUSA where I shelled out $2,200 for a new PC. Back at my place, Alex was helping me set it up when I checked my phone messages. There were eight. 'I'm watching the news...' 'I'm sure you've heard...' Finally someone spelled it out. I turned to Alex. 'Andrew's dead.'

We yelled and hugged each other.

The next day other emotions set in. Frustration that the biggest questions would remain unanswered. Disappointment that there probably would not be a $150K book after all. And – stupid as it may sound – sadness about Andrew. Though I still think of him as I always did, as a 'mad scary bitch', as you put it, in writing about him I came to identify with him a little.

I had more in common with him than I did with his victims. And he read my books.

For two months, people had been telling Alex, 'You must be so creeped out by this.' But the funny thing was, he wasn't. He wasn't reacting at all. With Andrew dead, it finally caught up to him. But then, how would you feel if someone you'd spent two years hanging out with, and grew pretty close to, suddenly became the most talked about man in the country, a superfamous 'sick monster', and died putting a bullet through his mouth? I found it gnawingly disturbing the way Andrew went out, mashed like a crab in the tacky seaside crevice of a fugitive German gay bathhouse owner who claimed to be a citizen of the Principality of Sealand.

I think Andrew probably loved 'Buckie', his pet name for Alex. He tried to make Alex happy.

In late summer 1994, Alex got out of the Marine Corps. He decided to move back to Wisconsin. His car was all packed up. I made a rare trip out to the West Coast for a last drink together. Andrew was there. I saw him studying me. Finally he came over, and said, 'You need to smile more.' I said that I was very sad that Alex was leaving. Andrew returned, 'But you'll be able to visit him.' I said that I wouldn't be able to afford that very often. He thought for a moment, then said, 'I'll pay for you to visit him.' Then, after just another few seconds, he added, 'I'll pay for us both to visit him.'

I had to laugh. At least he was trying to make things better.

Of course, had Alex moved to Wisconsin, he would have been living midway between where Trail and Madson (Minneapolis) and Miglin (Chicago) were killed. I assume that had I run into Andrew, his generosity may have extended to sharing a few bullets, if he still had some.

Finally, I feel a little sick about how Andrew has been represented in the media. Overnight he went from a cunning, criminal mastermind 'man of many faces' to a pathetic loser who spoke bad French and sloppily killed for cars. Is this the feeling of watching big assets force their way into small receptacles?

The Washington Post did the best job co-opting me. They appropriated my anemone and Xanax stories (just think – Bill and Hillary Clinton may well have read of my illegal drug use), but at least they got my quotes right and mentioned *The Masculine Marine*. *Time* mentioned my name three times, but misrepresented my story (conveniently substituting Jeff Trail for Alex), and used Alex's *Pulp Fiction* anecdote, without attribution.

Then there was the appearance of Andrew's former roommate on ABC's *Prime Time*, a week after the *Post* story. This is the guy I called 'The Teeth' in my essay, who subsequently sold his story to the *National Enquirer*. I faxed it to you: Andrew was obsessed with Tom Cruise, fantasized about him sexually, and took pictures of him to the bathroom – and killed Jeff Trail because he looked like Tom Cruise. (On the lam in New York, Andrew went to see *Liar, Liar*. Andrew would have loved your essays about Jim Carrey and Tom Cruise. Of course, he may very well have read them.) I didn't see it, but apparently The Teeth told millions of television viewers that he had just remembered his first glimpse of Andrew's sadism. Where did it happen? At the tide pools. He'd watched Andrew torture a crab.

Teeth is now number-one on Alex's and my list of Andrew's unfinished business. We know where he lives.

The night of Andrew's suicide, I gave Alex his first Xanax.

So anyway, you see why I began this letter with a cheap T-shirt slogan.

*

You left a phone message telling me you didn't think a book

about Andrew was necessarily dead. You're probably right. Even if I could only get $20,000, that's still more than I received from my interview books. But Alex isn't really in a condition to help me write it. And when he was down in San Diego last weekend for Pride, none of his other friends who knew Andrew wanted to talk about him. *The San Diego Union-Tribune* reported that the parade had undergone a last-minute *de facto* change of slogan, to 'Andrew Cunanan is not representative of the San Diego Gay and Lesbian community'.

It's almost too Mark Simpsonesque of me, I know, but my heartfelt response to that is: True. Andrew was more interesting.

August 7, 1997

This has been a really hard letter to write. I apologize that I haven't properly responded to your last letter, or talked about much besides Andrew, or even offered any serious conclusions. It seems like there have to have been stranger periods in my life, but I can't think of any. I wasn't exaggerating when I said thinking about all of this has given me nightmares. Yet when the stress and scariness abated, I felt a crushing *ennui*.

The Post piece concluded with a quote from a woman who said that Andrew was godmother to her kids:

'Andrew, wherever you are, please stop what you are doing … You still have a chance to show the entire world the side of you that I and your godchildren know … D.D. loves you, Schmoo. I bring with me a special message from our Papoose. Grimmy says she loves her Uncle Monkey, and hopes that you'll remember that always.' By the time the FBI distributed the tape, it was too late for Uncle Monkey. He had been seen by the houseboat's caretaker, and soon he would be surrounded. Andrew Cunanan's long [?] was over. He put the gun in his mouth.

In my essay, I misrepresented the Flannery O'Conner story I to read Alex at Christmas. This is how it really ends:

[T]he grandmother's head cleared for an instant. She saw the man's face twisted close to her own as if he were going to cry and she murmured, 'Why, you're one of my babies. You're one of my own children!' She reached out and touched him on the shoulder. The Misfit sprang back as if a snake had bitten him and shot her three times through the chest.

'She was a talker, wasn't she?' Bobby Lee said, sliding down the ditch with a yodel.

'She would of been a good woman,' The Misfit said, 'if it had been somebody there to shoot her every minute of her life.'

'Some fun!' Bobby Lee said.

'Shut up, Bobby Lee,' The Misfit said. 'It's no real pleasure in life.'

Love,

Steve

Urinals at Naval Station San Diego, where Zeeland had anonymous public sex with navy lieutenant – Cunanan's first victim

(Anti-)Gay Paris

London, 25 August 1997

Dear Steve,

Yes, the marketability of your letters to me would certainly have increased if you had somehow contrived to be Andrew's last victim. It would have been left to me at a press conference, clutching your letters in one hand and a tear-dampened million-dollar book-contract in the other, to explain to the world why Andrew singled you out, what your relationship was with him, and why I was far more interesting than either of you. I take it as further evidence of your vegetarian lack of business sense that you failed to do this.

However, *The Times* front page today does feature a strapline 'How I escaped Versace's killer', and the whole of page 17 is devoted to a reprint of your *Face* article with the title 'Cunanan offered to kill me'. As you know, the *Irish Independent on Sunday* will be running your piece this Sunday as well. If only I knew a few more serial killers...

I recently saw a TV documentary about Michael Alig, the NY party promoter who killed his flatmate Angel, chopped him up and dumped the bits in the Hudson. It featured all kinds of kooky club kids who had been waiting all their lives for their fifteen minutes of TV fame. Clearly, none of them gave two hoots about Angel, except in the sense that his death had got them on telly. However, there was one woman who really did have a heart – Screamin' Rachel, a washed-up middle-aged lady who's done too many drugs and not enough early nights, but who had the acumen to record a fantastically melodramatic dance record about the murder called 'Death in Clubland'; she told us, trying to look tortured but just looking bored, 'Well, I loved Michael, but I also liked Angel...' You see, it wasn't so much Angel's or Michael's story as *Rachel's*. An inspiration to us all, I think.

Actually, amidst all the shameless sensationalism and exploitation that is the way of the world, your article for *The Stranger* was a beacon. Your account is candid, personal, and consequently all the more objective – and humorous – in a way that most who write about these things never dare to be. *Never bother to be.*

And yes, even mad, bad, dangerous-to-know Andrew may have gone to his grisly end as a small receptacle raped by globally large assets, but at least he and one of his victims were humanized in one or two small crevices of the world by your writing. (By the way, I have to commend yours and Andrew's good taste, at least as far as his first victim was concerned – Jeff Trail looks scrummy in those photos.)

*

Have you ever thought of doing a book on policemen? I've never had any interest in them myself; I've always found them extremely unsexy. The British variety are ridiculous in those dickhead hats and shapeless tunics that were designed for walking puddings; the American sort in their tight trousers, shades and John Wayne fixation are just too macho and vain to even begin to allow yourself any sexual thoughts about them (they all remind me of the cop in John Waters's *Desperate Living* who holds up Mole, the outsixed black bulldyke at gunpoint and goes into ecstasies over her outsized knickers: 'Mmmmm!' he crows, 'I bet I can get my BIG BUSINESS into these!').

The only policemen I've found at all sexy are Irish Guarda. This is because a) No one, not even Henry Rollins, who I understand has 'cop issues', can call the Irish police 'fascists' and b) Their uniforms are so dinky and so retro they look like 1950s milkmen or guards on some kind of miniature private railway – which, come to think of it, is what Ireland is.

No, the reason I wonder whether you'll ever do a book on 'pigs' is that you might have to interview me – as someone who continually gets mistaken for one. A few weeks ago I picked up a lad in Brighton whose first words to me were: 'Are you a policeman?' When I said that I wasn't he looked disappointed, but obliged me anyway. Michelle and I were once mistaken by the manager of a gay Soho dance bar for plainclothes detectives (I think it's because we looked uptight, homophobic, and like we didn't want to be there). And then, last week, walking in the 'local park' of an evening I zeroed in on a bloke who looked a bit nervous (always an alluring quality). We exchanged several glances, and eventually, after

even more faffing around than is usual in such circumstances, he joined me in some bushes. 'Are you a cossie?' he
whispered, edgily, eyes darting from side to side.

'What?' I said.

'A copper. Are you a copper?'

I laughed, thinking that he was joking. 'Of course not!'

'You are a cossie, aintcha!' he said. 'I'm off!' And with that
he was indeed off – literally running away from me as fast as
his stocky legs would carry him.

Not so long ago I met another lad up there who afterwards
asked me what I did. I was evasive, as I usually am in these
situations. But he wouldn't give up. Eventually I confessed I
was a journalist. At this he said: 'I bet you're one of those
anti-gay journalists, aren't ya? I bet you write nasty stories
about gays for the tabloids!'

I told him that, alas, I didn't write for the tabloids.

*

In June I was in Paris, taking part in a literary debate called
'Impolitically Correct'. On my first night, I found myself attending yet another gay beauty contest – the Mr Gay Europe
Contest. My name had been mischievously put forward as
one of the judges by my journo friend, Stephane (perhaps as
revenge for my taking him to Russell Square). In the end the
event was so badly organized that there was no opportunity to
sabotage it – it did that all by itself. I almost found myself
waxing nostalgic for the Mr Gay UK contest I attended in
Birmingham.

I'd much rather have attended the European Lesbian
Beauty Contest, which was held in the same place the week
before. Apparently it was hosted by a huge transsexual who,
after introducing each hopeful, literally threw them into the
audience. The final judging was violently interrupted by a
gang of big Kraut femiNazi dykes who forced their way on
stage, announced that 'Zis cohntest ist demeaning to vim-
min!' and then proceeded to beat everyone up.

But I did discover something attractive in Paris.

'Why are the firemen in Paris so popular?' I asked my host
in the car on the way to his house, after he'd collected me
from Eurostar at the La Gare du Nord – driving in that
Parisian way which makes you wonder why they bother

painting white lines along the middle of the road. He shrugged Gallicly, taking both hands off the wheel as we approached a hairpin corner at high speed. 'Beecause zay all look like porn stars. Zay are all very fit, young, clean-cut and with short 'air.' (Even in France, 'porn' is defined by Matt Sterling rather than Pierre Cadinot.)

He screeched to a halt at a red light. ''Ere ze firemen are run as a branch of ze meeleetaree. Zay are 'and-peeked from ze ozzer serveeces, and 'ooever does ze 'and-peeking 'as great taste.'

Precisely on cue, a big, shiny fire-engine drew up next to us at the lights, throbbing seductively. A smooth, meaty forearm rested on the top of the red cabin door. Behind that, an anonymous square jaw and chin jutted out beneath a fetching blue cap, brim pulled rakishly over the nose. Suddenly I understood why my host drove so recklessly.

Emerging out of the Metro the day after my encounter with the forearm fire-engine, my eyes immediately caught a sexy stud in natty, tight-fitting navy-blue dungarees and cute cap pulled down over his snub nose ambling towards me. With a utility belt around his waist which managed to look like a gun-belt (nicely framing his pert arse which swaggered sexily as he walked) he was clearly as much in love with the idea of being *un pompier* as I was with the idea of him. As we passed almost lingeringly, our eyes met two or three times as we both turned to check one another out again (and check that we were still checking one another out).

I hovered on the pavement for a minute or two or three, watching him restore order and safety to Château d'Eau with perhaps an extra little swagger in his gait which I'd like to think was his gift to me. And then, whatever local emergency or neurosis had summoned him and his noble pals dealt with, they climbed back into their shiny engine, which revved into life with a sexy, stupid, but entirely competent roar, and sped him out of my life for ever.

*

The French gays attending the literary debate weren't quite so welcoming. 'And I most particularly object to the "penis fits vagina" quotation from Camille Paglia that Mark Simpson makes in his *offensive* book *Anti-Gay*.' The young French gay novelist with the shaved head on the 'Impolitically Correct' panel was offended by my book. He was offended by the concept. He was offended by the title. Apparently he was even offended by the typeface: 'It is the same as the one used by the police to type up their reports!'. But most of all he was offended by its reference to Camille's claim that the biological facts of our privates' plumbing make a nonsense of 'flimflamming' queer studies.

'Actually,' I interrupted him, 'the quotation appears in Bruce LaBruce and Glennda Orgasm's contribution, "A Case for the Closet". But now that you've brought it up, what exactly is it that you object to? Does the penis *not* fit the vagina?'

'It also fits a lot of other places!' he sputtered (and for a mad moment I wondered whether he might not have been the friendly chap with the expert lips on the other side of that glory hole at le sex club I attended the night before...).

'Yes indeed,' I said, recovering my composure, 'and I admire your sexual adventurism, but does it change the truth of the observation?'

At this point another panellist intervened, the Italian novelist Aldo Busi, an expert on meaningless sex and suicide (but in the universalist sense, you understand: fabulously, he once threatened to sue a bookshop that put his novels in the gay section): *'What do either of you know about vaginas? Eh!'* he exploded.

That shut us up.

*

I've been re-reading the preface Gore Vidal wrote for the 1994 edition of *The City & The Pillar*. It's classic Vidal: astringent, economical prose that conveys the impression of ease but which must have taken many, many redrafts. One particular passage caught my eye:

> Until then, American novels of 'inversion' dealt with shrieking queens or lonely bookish boys who married unhappily and pined for Marines. I broke that mould. My two lovers were athletes and so drawn to the entirely masculine that, in at least the case of one, Jim Willard, the feminine was simply irrelevant to his passion to unite with his other half, Bob Ford: unfortunately for

Jim, Bob had other sexual plans, involving women and marriage.

Well, no prizes for guessing what category of inversion we fall into, Steve. But isn't Vidal, in the light of what he reveals later in *Palimpsest*, also a lonely bookish boy who pined for a Marine 'who had other sexual plans involving women and marriage' – Jimmie Trimble? Jim Willard is of course a little bit of Gore and a little bit of his 'twin' Jimmie ('Willard' even sounds like a more wholesome, American version of 'Vidal'). He quotes a critic praising the subtlety of the character of Jim: 'Himself paralysed by romantic illusions, he is surprisingly perceptive about the illusions of others...' And so it is: Vidal's great cynicism about love is after all the product of a great romantic illusion.

Perhaps that romantic illusion wasn't Jimmie Trimble so much as the idea of an 'entirely masculine' sexual love between two men, fiercely held in the face of crude 40s and 50s Freudianoid orthodoxies. 'I knew that my description of the love-affair between two "normal" all-American boys, of the sort that I had spent three years in the Army with during the war, would challenge every superstition about sex in my native land,' explains Vidal.

But then, this is, is it not, Steve, the same romantic illusion that you and I both share as well?

Even inscrutable bald French philosophers are not immune. I was told, by Edmund White of all people, a story about Michel Foucault and how he fell in love with a boy in his year at school, how he sat at his feet, did his homework for him and generally made cow eyes at him. Of course, the object of his affections told him that he couldn't possibly give Michel the physical expression of love that he was looking for, since he was 'not that way inclined'. Sadly, Foucault resigned himself to his fate (something made a little easier no doubt by the probability that Foucault was half-hoping to hear this response anyway) but carried on his devotions for years until the end of their school career saw them separated. Then, years later, he ran into one of his old school chums. He asked after his *ancien amour*. At this the school chum laughed, and said 'Oh, that *tart*. Everyone shagged *her*. *Didn't you?*'

Doesn't this shed an interesting light on Michel's *History of Sexuality*?

Regarding Mr White: Steve, please *shoot me* if I should ever turn into him.

I have just finished *A Farewell Symphony*.

Well, what can I say? His prose style is frequently more overwrought than the most ambitious French pastries. The adjectives pile on top of one another until they begin to coagulate like one of those cakes left too long in the baker's window of a Parisian August afternoon.

The Farewell Symphony was originally a novelty piece by Haydn where the players and their instruments leave the stage one by one until only one instrument is left. White uses this as a cultured metaphor for the losses Aids has inflicted on his circle. The flaw in this conceit, though, is that in this book there is only ever one instrument on stage: a French horn played by an American who thinks that the problem with the world is that there aren't enough French horn concertos.

His romantic illusion? Well, however much Eddie might be in love with the idea of himself as a novelist, he's even more in love with the fatal idea of homosexuality. Writing about meeting his first big love (after Daddy), a jocko homo called Sean, Edmund complains, in an echo of Gore:

> Back then, in the 50s and 60s, I knew very few gay men, and many of those I met were tormented or effeminate, yearning after cops or Marines or moving men...

Plus ça change (except that *now* you're supposed to yearn after gay porn stars who impersonate – badly – cops, Marines and moving men). And I guess 'bookish young men' is interchangeable with 'tormented'. Sean was a revelation to Edmund in that he acknowledged his homosexuality but was neither tormented nor effeminate. In fact, he was 'strong as a moving man'. Alas, Sean's interest in Edmund didn't quite match Edmund's in Sean:

> Maybe he saw me as too openly gay – yes, that was what he disliked. He wanted to drink German beer with another guy and discuss Pythagoras with him and rugby

before, almost accidentally, deciding to stay over; once in bed they'd jerk each other off in the dark, wipe up, yawn and fall asleep, the only sign of affection being a muted, playful sock in the jaw and a whispered, 'Tiger...'

Sounds good to me. And obviously, despite the envy dressed up as irony, it does to White. As you've probably noticed, Sean is rapidly shaping up into Edmund's Jimmie Trimble. And indeed, the endless series of empty sexual encounters in *The Farewell Symphony* are haunted (and implicitly explained) by Sean, and Edmund's failure to make him into his husband. But at least White is, however, disarmingly honest about the reasons why he frightened Sean off:

> I was too histrionic with my big, pleading eyes, my oleograph fantasies of living with Sean as man and wife, my certainty that he alone could redeem me and confer humanity on me...

Or maybe it was the way Edmund would probably consult a thesaurus before shitting. At any rate, it seems that Edmund is aware that Sean rumbled him – deducing that Edmund's reveries had nothing to do with Sean and everything to do with Edmund. If Sean had turned around and reciprocated, Edmund would have grabbed his French poetry anthologies and fled.

However, having admitted the basically irrational and idealized, impossible, occasionally hellish, nature of his longing, White then spoils it by trying to extol a rational, practical, gayist line:

> Just as a woman of my mother's generation would have thought a 'hen party' a dinner with other women, an admission of 'old maidishness' and social defeat, in the same way the gay bars I'd first glimpsed in the 50s had been temples to despair, where self-mocking queens danced and 'rubbed pussies' with one another before they got up the courage to go out in search of the real thing, a bit of rough trade to rob and beat them. The clone look was a tribal look, a way of saying to one another, 'We're brothers. We're the men we've been looking for.'

Fortunately Ed is honest enough to allow his explanatory politics to be contradicted by his feelings, offering a more convincing reason for his promiscuity:

> ...with a gay man I always felt something indefinable was missing, whereas with a woman I *knew* what was missing: a man.

Gay men weren't the men he was looking for.

I recently met a gentle lad in his late twenties with biceps inflated to the size of baseballs by religiously attending the gym every evening after putting in a shift at the graphic design company he works for. He grew up in a working-class Liverpool family. He was the bookish sensitive sort, while his virile, waster brothers did nothing but play football. His parents encouraged him in his reading because they had aspirations for him. When he was fourteen, he plucked up the courage to buy *A Boy's Own Story*, but was terrified in case his dad, who was always going on about how much 'I 'ate dose fookin pooves', should find it. And indeed one day his dad did, but instead of tanning his arse (as he should have done) he showed it to his footballing sons saying, ''ere y'are lads, this is the kind a thing yous should be readin' – instead of playing fookin' footie all day!'

Fortunately, his father, who approved of learning in one of his sons at least, hadn't actually taken the trouble to open the book, or even read the blurb. He just saw the Picador imprint and the respectable packaging and thought *class*.

Ed White I think would have appreciated that.

*

Last Friday I got back at 1.10 a.m. from a Morrissey convention at the Institute of Contemporary Arts organized by the Duckie mob (I left early and missed the finale – a group singalong of 'The Queen Is Dead' outside Buckingham Palace) to find a message from some drunken Scottish bloke on the ansafone, recorded at 1 a.m., asking me to call him on his pager. I didn't recognize the voice until the owner of it remembered, just before hanging up, that it had been over a year since he last called and added, 'It's Jason'.

I wasn't sure whether to be insulted or touched by his presumptuousness. I decided not to return his call. Or at least wait a few days. After all, who does he think he is that after all this time he can just pick up the phone and call me in the early hours of the morning and have me come running?

After less than ten minutes I called his pager.

And I called the premium rate number again the next day. Twice. Once 'in case' he didn't get the previous message, and once again because that very morning a late birthday card arrived, postmarked *two weeks ago*. He wrote, 'I'll be thinking of you.'

All this happened a month ago. He never returned my messages. Which just goes to show: if you have a 'relationship' with somebody where you call them and they don't call you and you try to break out of it by not calling them, they'll find some way of arranging for you to call them so they can carry on not calling you.

The day after he left his message I was on national TV making fun of Pride on a Channel 4 documentary about London's annual GayLesBiTransWhatever Parade and Festival. Ironically, in sending gays up on telly I was not only seriously endangering my prospects of ever getting laid in London again, I was also probably scotching my chances of ever meeting my non-scene Scots squeeze again. Jason – who ex-lover ESP tells me saw the programme – will now be utterly convinced that if he were to be seen with me ever again, everyone would instantly know he was a turd-burglaring bum-boy pansy poof. Of course, he is paranoid – but in his case, as a serving soldier, it really doesn't mean that they're not out to get him.

I hope that Jason doesn't turn into my Jimmie Trimble, though it may be too late for that. The day after he left his last message I drove onto a traffic island, nearly writing off the used convertible I bought on tick to get over him.

I was stone cold sober, and I have never had an accident before.

Love,

Mark

It's About Power

Dear Mark,

Recently I searched for your name on the Internet and found a website featuring some comments on *Anti-Gay*. Did you know that you are part of the Simpson-Signorile-Rotello backlash, and that Daniel Harris has authored an antidote to you-all's anti-sex neo-con jeremiads?

– *Sigh* –.

And a bigger sigh as I realize that I am actually going to have to read these other books.

Scott O'Hara sent me a photocopy of a flyer announcing a 'Resist Attacks on Queer Sex' meeting to be held in San Diego in November. The authors refer to a nationwide 'sex panic' evidenced by increased policing of public sex spaces. I was pretty sure they had Gabriel Rotello in mind when they referred to 'anti-sex activism which arises within our communities' and 'the burgeoning demonizing of sex cultures appearing in current gay men's writing'.

But I have to say that I found *Sexual Ecology* a useful book. I came away with a new appreciation for just how right you are in pointing out that – like alleged watch queen Gore Vidal (and, depending on just how pre-gay we mean) – I am in some ways not so much gay or post-gay as pre-gay.

Rotello begins with an examination of how things used to be before gay liberation. He cites Chauncey's work on World War I era military chasers. 'Homosexuals back then did not necessarily seek or desire sex with each other ... Many fairies and queers socialized into the dominant pre-war homosexual culture/considered the ideal sexual partner to be "trade", a "real man", that is, ideally a sailor, a soldier, or some other embodiment of the aggressive masculine ideal' (Chauncey). And he quotes Allan Bérubé's work on World War II era military chasers: 'They had learned to prefer "servicing" straight men in semi-public places', and they often considered the masculinity and butchness [*sic*] of their partners one of the most appealing aspects of sex'.

By the 60s and 70s the category of trade had 'virtually disappeared as a sexual identity (if not a sexual role) within the gay world' ... Eventually, [Chauncey] writes, the lines were 'drawn between the heterosexual and the homosexual so sharply and publicly that men were no longer able to participate in a homosexual encounter without suspecting it meant (to the outside world, and to themselves) that they were gay.'

(Except in the pre-Don't-Ask-Don't-Tell military, Chauncey might have been able to add had he condescended to answer my invitation to update his Great War knowledge of the US Armed Forces.)

It was through the bathhouses, Rotello-quoting-Bérubé writes, that gay men first learned to prefer sex with gay men. Previously, men who enjoyed sex with other men were unlikely to play reciprocal roles. In the 70s, 'versatility was declared a political imperative.' By the 1980s, anal sex 'had come to be seen as an essential – possibly the essential – expression of homosexual intimacy.' Rotello argues that it was the new popularity of reciprocated anal sex among 'core groups' of gay men that provided an open invitation for epidemics of viruses that may have been quietly operating for years.

For my selfish interests, so far so good. No dully reciprocal gay sex, no disco divas. Fine. For a moment I almost thought that Rotello might at least by implication endorse a return to the glory days of trade-chasing (though, on reviewing the pages of this library book I marked up with pencil, I now see that his comment on the pre-gay era is: 'It seems so debasing, emotionally empty, self-loathing').

No, Rotello's plan for us late-90s gays is to construct a whole new culture in which public sex is *streng verboten*. He warns, 'Only direct intervention and regulation by the gay community or, as a last resort, the government, is likely to have any impact.'

Rotello's vision: enforced monogamy.

To show that gay men can be monogamous, Rotello makes a surprising detour to ancient pre-gay worlds. But don't even think about the possibilities inherent in that, for he quickly cautions: 'This is not, by the way, to suggest that modern gay men ought to look to ancient Greece or samurai Japan as models of any kind.' That would be 'absurd'.

Rotello's demand: a new gay world of happy gay couples who centre their wholesome gay lives around the gay community centre and the 'growing networks of gay religious organizations ... ranging from gay synagogues and churches to New Age groups and meditation centres.'

'Mark!' I cry, echoing Divine's Hare Krishna-convert daughter in *Female Trouble:* 'Come with me to the temple!'

I suppose you remember how Divine responded. She strangled her daughter.

I skimmed ahead to the sub-chapter 'The Greening of America'. 'The creation of a sustainable gay culture is almost by definition the opposite of reactionary. A reactionary agenda would call for gay men to return to lives of shame and fear in our place of psychic exile, the closet. Make them stop having sex. Bring back the silence and invisibility of the past.'

So Rotello can't imagine that the sailor-chasing Chauncey queens ever had any fun. Though he does favour the return of Chauncey-era police persecution. (If gay self-policing fails. The next time you cruise Hampstead Heath, watch out for a frowning sister Gabriel and the ghost of Randy Shilts.)

Brimming with all the cheerfulness of the sadistic male nurse who catheterized me when I was hospitalized at twenty-one, Rotello enthuses: 'The strictures of gay men's gym culture often sound a lot like the advice that doctors urge most Americans to follow ... Sort of like the benefits of safer sex for gay men ... A glance at the hard-bodied, flat-tummied musclemen in most gay neighbourhoods illustrates how powerfully such social inducements can work among gays, and how quickly they can produce shifts in behaviour that under most circumstances people would consider extremely difficult if not impossible to maintain.'

Rotello's plaintive closing hope is that homosexuality 'may finally be accepted for what it is ... the left-handedness of love.' Well, he's pre-gay studies, anyway. He offers 'a vision in which homosexual people accept themselves and are accepted by others for who they are.'

I guess I should be glad. Suppose Rotello had advocated a return to pre-gay days. Do I really want thousands of crystal-crazed roid raving gym culture circuit queens emptying out of White Parties to compete for my trade?

*

But then, trade isn't what it used to be either.

Recently, I ran into a man who closely resembled the proto-type military-boy ideal I developed fifteen years ago. It happened on another trip to Fort Lewis with Navy Davy.

For long hours of a Friday pay-day afternoon I watched a parade of painfully beautiful young soldiers enter the PX mini-mall men's room. At five-minute intervals I trailed after them. Unfortunately, the two toilet stalls joined by a glory hole remained steadfastly occupied by two admirably persistent grumpy old men (or, at intervals, one persistent grumpy old man and alternately me or Dave). In desperation, Dave and I left the base to visit the adjacent Fort McChord Air Force Base. Finally, we sought out the one surviving video arcade on the once busy adjacent strip of pawn shops, gun shops, massage parlours and sleazy motels. There were no military boys, and in the maze of video stalls red lights lit up only one or two of the 'occupied' lamps, which were shaped like pine-cones. Built into each booth door was a rectangular window. The men in the booths hunched close to the video screens.

Evening approached. I suggested that it was probably time for us to concede. Dave agreed, but said that he wanted to give the cruisy latrine one final try.

Yawning and fidgeting in my uncomfortably toilet-seat-like PX food court chair, I looked up to see a handsome mid-/late-twenties beefy dark-haired almost Oliver North-scowling guy in civvies march by and nod at me.

I passed Dave on my way into the latrine.

The soldier had taken the unoccupied stall, the one without a hole. I stood at the urinal, looked behind me to catch him studying me through the crack in the door. I turned around and indicated my interest. He signalled his. Then he stood up, zipped up, exited and nodded for me to follow. To Dave's thrilled disbelieving stare I exited the mini-mall and climbed into a beat-up low riding Camaro.

Off we sped. Breaking the silence, he asked me my name. His was Alan. Beaming almost too little-boy winsomely, he told me he was from 'North Dakotey'. With a balled fist, he reached over and pounded me on the thigh, laughing: 'You aren't going to give me any trouble, are you, Steve?'

I told him that I would not give him any trouble.

It was raining hard. He drove me into the woods – down a tank trail. Deeper and deeper we sped into the dense dark Douglas Firs, him muttering that he needed to find a place to turn around. I thought of the phrase, 'remote, densely-wooded area'. (Too much pondering over Andrew, probably. Good thing that this was the day before I saw Arthur Dong's documentary on 'men who kill fags', *Licensed to Kill*.) I glanced over the back seat and saw some kids' toys ... and some military gear, including an MP armband.

Finally he wheeled the car around and ground to a stop. He rolled down the already steamed-up window. His face was stern. What was he going to do with me? My super-macho Army MP leaned over, and in my ear whimpered, in a scared little boy voice: 'Be mean to me, Steve.'

He pulled up his shirt, revealing a muscular torso shaved below the nipples. He instructed me to twist and bite his nipples.

He whined, 'Talk to me, Steve.'

But I could only come up with compliments. (Snarling:) 'You! You ... got a big dick.' To get his big dick sucked was not, however, what this soldier drove me into the woods for.

I know it wasn't unpredictable. So many of my friends would have been in heaven. But I was disappointed (if not as disappointed as Navy Davy when I told him this story).

I guess I could have insulted him in German. On the ride back his disappointed face perked up when I told him I knew how. But that would have cost me my own erection, which began flagging anyway when he pleaded: 'Do you got any-thing to sniff?'

Dropping me off at the PX, Alan was polite. Maybe he would see me again, he said. But really he didn't cruise there that often. You see, he was married.

And people wonder why I've lost my faith.

*

Of course it's high time you lost Jason's number. Of course you won't be able to replace him. Of course you really shouldn't want to put yourself through another Jason. Of course you probably will. Unless, of course, you're that different from me.

On second thought, maybe you are more pre-gay than me. At least Jason stayed in the barracks. You haven't taken military boys and made them into gay roommates and Ikea shoppers.

Honestly, though, I don't know if I could survive another Alex right now. My Marine ex, for his part, now lives with an established, older gay man who has a crush on him and leaves little notes around the house signed 'love'. I met the guy that night I went to Alex's hang-out, The Cuff. My moustachioed replacement-to-be happened to be standing nearby when I nodded at a tasteful work of art on the wall depicting a lion fucking a leatherman. 'It's not about a lion fucking a leatherman,' he informed me with terribly earnest solemnity, 'it's about power.'

More recently he has proposed that Alex should fuck him. (Was he perhaps inspired by the 'steak knife' passage in my Andrew article?) Chagrined, Alex explained that because of his background he prefers to keep friendship and sex separate. Leather roommate appeared at Alex's threshold at bedtime, curled his lip and demanded to know whether a towel on the floor was Alex's 'cumrag'.

Alex has since compared notes with former occupants of his bedroom. It seems that leather roommate's M.O. doesn't vary too much. He listens to young men tell their stories, smiles at them, invites them to share his townhouse, then –

*

'At first one shouldn't talk too much, for talk reveals character, and unless one is simple and artless and appealingly boyish, it's best not to talk at all, to remain silent and smiling, enigmatic, waiting for the proper moment to assume the character of the other's dream.'

A colonel who teaches at one of the service academies (and referred to you as his 'beloved Mark Simpson') mailed me a photocopy of Gore Vidal's 'Three Stratagems' from *A Thirsty Evil*. He said it had special bearing on recent events.

The story is set in the southernmost reaches of Florida and concerns the interaction between a suave young enterprising man and an older very rich fag.

Did I ever tell you my Gore Vidal story? There's not very much to it. Sometime in early 1995 I passed by The Blue Door bookstore in Hillcrest and noticed a crude colour photocopy in the window announcing that the author of *Live from Golgotha* would be appearing that Saturday evening. The event was not listed in any of the papers. When Saturday came around, I walked into the dishevelled, fluorescent-lit hole-in-the-wall with a sceptical expression on my face and found all the folding chairs occupied by an odd, uncomfortably silent assortment, typical for San Diego. Behind the counter, the bearded owner stood beside his worried-looking long-haired daughter, stoking a pipe. 'There aren't any more chairs?' I demanded. 'We'd put out more if we had any,' he answered, somewhat defensively.

Soon after, Gore Vidal was led into the store by a half dozen scruffy-looking young people. It looked for all the world like he'd been taken hostage. On the end of his nose was a small bandage. His first pronouncement was: 'I've just had a cancerous lesion removed from my face. I guess that qualifies me as a native San Diegan.' He sat down on a wooden chair and glowered. A bald young man in his twenties took the microphone and explained what was to happen: he and his friends would take turns reading from the great man's works. Afterwards, we could ask him questions.

A chunky guy with goatee (before it had spread from Seattle), whom I'd previously observed at Flicks gyrating in crystal ecstasy to Billy Idol's 'Heroin', read from *Golgotha*, mispronouncing words, which Gore testily corrected from his folding chair.

The simpering Hollywood gossip columnist for the *Gay & Lesbian Times* read from *Hollywood*, then asked the first question: 'I'm told you didn't get along with Truman Capote. But wasn't it more just a friendly rivalry?' Gore grimaced/smiled: 'There was nothing friendly about it. And I certainly never saw him as a rival.'

But midway through the proceedings Gore appeared to start enjoying himself. He rose to his feet, puffing up magisterially as he railed against the shortcomings of our state, which he predicted would soon go the way of Yugoslavia. Southern California would ally with Arizona and Nevada. Northern California would unite with Oregon and Washington, and perhaps British Columbia, to form Cascadia, which he said would be a very nice place to live. The new capital of the loosely allied federation would be Denver, pretty mountain country infinitely more hospitable than Washington, D.C. The audience posed some surprisingly good questions.

'Why do you live in LA?'

'Because it isn't there.'

'Tell us about the screenplays you wrote.'

'They were all pretty lurid.'

'What about the movie *Myra Breckinridge*?'

'I never saw it.'

'Tell us something about your grandfather.'

'He always said, "Is there any sound more horrible than the laughter of women?"'

As the questions wore on, however, Gore began to sag again. And by the time the end of the line of autograph seekers reached him, he had turned very grouchy indeed. Gushed the man ahead of me: 'I didn't even know you were going to be here! I just happened to see the crowd and come inside!' Spat Gore: 'What an ugly surprise for you!'

I thought Gore and I had been making eye contact the whole time. Despite his irritation, I almost felt he expected something of me. But as I handed him my Vintage paperback of *Myra/Myron*, all I said was, 'Just sign it, "Steve".'

I didn't offer him the galleys I'd brought of *Sailors and Sexual Identity*. Though after the autograph I did contemplate throwing it into his limo like a bomb.

Obviously, I kicked myself for never having bothered to ingratiate myself with any of these (civilian) bar queens. Later I saw the bald young master of ceremonies at a 'military haircut' party. He turned out to be a masseur at La Costa, the N. San Diego county spa where (Gore confessed to the Blue Door audience) he annually checks in to dry out.

Andrew Cunanan had disdained my invitation to attend the Hillcrest bookstore appearance by Gore Vidal. He told

Alex that he had already stayed with Gore Vidal in his Italian villa, and that his host had behaved like a monster.

*

Thank you for sending me Frank Rohan's *Lovely*. I found it a pretty good read. Certainly there are some aspects of the Nick character that seem alarmingly reminiscent of my (and your?) love interests. '"So maybe you associate being fucked with being abused, and maybe you can't take it from someone who loves you." That sounded a bit simplistic to Nick, and he was about to tell Aaron that he'd been fucked by plenty of people who loved him, but then he realized that it would only make things worse, so he said, "Maybe."' Recovery counsellor: 'Admit it. You are supplying him with the thing he probably fears most, which is love.'

But I have to say I found the saintly writer-protagonist Aaron less than convincing. His sole shortcoming was that he thought he could never be wrong. I felt strongly that he had to have been selfish in ways that went unprobed.

Still, my identification as reader was not restricted to Aaron. In fact, one scene reminded me of a real-life episode where I played out the role of the younger, shallow gay sex-driven opportunist.

As you know, I recently went back down to Southern California. Landing at Lindberg Field, I couldn't help but recall the first time I arrived in San Diego. It was five years ago, and I was also coming from Seattle. Then, too, I was met by my old cruising buddy Phillip.

Phillip is the dullest person I know. This is precisely his charm. He's like a glass of water. Which, of course, is a nice thing to be able to reach out for in the night. But he sure does love military boys, and when I moved to San Diego, he had just 'married' one. After years of desperate video arcade all-nighters, and publishing and responding to classified ads and toilet stall graffiti, and dating the occasional blond, blue-eyed Army lieutenant from Texas who ended up betraying him in a public toilet with Phillip's friends (me) present to witness his humiliation, Phillip finally moved in with the man of his dreams. Tim was a former Marine and Army Special Forces soldier. He was blond, in-shape, conventionally masculine, smart, and very much in love with Phillip.

This better-looking gay version of Timothy McVeigh also beat Phillip, and on Christmas Eve put a knife to his throat. But I didn't find out about that until much later. All I gathered my first evening in San Diego was that Tim was maybe a little possessive. After picking me up from the airport, an uncharacteristically nervous Phillip had just enough time to buy me a Mexican dinner – to go – and dump me off with my new roommate, an old friend of Phillip's named Todd.

Todd lived in Golden Hills, which is on the other side of Balboa Park from Hillcrest. This wiry, bird-like, Tony Perkins-ish thirty-year-old gay man had rented a nice little cottage on a mostly lesbian street in an otherwise sketchy neighbourhood.

Todd was like a glass of strychnine. He suffered from Tourette's syndrome. Cooking, cleaning, or puttering about the lawn, he was for the most part a very quiet person, until suddenly, when you least expected it, he would scream out some improbable weirdness, usually something scatological. A notebook I recently rediscovered lists his utterances on the day Bill Clinton was elected president:

'She had a shiny butt!'

'Put on some new panties!'

'And cow secretions!'

'We love it with gravy!'

'We enjoyed his dome!'

And, finally:

'Something's wrong with me!'

Todd explained that usually a certain sensation preceded such exclamations; he started to feel 'all rubbery'. I asked him how his co-workers reacted (Todd worked as a welfare agent for the county). He replied that most of them found it amusing, but one woman had requested to have her desk moved to another office.

For the most part I too was more entertained than put off by this habit of Todd's. Unfortunately, it wasn't his only quirk. He was hearing-impaired and watched TV a lot with the volume CRANKED. In my room with the door shut, there was no other option but to turn on the TV to the same channel, with the volume turned down. Todd was also subject to unpredictable fits of rage. He didn't have a waste basket, so I bought one. Walking home one day, I observed him smashing it to pieces against the side of the house. He offered no explanation.

But Todd could also be intelligent, genial, and generous. On his day off, he took me to Point Loma National Seashore. I photographed him standing against the Juan Cabrillo monument. Like Aaron in *Lovely*, Todd had an encyclopaedic knowledge of flowers and plants, and proceeded to give me an in-depth walking tour of the Point Loma flora. At some point I observed a Navy destroyer steaming into the harbour. I excitedly asked if he would please take a picture of me with the ship in the background. This Todd did. Then I asked him if he would drive me to the nearby video arcade that Phillip had told me about.

Todd thought about it, frowned, and said no.

One morning Todd saw me open the door to my bedroom and groggily make my way to the coffee machine. Wordlessly, my eyes met his. He screamed:

'SHUT UP!'

After I had my coffee I gave notice.

'Just because of that?' he asked, sadly. I told him the truth: his yelling just made it easier to tell him that I was moving anyway. In 1992, I couldn't handle being two slow bus rides away from the gay ghetto.

I moved in with Ken, Phillip's abusive ex-Marine lover's abused ex...

A year later – the night of the O.J. Bronco chase – I received a surprise phone call from Todd's sister. She'd found my name in Todd's address book. Todd hadn't told me or Phillip or any of his friends that he had Aids. I guess that's why he wouldn't take me to the peep show.

Alex never met Todd, but his favourite utterance, of the ones he heard me recount, was:

'Dee-dee, you need to clean your anus!'

*

After five years, Southern California was not the way you remembered it. After eight months, to me it still felt like home. And it felt like being washed up dead on the beach. I think a lot of people must feel this way.

In Seattle, people often look to have even less of a pulse,

and certainly less of a tan. Yet I think San Diego may actually be the most George-Romero-film-perfect of American cities. *Bronzed Zombies*, Alex suggests. Except really it's more a surrender to mummification. Nothing can decay there. There isn't enough humidity.

Which, of course, makes the beautiful young military men all the more like (as military-chaser newsletter publisher Dan Devlin recently told me) 'flowers in the desert'.

Riding through Balboa Park from downtown, a woman sitting ahead of me on the number 7 bus announced to her seatmate that she had scars on her brain stem. My seatmate was so disturbed that he spoke to me: 'Did you hear what she said? She did not say on her *skull*. She said scars on her *brain stem*.' I answered that riding the bus in San Diego I'd picked up a lot of second-hand information on disease, senility, parole boards, and mental illness. If only I'd written all the incidents down for my novel *The Cat Masseur Who Lost His Touch*. Believe it or not, I once boasted to Alex before that I had 'the touch' for cats. Soon after I overheard a woman with an East Coast accent complaining that her ne'er-do-well son was trying to massage cats for a living. In La Jolla. And it was hazardous work. But most of the things I heard on San Diego buses I did my best to forget.

I spent three of my four years in San Diego (first with Ken, then with Alex) at Spanish Court apartments, Casa de Las Pulgas. The concierge was a welfare mother of trailer park origins. Kelly is like a glass of isopropyl alcohol (which by the way I drank one time in San Francisco. I was trying to summon nerve to call my family, and without looking reached for Troy's bottle of Absolut, which was right beside the bottle I used to clean my tape heads with. I called Poison Control. They told me I'd be OK, but made me tell them my zip code and my age).

Kelly has since moved to an ugly concrete apartment complex one building down. Clintonian changes in welfare policy have forced her to find a job. She's put her busybody talents to use working for the local Citizens' Patrol organization, which recently launched a controversial vigilante campaign against gay men cruising for sex in Hillcrest. I found her in the back of her new building, by the swimming pool. She'd organized a birthday party for her three-year-old daughter, Amber. She asked me about Alex, about Andrew, about my cats, and whether I had any psychotropic prescription drugs she could 'borrow'. Out of the corner of my eye I saw a woman emerge from the pool, in soaked party dress, face drained of colour, clutching a sputtering and coughing two-year-old boy. None of the other guests paid any notice. In a later phone conversation I confessed to Kelly that only on leaving the party did it hit me that the woman had rescued the child from drowning. 'Oh,' she said, 'She acted like it was such a big deal. After you left, Amber started drowning, and I had to jump in the pool too.'

(Todd's memorial service was conducted in Oceanside. I rode there with Phillip and a large lesbian, with whom the young crystal-taking Todd had enjoyed an experimental three-some. Todd's family were dressed in linen and sandals, and silently grimaced as a self-important queeny welfare office co-worker eulogized that really Todd didn't suffer from Tourette's, it was just his way of getting attention.)

Phillip drove me to the Hi-Lite Video Arcade. With the closing of Naval Training Center in April of this year, the trade has all but disappeared. I recognized only one compulsive cruiser from the 'old days'. He confessed that he has had to branch out to civilians, sometimes even with long hair, and that only maybe once a month does he hook a sailor or Marine. Outside, under the neon, stood a minuscule man I recognized as the long-time peep-show mop man. This straight Mexican, who told me before that he had a wife and kids, was always unfailingly cordial, and with the least encouragement used to perform a kind of stand-up comedy routine, mimicking the various regulars. There was the octogenarian whom he once caught boring a glory hole with a circular saw. There was Boris, the most viciously territorial of the young queens, who carried a customized cruising kit: notes to pass under the doors, a video booth token worn thin from years of exhibiting his intent to spend money at the place, etc.

Tino appeared oddly uncomfortable to see me. He explained that he no longer worked at the bookstore. He had been sick. I remembered that the last time I had seen him he had just got out of the hospital for an undiagnosed ailment. A year later, he still didn't know what it was. 'Fumes,' he told me. 'I start to smell fumes.' He had gone to a neurologist, a psychiatrist, a psychologist and other specialists. He had taken sixteen different kinds of medications. Still he could not break free of a panicky sense of being poisoned. (Did you see Todd Haynes's *Safe*? 'Are you allergic to the twentieth century?') Listening to him, I almost started to feel the same sense of panic (and thought of your recent paranoid pick-up). The only thing that helped, he said, and that only sometimes, was long walks.

Needless to say, I struggled for words to wish him well and excused myself. But when I was otherwise occupied, so Phillip told me, the little man was trying the doors to occupied booths...

Of my old military friends, I met with only three. Anthony has been in recovery for over a year now. He told me of a recent night out at Rich's. A young man, who appeared to have taken both crystal and ecstasy, disrobed and paced back and forth along the stage, casting longing looks at the dancers below. Rich's and other gay bars in Hillcrest now employ full-time security guards. But in this case they called the San Diego Police to arrest the nudist.

'Was he cute?' Phillip, who accompanied us to dinner, asked Anthony.

'Obviously not,' Anthony said. 'That's why they called the police.'

*

I read Edmund White's *Genet* but can't remember a single cool anecdote. Just that in middle age he needed pills to get to sleep. Some other even less funny author wrote a biography of Wittgenstein, but at least it had one memorable bit. At some inn where he once lived in Austria or Norway or some other such place Wittgenstein told the landlady that he didn't care what she served him for dinner, just as long as it was exactly the same every night.

Love,

Steve

PS I relished the enclosure your sister sent you about the personality traits common to persons who share your birthday. 'July 4 people feel most fulfilled when representing a group of which they are proud ... Characteristically, those born on this day will make a strong or renewed commitment to a well-defined group at some point in adult life: either they will strive to become its leading representative, or simply be content to function as a devoted member.' I just checked my e-mail and found the following unsolicited message: 'Come home to PlanetOut. All of your friends are waiting for you.'

Funereal Themes

London, 5 October 1997

Dearest Steve,

Greetings from the Kingdom of Diana.

I never thought that I would live to see a revolution in this country, but that is almost what happened here after the Princess of Wales took a ride in a car driven by one of those Parisians who make you wonder why they bother painting white lines down the middle of the road. The infamous stoic stiff upper lip of the English has quivered, cracked and broken into public sobbing. And who has achieved all this? A bulimic, self-mutilating, manipulative blonde bimbo from a broken home.

After our own (black) Velvet Revolution, Princess Diana is the drama-queen of all our hearts.

OK, so I exaggerate a tad. But by sheer pressure of public outrage over their silence after Di's death, the Queen was forced to return to London early from Balmoral and address the nation on television. In the British context it was as if they'd returned in a cart lined with straw and rotting vegetables. In her address she said something that no one can remember a British monarch saying before and the very utterance of which is a kind of abdication: 'as your Queen...'

Well, baby, you know you've lost it when you have to spell it out.

I visited Kensington Palace (Di's former royal residence) the Day After, escorted by tranny Michelle and her male model and male-to-male transsexual friend Enzo (Pierre et Gilles have painted a picture of him, but this was an exercise in redundancy since the flesh-and-blood Enzo is so perfect, so airbrushed and colorized already – he's *post-production*). Both Michelle and Enzo adored Di. They recognized a kindred spirit. But that didn't stop Michelle joking

Enzo, Mich and Mark
frightening human beings
at a wedding

as we approached her former home, 'It's a good job she sold those frocks, otherwise William might have turned into a Norman Bates!'

Hundreds of candles guttered in the wind at the foot of the railings in front of the palace; thousands of bouquets of flowers and messages fluttered on the railings; an ocean of flowers in front of the gates gave off a shockingly strong smell of sweetness that filled the eerily silent air. A long, respectful procession of people clutching their own tributes inspecting those that had already been left there shuffled past (giving murderous looks to Mich and Enzo who were kneeling in front of the candles singing, *à la* Madonna, 'Life is a mystery...').

Of course it was one of those occasions when people mourned their own losses. One middle-aged woman interviewed on the radio explained why she had come to lay flowers: 'It seemed such a fairy-tale marriage – *and it turned into such a nightmare!*' Well, we've all been there.

The next night I took The Divine David to Ken Palace. At the sight of all this sombre devotion he burst into tears and croaked in a small, hardly ever heard un-ironic voice, *'This is what love looks like, Mark.'* The implication being that this was the closest he or I would ever get to it. He cheered up, however, when I drew his attention to one of the madder messages pinned to the railings:

'YOU who are responsible for the death of DIANA will find no hiding place, you will DIE in agony and be sent straight to HELL – the CURSE of TUTTENKAMON is upon YOU!'

A week later, the night before the funeral, I accompanied David to the gates of Buckingham Palace, where a different kind of demonstration was happening. Initially I hadn't understood why people were placing flowers there, but it rapidly became apparent that for some it was a calculated snub to the Battenberg Cuckoos who were considered to be covered in Diana's blood. David harangued the CNN cameras, shouting 'LIARS!' as they interviewed hand-picked people to announce how satisfied they were with the Queen's humble-pie speech earlier that day.

He also confused unsuspecting bystanders by asking them what they thought about the (non-existent) second broadcast she made: 'Personally I think she did the right thing,' he'd say, looking serious/sympathetic. 'It's best for the country. I mean, abdication was the only thing she could do...' Or: 'Apparently they've announced open house and the Duke of Edinburgh's having a barbecue in the back garden. Liz has also agreed to allow people to sit on 'er throne and try on 'er crown so that they can get some idea of what it's like being Queen.'

Then he produced, from where I have no idea, a pair of big inflatable red lips with a flashing torch attached to the back of them. Clambering clumsily over the floral tributes, he hung them on the palace gates, making the large round ornaments above the hinges look like eyes and the whole gate like one huge crazy cartoon. As David put it, for a moment, before the police removed them, the Battenberg-Saxe-Coburg-Gothas had a human face.

Sadly, the evening's jinks came to an end when the police, who had been eyeing us warily since we arrived, suddenly accosted us, asking threateningly, 'Planning to 'ang around, *Sir?*'

'No, I think not, officer,' said David tactfully. 'I'll be on my way.' (Like a lot of anarchists, when it comes down to it, David is *very* respectful of authority.)

Outside Westminster Abbey the next day I saw the coffin arrive on the gun carriage (David: 'How *offensive* that they should put a woman who campaigned against land-mines on a *gun-carriage* and wrap her in the *Royal standard* when they deprived of her royal title coz they thought it'd be a laugh that she would have to bow to her own kids!'). Sweltering in the sun, we listened to the service, clapped loudly at Spencer's bitter speech. Some people cried quietly. I didn't.

Which is just as well. A CNN camera was inches from my face. If I had allowed a tear to form, it would have been instantly beamed around the world. Not to worry though, CNN had apparently arranged for a couple of girls next to them to weep and sob openly throughout the service (when a woman fainted, the cameraman leapt down to clear people away, shouting, 'Give her some air!', only so that he could start filming her. At this the crowd turned into a lynch-mob: 'STOP FILMING HER!' they yelled as one. And he did.)

After the service ended, I went home and watched on television the funeral cortège drive through North London, along Hendon Way (a mile or so from here) and up the M1 to the Spencer estate in Northampton. All along the route, which was over 50 miles, people lined the sides of the road and threw flowers in her path. *Then*, in the privacy of my own home, I cried. Who wouldn't at such a image? Life goes on however – an hour or so later I went to the supermarket. Which meant driving along Hendon Way. Already the flowers had been crushed into the road by the traffic, forming ghostly flower-shadows on the tarmac. It's astonishing how flat flowers press, how little substance they have.

The next day in the gym, a young football-crazy lad I often chat to there spoke to me about the funeral and how he watched it on telly. 'I had a little cry,' he told me. Strangely, I couldn't quite bring myself to tell him I did the same. I also spoke to another gym-romance of mine, a twenty-something squaddie farrier (two fantasies for the price of one) with the Kings Troop RA – who provided the cortège and escort for Diana's coffin. He had shod the horses that drew Diana's coffin himself. How did he feel about it all?

'Very sad,' he said, fixing me with his guileless clear green eyes. 'She was the best we had. You couldn't help but cry.'

Like my Anglo-Turkish barber told me: 'To fink that there were all those millions of people on the streets and none of them were pushing and shoving – they were all being dignified and well-be'aved. I tell you, Mark, it makes you realize that there are nice people in London; it's just that they keep themselves well 'idden most of the time.'

*

I was in Torquay, Devon when I heard the news. Sunday 30 August. The last day of summer. It was also the last day of a weekend break I'd taken with a friend of my called Lee who grew up in Torquay and now lives in London. Torquay is a strange place. In fact, the whole of the West Country is a strange place. The people down there talk with clotted accents, and because it's a fairly inaccessible part of the country, they are trapped in a time warp. Torquay was the setting for *Fawlty Towers* – have you ever seen it? It's the sort of Brit comedy that gets played endlessly on PBS.

Torquay itself, though pretty, doesn't hold many attractions for me. So Lee and I visited Plymouth, about an hour's drive away, which does. Plymouth is Britain's major Naval port. Lee needed to be cajoled to take me to Plymouth: he doesn't really share my interest in military trade. Instead Lee prefers public schoolboys. But that doesn't appear to include me, alas – I'm too old and too butch, apparently. Lee is an ex-life-guard/current drifter, blond, blue eyed, boyish, stocky, and with an Antinousian/Irish boxer profile (his father is Irish). The boys he ends up with are always effeminate, huffy eighteen-year-olds who are usually on the game (is my jealousy showing?). In fact Lee himself is always complaining about their effeminacy and enacting savagely accurate impersonations of their nelliness and yet stays with them, or replaces them with someone just as Mary. When I asked him why he answered, with disarming honestly, 'They make me feel like I'm the boy.'

Plymouth is a fascinating town. When you finally come to Britain, Steve, I will have to take you there for a couple of days. Or maybe a month. Essentially, it has no industry except the military, and hasn't done for hundreds of years. Building and defending the Empire and annoying the French was the job of this port.

Union Street on a Friday or Saturday night is where the real action is: here the local girls conduct their drunken courtship rituals with sailors who have just been given their pay packets. Lee refused to go near it. So instead we made for the Hoe, the natural harbour created by two comforting green arms of land which reach out into the English Channel, and the place where Sir Francis Drake played bowls before departing to thrash the Spanish Armada. It was also a port for the precious convoys of arms and butter from the New World that sustained Britain during two World Wars. And, of course, where your Puritan Pilgrim Fathers set sail for the New World.

It's also the place where men go looking for cock.

The cruising area of the Hoe is by far the most beautiful trolling ground I've ever visited. Set into the cliffs above the western side of the Hoe and beneath the old Napoleonic fortress which is now the home of 29 Commando RA, it's a

series of paths and terraces built in the 1930s, painted a tasteful Marine blue and ice-cream white. The further down the
cliffs you go, the more intricate the design – arcades, awnings,
nooks and crannies present themselves, beckoning saucily,
until you reach the water's edge, where the Atlantic laps
against concrete steps descending lazily into the sea. The
steps rise out of the water and into a recess in the rock with a
columned awning in front. It looks as if it were built as a
throne-room for Neptune himself, climbing with nymphs in
attendance out of the sea. Or perhaps his bedroom. At night,
this is apparently where most of the 'action' takes place. No
one could have devised a more romantic setting for the exchange of briney body fluids.

'Every so often the Military Police drive along the top in
their Land Rover,' Lee informed me, 'sweeping the cliffs with
their searchlights, and everyone ducks down. They never
really do anything, though.' Adding, 'But it does scare the
military lads I've met here.'

A little further along, stretching out a few yards into the
bay and creating a mini-harbour around the cruising area, is
an abandoned seawater swimming pool, a leftover from an
era of public health and hygiene municipalism that has long
since ebbed, melancholic in its decayed obsolesce and neglect. East of that is the main Hoe area, which is better maintained – and attended – but exudes the same tempting aura
of faded glory, with its candy-floss, hot dog and palmist stalls.
Despite the chilly wind that afternoon, a diving platform at
least thirty feet high was being used by some local tattooed
toughs who cheerfully disregarded the warning signs and the
fact that the bottom ladder had been removed to discourage
use. They just scrambled up the steel girders. Their girlfriends cheered from the promenade, tongues eagerly licking
'99' ice-creams. These lads are the sort of brawny, lovable,
completely disposable fools they built an Empire with.

The whole place is exquisitely English in a way that
England stopped being even before I was born. Here time
stands still. The tides come and go, but here England remains. Flaking in the prevailing southwesterly breeze – the
trade wind that made England rich.

Lee wanted to go back to Torquay and hang out at the local

gay nite-spot, which is literally two rooms in somebody's terrace house, one upstairs with a sticky carpet, beer kept in a
kitchen fridge (complete with 'tasteful' framed black and
white prints from the early 80s of the Soloflex boy and that
guy lying face-down on that white sofa, one leg on the floor,
white ankle socks still on, who I've always suspected was
dead – strangled by a necrophiliac). It's a perfect microcosm
of gay life: upstairs is disco disco; downstairs is torch songs
for alcoholics too old and too lush to go upstairs. On my one
and only visit I hovered half-way up the stairs.

The journey back to Plymouth after dropping Lee off in
Torquay took longer than it did earlier and felt a lot more
forlorn: it was dark, and a driving rain that a western cold
front had brought in from the Atlantic was battering against
the windscreen. I reached the Hoe at midnight. Here the rain
was almost horizontal, there being nothing between me and
the New World and you, Steve, except thousands of miles of
cold, wet, lonely ocean.

I wandered around in the rain, without a jacket. No one.
Except a mincing young man with heels that clicked loudly
and annoyingly and an old man who shuffled around fur-
tively. I went and sat in my car and waited for a while.
Eventually the droplets on my windows lensing the orange
light of the street lamp got smaller. I left the car and wandered around again. A tall, skinny fortyish man who had
been following me for a while despite my carefully signalled
uninterest began talking to me as I leant on a balustrade,
gazing out at the Xmas-tree-like lights of a couple of Royal
Fleet Auxiliary vessels anchored out in the bay, which came
in and out of focus according to the level of moisture in the
air, a mirage of warmth and cosiness. I can't remember what
he said, but it was sufficiently sex-neutral and friendly to lure
me into conversation. It turned out he was from Surrey, near
London, and was married. He was in Plymouth on holiday.
After about ten polite minutes I thanked him for the chat
and moved off. He then crazily clutched my arm and asked
me if I'd wank him off.

'Please,' he said, 'I'm not into anything heavy. Just *hand
relief*.' Only a married man would say, 'hand relief'.

'No thanks.'

'Oh, *please*! I'll pay you £30.'

'No thanks.'

'All right then, £60!'

'No *thanks*,' I blurted over my shoulder as I walked quickly away, now very embarrassed.

Of course, a few minutes later I found myself thinking about what I could have done with £60, and that this might have been the last chance I had to get paid for sex.

Eventually I caught up with someone I'd seen while talking to Surrey Hand Relief. With short hair and a military manner he looked quite promising. Behind the swimming pool we began our exploratory gropes. 'What's your name?' I asked.

'Jim.'

'What do you do, Jim?' God, I'm so predictable. But the Commando base was right above us, and a boy can dream, can't he? His reply served me right:

'I'm a military historian.'

I suppose that's the nearest thing to going to Oceanside, cruising the bookstores popular with Marines and picking up you, Steve.

Turned out Jim had a live-in sailor boyfriend. He was the reason we couldn't go back to his place. 'It's an open relationship, but we have an agreement that if one of us is already home the other can't bring somebody back.'

'It's true love then,' I said sweetly.

'What's that?' he said, not catching my nasty quip.

'Nothing,' I replied, innocently. I wanted my dick sucked more than I wanted to be judgemental.

But he was a mediocre cocksucker, if enthusiastic and full of exclamations at the 'huge size' of my dick. This, Steve, is how you know you're in the provinces: people give bad blow jobs and think that your moderately large dick is *the biggest they've ever seen*.

The next day, before driving back to London, Lee and I attended a party held by a local millionaire in his house overlooking Torquay bay. It was, I suppose, his 'coming out' party. For the first time this middle-aged bisexual businessman had invited his straight and his gay friends to the *same* party. His two live-in teenage sons were also there. It was a revelation to see how close they were to their father, how much they had to talk about and how few secrets. They also understood all the gay in-jokes, but I don't think they're 'so' themselves. An advert for bisexual fatherhood if ever I saw one.

One of the guests, Steve, the gardener, was very 'straight acting'. He told me that all his straight mates had accepted him, and how this might have something to do with the mutual masturbation sessions he had as a lad with 'every single one of them': 'We'd have a wrestle and then we'd tug one another off.' (Love that word 'tug'.) His boyfriend, John, was a pretty Italian-descent boy from Liverpool with big brown eyes who got camper and camper and more and more flirtatious with every glass of dry white wine. Eventually he came up to me and gabbled without taking a breath: 'WellI'vegotyournumberfromLeenowandI'llgiveyouacallabout comingup toLondonI'llcomeupverysoonprobablynextweek we'llhaveagreattimeI'llgiveyouacallI'mreallylookingforwardto itspeaktoyoulaterI'llgiveyouacallwantsomewhitewine?'

Having just spoken to someone in the kitchen who had been beaten up for sleeping with John by straight-acting Steve and his straight mates-that-he-used-to-tug-off, I was less than taken with the idea (though, maybe it might have been a risk worth taking if he'd been a bit blonder and a bit butcher).

Provincial life can be even more desperate than the urban variety. Sometimes the jism prison can look quite appealing. The homewrecker had poured his heart out to me in the kitchen as he poured himself another half-pint glass of cheap red wine. Not bad-looking, young and 'gym-toned', he was probably quite a prize in Torquay. But precisely because of this and the fact that he was unattached, he was T-R-O-U-B-L-E.

'John told me he was single and I believed him,' he complained sorrowfully. 'But after we shagged, he went back to Steve and told him about it, so Steve and some straight mates of his waited for me outside a club one night and kicked me about, telling me not to go near John again. The worst part is that I've being trying to get along with Steve tonight because I don't want to have to be looking over my shoulder for ever.'

'It's a pretty nasty state of affairs,' I commiserated. 'And clearly you're caught in the middle of some couple's jealousy game. But on the other hand,' I offered, trying to look for a silver lining inside a hangman's hood, 'at least down here people go through the motions, at least things *matter*. In London, nothing matters. 'Cept how big your dick is.' (Yes, I actually said that).

'Yeah. I lived in London for a while,' he said wistfully. 'I tried that. But it didn't work out. Casual sex is great if you can keep it going, if you can keep scoring. But if it stops for some reason – you're in the shit. You realize that you're in the same boat as everyone else...'

At this point we were interrupted by a fat drunken man whose main sport seemed to be putting his fag ends in other people's drinks and pinching the bum of any male under forty. Earlier he'd asked me to put my arm in the air; when I stupidly complied, he licked it with his cow tongue before I could hastily put it down again and 'accidentally' knock him over the head. Hard. His boyfriend, wearing another lycra all-in-one, was behaving towards his appalling 'husband' like those timid people who have badly-behaved dogs – giggling shyly, apologizing half-heartedly and pretending to be embarrassed but quite obviously enjoying every vicarious minute of it.

It took some time to leave the party as Lee was very drunk on punch and having fun with the wig and glasses of the cabaret drag artiste, The Dame Edna Experience. The drive home took three hours, Lee snoring sweetly on the passenger seat. Asleep, of course, he is even more gorgeous than awake.

All the way back I listened to sad ambient music on Radio 1, a special playlist without inane DJ intervention, only broken by hourly news updates on the return of Di's body to Britain. Perhaps I was brainwashed by this experience; perhaps my emotion in the following week was merely Pavlovian (the psychologist; not the overwrought dessert) and my 'radical' friends who thought the whole business ghastly and reactionary were right. All the same, I didn't think that one person's death could stop that *noise*. Even for just a little while. The Princess of Wales should die more often, I thought.

It sounded as if they had a couple of moody CDs on random play: the same tracks were played repeatedly, but never in the same order. Funnily enough, the track which cropped up the most was an instrumental of Riuichi Sakamoto's 1983 single 'My Love Wears Forbidden Colours' from the film *Merry Xmas, Mr Lawrence*, a film notable for another teeth-enamel-peeling screen performance by David Bowie, this time in his 'Let's Dance' period bleached blond hair and shiny orange face. And the homoerotic story-line in which a handsome, dark-haired, capable young commandant of a Japanese POW camp is 'bewitched' by a British sergeant, played by Mr Bowie – who destroys him by striding up to him at roll call and kissing him (the film begins with a Jap prison guard disembowelling himself after being discovered fucking a blond Dutch prisoner).

When I wrote in my last letter about Ed White and Gore Vidal, I neglected to point out that both their Jimmie Trimbles were blond. I wonder if the world would have grieved for Diana so much if she were a brunette?

*

A dark-haired lad in Adidas track pants I picked up at a performance of The Divine David's at the Vauxhall Tavern, wearing an Umbro T-shirt myself (whilst The DD denounced queer sports casual wearers and their pathetic attempts to look like the boy next door) provided an experience which parallels, in its own way, your MP disappointment. His handshake was like a car crusher, and he walked like a sailor in a force 8 gale. He was very drunk. Too drunk. But how could I resist? Before we even spoke to one another, he positioned himself in the audience in front of me so that his eminently biteable sportswear-clad bum pressed against my packet, and his thick, clean neck smelling of soap distracted me from David's scrawny drug-ravaged body on stage. When we did speak and he turned out not to have very much to say, I somehow found it in myself to overlook this particular defect. Except in the way he walked, this boy seemed artless, not dull.

I brought him back here in my car, dropping Michelle off on the way. He kept having the same exchange with Michelle, over and over: 'But thing isss, right, not being funny, but you look like a woman.'

'But I *am* a woman.'

'Yesss, I know that, but most of 'em, they don't look like women at all. But you do.'

'Thank you.'

'Yeah. I'm not being funny like, but . . .'

At my place things didn't go much better. First he wanted to *box*. I declined, thinking that it wasn't a good idea getting into a fight in the early hours, even a mock one, with a complete stranger who was completely paralytic. 'But I like to box with a bloke. I like *blokes*, y'know what I mean? I like being with blokes, doing bloke things. Like boxing.'

'Yeah, so do I, mate, but I don't want to box you tonight.'

'Got any poppers?'

'No. Sorry, I don't have any poppers.'

'Got any porn, mate? Men fucking each other up the arse, that sort of thing?'

'Yeah,' I sighed and reluctantly dug out my dusty ancient Yankee porn tape featuring Jeff Stryker before he could travel free on the buses. He seemed to like this and wanked himself for a while staring alternately at it, my cock and my chest.

'I wanna fuck you,' he said at last.

'Not my cup of peculiar, mate. Sorry.'

'Oh right, you're like me then. I know you want to fuck me, but I don't get fucked either.'

Well, what can you do? You can hardly say, 'Oh yeah? Then why were you rubbing your arse against my dick for an hour before we were even introduced then?' Can you? It's against the rules. Anyway, he really was too drunk.

'Can I spank you?' He wouldn't stop.

'You'd wake the neighbours.'

'You can do the same after I've spanked you.' Obviously he liked the idea of reciprocity. He'd come to the wrong place.

'It'd wake the neighbours,' I said, deadpan.

'Oh right. Got any poppers?'

'No, mate, I've just told you I haven't got any poppers.'

'Oh right. Got any football shorts?'

'No, I don't have any football shorts.' But I found myself going to look for some all the same, just so that I could get away from this maniac. Mr 'artless' savage had turned into a fucking academy of fucking fetishism.

I returned five minutes later without any football shorts and no idea how to salvage this hopeless situation.

The lad took the news well. 'Have you got any poppers?'

'No, I still don't have any poppers.'

'Let's go into Soho and get some from a sex shop. I don't usually do poppers with most blokes, only with the ones I really fancy, like. Let's get some poppers mate. I'll wank you off in the car on the way.'

Is all sex like this? Is it just that most of the time we don't realize it?

Grateful for an excuse to get him out of the house I got him into the car and we drove off. But instead of taking him to Soho I took him home (right on the other side of London). He tried to play with my dick on the way, whilst I was driving, but couldn't get it free of my jeans and I wouldn't let him undo my belt. 'The police might stop us,' I cautioned, praying they would.

Yeah, I realize that the poppers 'he doesn't do with most blokes' was probably the key to anything approaching a 'successful' sexual exchange: that 'poppers' was something that gave him permission to get fucked. But, frankly, I couldn't be arsed.

As we were leaving the house at 2 a.m., I remembered I'd left my car keys upstairs. While he was waiting for me, leaning against the wall downstairs in the hall I heard my seventy-five-year-old yoga-teaching landlady who lives on the ground floor demand in a querulous but firm voice: '*Who are you?*'

'Oh, er,' he slurred, 'I'm a friend of, um, er, whasisname ... upstairs?'

'Oh, you're a friend of *Mark's*,' she said, like someone solving a puzzle they really didn't want to solve, and I heard her door close.

'That was your landlady?' he said to me as we were getting in the car. 'I thought she was a geezer.'

An evening of confusion all round.

*

On the subject of confusion, I was recently accosted in Highgate High Street by the artist formerly known as Della Grace but now known as Del La Grace Volcano. Del used to be a boyish dyke photographer of some note, and extraordinarily hypnotizing narcissism, but got carried away by the idea of her body as her own canvas. She went to SF a few years back when it was fashionable for some dykes to take testosterone, grow beards and cultivate acne.

So this battered van pulled up in front of me and this Irish navvy rolled towards me, accompanied by a typical German leatherish gay.

'Hey Mark! How you doing?' When I heard the American accent and saw the eyes up close, I realized the Irish navvy was Della/Del. 'Listen, this is Hans ... a German film-maker and we're going up to the Heath this afternoon to make a documentary about public sex. Do you wanna be in it?'

'Oh, I'd *love* to Della – err Del – but I've got to be somewhere else right now and I'm already really *really* late...'

Recounting this story to Paul, my gay journo friend, a friend of Della's (before Del killed her), he said of the German accompanying Del, 'Oh, *Hans*, that's not a German leather queen, that's just another lesbian friend of Del's on *testosterone*.'

*

Roles are reversing too much these days. The last three men I've met have all wanted to fuck me. Why should this be? I'm thirty-two, they've all been in their twenties – it's *un-natural*, for heaven's sake! There was a lad in Worthing I saw for a while who wouldn't let me fuck him and kept trying to persuade *me* to let *him* have a ride; he thought he had me sussed: 'Are you sure you don't want me to fuck you? They say that butch men like getting fucked...' (I didn't have the heart to tell him that it was *me* who put that rumour around). And then there was the ex-Royal Navy lad who lured me round to his place with a promise to let me fuck him and then reneged, instead proceeding to spend the entire evening trying to jam most of his fingers up there despite my repeated brush-offs.

I'm beginning to think that I should just go with the flow and be thankful that at my age there are sexy young bucks out there who are willing to do all the work and give all the attention.

*

Since I last wrote to you about firemen they seem to be everywhere (except in my bed, alas). They cut Diana free from the concertinaed Merc in Paris. They put out a fire in a window box belonging to a flat beneath my crazy friend Justin's place in Westminster, where I was staying the night before Di's funeral. And they were on my street just a few days ago, putting out a blaze in a house three doors along and which claimed the life of an old lady who might still be alive if Michelle wasn't so romantic.

Last Wednesday, Michelle was waiting for me on the steps of my house at 8 p.m. I was about fifteen minutes late. No sooner were we indoors then all hell broke loose and sirens sounded, lights flashed and pump engines roared. We looked out of the window in my third-floor flat and saw eight firemen running towards a house three doors along. Michelle screeched: 'I thought it was *mist*!'

'*What* did you think was mist, Michelle?'

'The smoke – well, now I know it must have been smoke. But I thought it was *mist*, coming from the Heath!'

'Just because you're a character from a Gothic novel, Michelle, doesn't mean the rest of us are.'

After the fire had been put out, there were about ten or twenty firemen milling around in the street outside. Michelle showed her appreciation of their sterling efforts by pulling up her jumper and flashing her tits at them through my living-room window shouting GERRA LOOK AT THESE LADS!!! She wasn't wearing a bra. All hell broke loose again. The firemen looked up, roared their appreciation, and flashed their torches and searchlights up on my window.

'Gerrum orrff!' they shouted.

'YOU GET YOUR COCKS OUT FIRST AND I'LL FLASH 'EM AGAIN!!!' she hollered back, in her coy way. And for a moment I thought they were going to. Or storm the house.

When it seemed like twenty or so firemen might knock down the front door and come charging up the stairs, all I could think of was: Where can I get a pair of tits at this time of night?

*

I was interested to read your précis of Rotello's argument about bathhouses and disco and the spread of HIV. You might be interested to read mine from my essay, 'Parading It: A revisionist history of homosex since Wolfenden' published in 1994, in a collection called 'Stonewall 25' at a time when I hadn't yet grown sick of epidemiology:

It was in the 70s that gay men began sleeping almost exclusively with other gay men instead of 'straight trade', as had previously been their habit. The clone look distinctive of that era was about eroticizing/masculinizing the homosexual body and making a self-sufficient economy of gay desire. As a result of this, anal sex – fucking – went from a minority activity to a majority activity. Meanwhile, the commercialization of the gay scene provided gay men with a much increased opportunity for casual sex – but with a largely closed group of men travelling between the main urban gay centres of the world. Thus the very self-sufficiency of the gay male economy of desire provided the perfect conditions for the extraordinarily rapid and unseen spread of what was later to be identified as the Human Immunodeficiency Virus.

So perhaps there *is* a Simpson–Rotello axis after all.

My guess is that Rotello isn't the best lay in the world. His idea of a sex police state, seems like a rather elaborate way to make sure your bored lover comes straight home after work, without taking a detour through the tearoom. Or maybe Rotello is actually motivated to save public sex from banality – after all, such a crackdown would make it *much* hotter.

Actually his suburban totalitarianism is just gayism taken to its logical conclusion. Rotello just takes the next step that even Kramer, Signorile, Andrea et al. don't have the censoriousness to do: finally replacing nasty, messy, scary same-sex desire with a smothering, goody-goody, mumsy-wumsy, *gay identity*. Sex into identity doesn't go – Lord knows, it doesn't even go into *straight marriage*.

Though Rotello is absolutely on the money to predict that he'll find some powerful allies for his project. Writing in the mighty right-wing national *Daily Telegraph* recently about how all his political certainties have been undermined in the wake of the Labour landslide and Diana's funeral, Peregrine Worsthorne, a veteran reactionary anti-gay (in the old-fashioned sense), conceding defeat in his war against homosexuality, had this to say about gay marriage:

It is no good denouncing homosexual promiscuity if

220

church and state refuse to allow homosexuals to choose to give up the hurly-burly of the *chaise-longue* – as Mrs Patrick Campbell put it – for the peace and quiet of the marriage bed. At a certain point the sensible thing is to make the best of a bad job, and it would seem to me that today even those who disapprove of homosexuality – indeed especially those who disapprove like myself – should stop fully denouncing the practice and start purposefully to civilize it...

If homosexuality can't be defeated – let's just concentrate on eliminating those features of it which distinguish it from heterosexuality! Sometimes, just sometimes, I'm tempted to join such a crusade. But I think 'neo-conservative' is such an ugly word and besides I haven't got a tuxedo, or even a mortgage.

I have an agnostic relationship to casual sex: I practise it, but I don't believe in it. The Italian novelist on the 'Impolitically Correct' panel in Paris exhorted homos to be thankful that they can worship sex in the park, on the beach and at the cinema and escape the 'womb tomb' (I think I read somewhere that he lives with his mum). But what if you don't want to spend your life on your knees in the jism prison? Maybe homos need to create some institutions that will protect them from sex, or at least *mitigate* some of its worst effects. Not many are cut out for the life of John Rechy, not even John Rechy. But isn't it in the very nature of homosexuality as a condition that it is a rebellion or at least a protest against institutions? Isn't it essentially irresponsible? Isn't this irresponsibility more than an embarrassing 'defect' that can be tidied up by some social engineering; isn't it in fact *the whole point*?

'Do you ever wake up in the middle of the night screaming and wonder why there's no one next to you?' asked The Demented David from the stage of the Vauxhall Tavern the other night as I ground my hardening packet against the drunken sportswear lad. 'Do you wonder how long you're going to be on your own? Well, the answer's very simple. ALWAYS BABY, ALWAYS! UNTIL THE DAY YOU DIE! Isn't that lovely, ladies and gentlemen?'

Alex's roommate should come to see David. 'Some of you in the audience tonight might be into S&M,' he announced, glaring at some of the pierced people hanging on his every word at the front of the stage. 'You are probably thinking you're really funky, that you're *really pushing out the boundaries*, that you're really getting to understand and *deconstruct power*. But you're not. *You've just got a mental health problem.*'

Isn't that lovely, ladies and gentlemen?

Love,

Mark

Following the Fleet

Seattle, October 31, 1997. Halloween.

Dear Mark,

Time again for another Tennessee Williams quote:
'Death never was much in the way of completion.'

I read your dispatch from the Kingdom of Di on a flight to San Francisco. I know that some Americans identified closely with Diana. Two gay male acquaintances stayed up all night to watch the memorial service. The mutual friends who reported this were puzzled. Like me, they didn't have anything against Diana; it's just that the whole idea of a princess seems, well, foreign. My Texan novelist friend D. Travers Scott said, 'Didn't we put all that behind us that two hundred years ago?' Reading your letter made me wish I'd paid more attention. If nothing else, to have a better understanding of what was going on in your world.

It's good to know that you can still cry.

*

Two weeks ago I flew to SF via Oakland. The airport shuttle took me right past where Troy used to be stationed. When it closed in April 1997, Naval Air Station Alameda was the last major military installation in the Bay Area. According to some sources, the Navy pulled out because of the popular equation *San Francisco = Gay.* (They thought their sailors would be safer in San Diego and Seattle.) But every October the US Navy returns for Fleet Week.

Riding across the Bay Bridge, I noticed, very high up in the pink-brown haze over the city skyline, four tiny arrowheads flying in formation. I remembered that it was five years ago to the day that I fled Troy and Washington state for San Diego, with a stopover in SF.

I tipped the van driver and found that my keys still fit the lock to the building that has always been SF home base to me: Bart's apartment. Bart, you may remember, is the friend who used to lecture that my desire for military boys could only be explained by my internalized homophobia.

Back when I lived in San Francisco, Bart was militantly

queer nationalist. Having at age thirty only just escaped Grand Rapids, Michigan with a degree in film production, Bart very quickly wormed his way to the epicentre of queer San Francisco. He worked as a doorman at a Castro bar (he is mentioned in the first edition of Betty & Pansy's *Severe Queer Review* of San Francisco), humped the late scary drag queen painter Jerome Caja on cable TV, and accidentally set his car on fire while cruising Dolores Park in a Skyy vodka stupor.

Bart used to sometimes be mean. For example, he urged my Navy ex, Troy, to cheat on me. He advised Alex to take up hustling. When he visited me in Germany, Bart kicked my cat and denounced me to the Polizei (I was wanted for riding the U-bahn without paying).

But I love Bart. And it's *because* of his edge that I love him. I reminded him of this when he sent me his comments on *Anti-Gay*.

He said that he was disappointed that you were so bitter.

I think Daniel Harris, whose lament for the dying 'aesthetic of maladjustment' I started to read (following the example of my male prostitute pal Matt Sycamore, I shoplifted it from Tower Books) may be on to something when he mourns the disappearance of old, alcoholic queens. Even if, like Signorile and Rotello, he feels compelled to pity those sad pre-gay homosexuals who were inevitably demeaned by their desire for straight and military trade (he quotes *Physique Pictorial* as an especially pathetic example of gay self-loathing).

These days Bart is older, freely admits to having lost a lot of brain cells, and in this second Clinton term finds it a lot harder to be dogmatic. Also, his two and a half years with Lee have mellowed him.

Lee just became an American citizen. His English has improved dramatically since the last time I saw him. He told me that he chose not to attend this year's Folsom Street leather fair.

'Conflict with my character.'

'It does for me too,' I assured him.

We talked about Fleet Week and the Blue Angels. I confessed that, watching the air show, I experienced an unconscionable ache to see one of the fighter jets crash. Lee said he felt the same way.

'I want they fall down.'

They took me to an excellent dive Vietnamese restaurant on Sixth and Market; then we said good-night.

Bart's dance club years are over. These days, he has a real job, and has to get up at 5 a.m. After he went to bed I wandered the streets.

Ah, the above-ground queer sex opportunities in San Francisco. What do you think I did my first night in Mecca?

The big gay bookstore on Castro Street is open until midnight. At the checkout, I had to wait while the clerk made an announcement over the store's intercom. 'A Different Light will be closing in ten minutes. Please make your final selection and bring your purchases to the cash register. If you're cruising, we just want to let you know: *it's OK*. There's no need to feel guilty or embarrassed. Why should you be furtive and ashamed? This is San Francisco.'

I paid for my three-volume copy of the collected works of AMG Physique Pictorial (offensive pink cover and all), took it back to my TraveLodge room, took a sleeping pill and beat off.

*

But I didn't sleep. The whole point of staying at the TraveLodge and not Bart's was so that I would have quiet. The next morning, I asked the desk clerk if I could move to another room. He hissed at me: 'There's no such thing as a quiet room in San Francisco!'

I had five cups of coffee and a $3 spirulina and wheat grass juice concoction. But I still wasn't awake.

My editor picked me up and drove me to his condo in a somewhat surly mood. His doctor has put him on a starvation diet – 500 calories a day. My editor is an Epicurean. In my sleep-starved state, I still hadn't made the adjustment as we drove down Sixth Street.

'Oh – there's the restaurant my friends took me to last night. It was *so good*. I had this "crispy noodle" dish. You know, shiitake mushrooms and vegetables over this cake of noodles. The noodles are crispy, but as you start to eat, they begin to soften, from –'

'The juices?' he whimpered.

I came to my senses and apologized.

At his condo, my editor poured me my sixth cup of coffee.

When he dropped me off at the TraveLodge, I had exactly thirty minutes to rest up before meeting Leo Bersani.

I would have cancelled if I could have, I felt so debilitated. But it was too late. Café Zuni was only a block away. I scanned the customers but did not find anyone resembling the book jacket of *Homos*. I waited outside.

When he showed up, we recognized each other at once. Dr Bersani surprised me. He was charming, down to earth, and a lot of fun. He also looked better in black leather than anyone else I noticed in San Francisco.

But he wasn't hungry, so we just ordered cappuccino.

Bersani kindly indulged my caffeine-OD chatter, and, when it became apparent the waiter was not going to fulfil my desperate request at one point (I was about to faint) for some bread, he ordered chocolate cake for me. I asked him about his comments on Marines in *Homos*, and told him I expected that he probably had some stories of his own about military chasers. He said that, on the contrary, he doesn't know very much about the military or military chasers; that isolated passage in *Homos* was mostly just a fantasy inspired by the gays-in-the-military debate.

So I told him about the kinds of men I have been interviewing for this book. He said that it sounded to him like they could be divided into two crude overlapping categories: men who ended up as chasers for largely opportunistic reasons (as an amateur porn videographer I interviewed put it, 'Marines are easy prey'), and men who are drawn to the military for complicated psychological reasons.

I said I hoped he wasn't offended by the porn photos I sent. He said no, on the contrary; he'd shown them to all his friends and told them, 'At last my work has resulted in some worthwhile mail.' But he said that there were certain physical qualities about the Marine that he disliked. It was the ass. It was too big.

*

Energized by the encounter, I headed for the tourist areas.

There were a lot of sailors hanging around Fisherman's Wharf – and almost as many Marines. Because it was the first night of Fleet Week, all were in full dress uniform.

I followed two Marines into a Pier 39 men's room. The

huger of the two men, standing before the mirror, uttered the first words I heard a Fleet Week military boy speak:

'Damn, I look good in uniform.' I resisted the temptation to second him, contenting myself with silent admiration of his big ass.

I made my way to North Beach, where the streets were teeming with hundreds of uniformed Marines and sailors, many of them drunk, several pissing in alleys, a few squaring off to brawl. Groups of them stood clustered under the neon looking almost like corny Tom of Finland drawings come to life, hands grabbing at very visible bulges.

Feeling faint again, I prowled one sex shop after another. I had no hope of sex. Military men no longer travel in groups of three. They come in nines. And these days, the sanitized 90s video arcades of San Francisco are geared strictly for tourists, with $3 minimum token purchase, surveillance cameras, electric-eye beeper devices, and blinding banks of fluorescent lights.

Inevitably, inexorably I ended up at the last refuge of sleaze, The Lusty Lady. In the remote dark back corner I found my old sailor-chaser buddy Melvin.

Melvin has been hard hit by the closure of Bay Area bases. For years he fed off Navy trade. Now, his sole sexual sustenance is this annual event, and that has proven increasingly dismal. But, he told me as I called him up from Bart's, he still takes off work so that he can spend every night of Fleet Week on the streets – all night if necessary. He called it 'the drive'. He said he feels 'like a salmon – swimming upstream against almost impossible odds'.

Melvin was not as happy to see me as he would have normally been. I guess I caught him in mid-leap. I wandered back outside and walked around the block, stopping to admire one group of almost 50 jarheads and squids, staring just a little too hungrily. I went into a bar where there were a lot of military boys, but though I followed several in the pisser ('You can come on in, man. There's another head in here.') I didn't talk to any. I decided I would try to find my friend and say good-night. Back at the peepshow there was no sign of Melvin. Almost as an afterthought, I tried the door to one of the occupied video booths. It was unlocked. A short, blond sailor with glasses was just buttoning up his trousers. He looked at me and closed the door, but not completely. I stood there for perhaps half a minute.

With the door locked behind us, the sailor took out some dollar bills and fed them into the video. Like how many thousands of San Francisco sailor chasers before me, I fell to my knees on the filthy Lusty Lady floor as the sailor undid his 13 buttons.

Luckily, the encounter lasted long enough for me to recover from my shock and enjoy it. The sailor pulled up his 'blouse' for me to admire his flat stomach. He wanted me to play with his ass – just a little, then returned my other hand to his balls. His pubes were untrimmed, and there was lint in his belly button. I half-swallowed, half-spat as he (and I) came. I stood up. Drunkenly, he threw his arm around my shoulder. For a second I was almost afraid that he would kiss me (not because that would be so bad, but because it would have been so unexpected). Instead, he just said, 'Thanks, man. How are you doing tonight?'

I said the only word I ever said to him. 'Good.'

'Take care,' he said as he left the booth.

The sailor was gone as I staggered outside. Immediately I found Melvin. He was ready to talk to me now. 'So, not too much going on here. How about with you?' he asked, doubtfully.

Dazed, I had no choice but to tell him.

'Oh.' He looked incredulous, and a little hurt. 'Maybe that means there's hope for me.'

I felt salmon survivor's guilt.

*

Maybe I should limit my book to interviews with rock stars who love military men. In September, I flew back down to San Diego to interview a famous British heavy metal singer of the 70s and 80s who has a thing for Marines.

Arriving in the hotel lobby, I came face to face with a huge, gorgeous, red-headed Marine and a tiny, gorgeous, blond twink. At the front desk a man stood with his back to me registering for a room in a British accent. This, I decided, must be Rob 'Wormcan'. Turning around, he recognized me at once.

Up in his room, the boys stripped off most of their clothes and rolled around on the two beds, then rolled around with each other on the same bed. Wormcan inspected the furnishings and lectured his young companions. Rolling his eyes, he turned to me: 'Everyone has ailments.' The small one was on pills for stomach trouble – and he had better not drink.

Blond Boy flashed his eyes at me: 'Where's the bar?'

And Tom was suffering from sleep deprivation.

'I only got two hours last night,' the ex-Marine confessed with a sheepish grin.

'*And your point would be?*' Wormcan demanded. 'I get my sleep in *before* I come to San Diego. Two hours a night is all I need.'

Changing the subject, Tom announced that he dated one of the guys in my last book. He asked me if I keep in touch with the men I've interviewed. Ever since he first read *Barrack Buddies* he's had a crush on 'Doc', the punkboy signal corpsman. He liked that book best, he told me; it felt the most representative to him. Reading the last one, he had to wonder where I'd found these Marines. He disagreed that the camaraderie was an illusion. But then, he was a grunt, and I hadn't interviewed any grunts, had I?

Um no, I said. That is, I did interview one, but I disqualified him after he boasted of all the *Saudis* he killed during the Gulf War. (Bersani, too, was a little suspicious about the representativeness of the Marines who made it into my book.)

Tom told me that when he was at sea, the guys in his berthing used to watch porn videos together – with the curtains to their individual berths mostly closed. One of the best-looking Marines on the ship noticed that Tom's gaze was more often directed at the gap in his curtains than at the monitor. Night by night, he left the curtain open progressively more, so that finally Tom had an unobstructed view. The last night of the float, he gave Tom a kiss on the neck and said: 'I'm going to miss puttin' on a show for you.' Tom replied that he was going to miss watching it. But nothing more was ever said.

Interestingly, Tom expressed scepticism about the anecdote in *Sailors and Sexual Identity* about the four Marines getting fucked by a sailor in a hotel room with a sugar-daddy watching. I had to wonder whether a similar scene might not play out in this very room later that same night. When Wormcan mentioned that a young Marine he had met on-line would be stopping by, Blond Boy and Tom speculated whether the boy would want to play with them too, or only Wormcan.

When Wormcan was ready to be interviewed, Tom and Blond Boy took off cruising.

The friend who'd introduced us cautioned that all Wormcan liked to talk about was sex, in the crudest, lewdest manner. My challenge, he said, would be to get the old rocker to be more reflective.

We found a spot on the outside terrace. Wormcan seemed relaxed and ready. He told me that ever since he had been in recovery he had become more ... reflective. This seemed my cue to push 'record'. At just that moment up walked Wormcan's newest love interest, Daniel. Though I protested, Wormcan insisted that the interview be conducted in the presence of this blond, sunburnt, ultrawholesome Mormon Marine who stared at Wormcan radiating a beatific, barely corrupted smile.

When I asked Wormcan why he liked Marines, he said: 'See, for me it's not all sex. It never has been and it never will be. It's a lot of other things, like tradition, um, the mind-set of being involved in an organization that requires some discipline, some intelligent comprehension of what it means to be a particular kind of a person, to do a specific kind of a job. It's all about what military service is capable of doing in terms of maintaining democracy and a free world.'

When I repeated this to Leo Bersani he said, 'That never got anybody hard!'

Channel surfing the TV that night, I saw bits of *Spinal Tap*.

The next day, I met up with Wormcan at Starbucks. I'd forgotten to have him autograph some CDs for Troy. Blond Boy studied the CD covers as though he'd never seen them before. I asked Tom if he'd been a fan before he met Wormcan. 'No,' he said, 'but my mom was. She was a headbanger.'

As I rode off with the friend who introduced me to Wormcan, I watched the forty-seven-year-old 'metal god',

head shaved with lightning bolt tattooed on his scalp, marching up the street underneath the Hillcrest sign with three
beautiful young men following after him like baby ducks.

'I get more maternal every year,' he'd said in the hotel
room.

*

Still, I was disappointed that I didn't get to hear the story
Wormcan told my friend about the time when he was on the
road with his band in Texas and he blew some guy in a rest
area without ever seeing his face. Afterwards, he hung
around outside until the guy emerged from the stall. He saw
a Marine wearing a T-shirt emblazoned JUDAS PRIEST. The
Marine saw a rock star he'd travelled across Texas to see perform the night before.

When I called up Wormcan's 'sidekick' to get the full story
on the barracks 'ballsac' ritual, I mentioned the tearoom
story. Tom was sceptical: 'I never heard that story. And I
thought I'd heard 'em all. That sounds like something out of
a magazine to me.'

Needless to say, what most impressed me about the rock
star is his taste in former Marines.

*

Earlier this month I went to see Morrissey. He was on good
behaviour. And he looked in excellent shape for thirty-eight.
I think he was the only person older than me in the
auditorium.

It's been a while since I've attended a rock concert. At the
door, I had a weapon confiscated. I'd forgotten about the
(tiny) Swiss Army knife on my keychain. There was no place
I could check it. The security guards made me throw it away
– in front of Alex, who gave it to me on Christmas (the day
he 'broke up' with me).

Still shaking from the confrontation, I found our seats ...
behind three Army boys. My amusement soon dissipated. I'd
forgotten how stupid and – sad to say – *ugly* straight military
boys can be. As Alex said about the loudest, 'His ass is even
fatter than his head.' I actually found myself turning around
and gazing sympathetically at a pretty teen queen Morrissey
lookalike who, cocking his head dreamily, mouthed along

every word to every song from the last three albums, none of which the ordinary boys knew.

The next night I rode the ferry over to Bremerton to address fifteen gay men, half of them sailors, in the basement of an Eagles fraternity lodge. I read ex-grunt Tom's powerful, important and sad stories of straight buddies who licked the fruit and put it back on the tree. Nobody seemed to get it. Except for Alex, who just looked sad.

'. . . and I'm not too keen on anyone else . . .'

My favourite moments from the Morrissey show: In 'Reader Meet Author', after the line 'Have you ever escaped from a shipwrecked life?' he bent down with his head buried against the monitor for the rest of the song. Is this song about me? 'You shake as you think of how they sleep / but you write as though you lived side by side.' Having never seen The Smiths, it was a great thrill to hear 'Paint A Vulgar Picture'. But weirdly, the song I most lost myself in was the close, 'The Teachers Are Afraid of The Pupils', an intense version of a track I never thought that much of.

It was somewhat hard to immerse myself because, seated between two of the ugly Army boys was a child who looked exactly like Becky from *Roseanne*. Hair and all. When Morrissey walked on stage, he sprang up and flailed about, shaking his crustacean-infested locks for 80 minutes. The only person standing in the entire balcony was sitting directly in front of me.

I'm going to strive to be a better person.

*

Last weekend I had Max euphemized. Alex went with me. It was the first time we ever cried together. Everyone tells me I 'did the right thing', but I'll tell you this: I'll never mercy kill again. Not even for you, so don't even ask.

Love,

Steve

The One That Got Away

London, 3 December 1997

Dear Steve,

If boys are like cats, cats are like queens – at least in terms of their entertaining vanity.

My landless aristo friend Simon (who lives, I kid you not, on Great Queen Street) is writing a play about his uncle Stephen's life. He thinks it should be based around Stephen's bed, to which he retired in his forties and from which, as I mentioned in an earlier letter, he never arose – living on ice-cream, surrounded by empty perfume bottles and sketches of sailors in Marseilles. Illustrations for the classic novels about romance and betrayal on the Côte d'Azur that were never written. On the rare occasions that he received visitors they would be ushered into his bedroom and then asked, by a purring, delicate, slightly *worn* voice straining to be sultry, 'How *old* do you think I *am?*'

Of course, there was only one answer that was even thinkable: 'Why, Stephen, twenty-one years if a day!'

Simon planned to have two actors play Uncle Stephen, one for youth and one for bed-exiled middle-to-old age. I suggested that he would save money on actors' fees and strike a more poetic, tragic, *homosexual* note if he had the one old actor play both roles, leaving his bed to act out the youthful reminiscence – sagging face and belly be damned. He seemed keen on the idea. After all, Simon recognizes stagy drama when he hears it: his alcoholic, divorcee mother was over-fond of Judy Garland. Apparently she used to force visitors to listen to the whole soundtrack to *A Star is Born*, exclaiming, 'This isn't art – this is *life!*' She would sing along to 'The Man That Got Away' ('The man that won you has run off and undone you') at full tilt late at night, waking young Simon and his little sister and big brother – who were probably glad they weren't being woken by the more usual shouts, screams, curses, crashes and the sound of a drunken man methodically and pitilessly beating up his hysterical wife. As Simon puts it, 'I had no chance really, did I? I was sentenced to homosexuality from day one.' (The childhood memoir he's writing is called *No Time To Grow*.)

He's promised to cast me as one of the soldiers that the young Stephen has sex with in his play – and as the sergeant in his yet-to-be-made movie about his grandfather, whipping a deserting First World War soldier while Lord Kitchener looks on, gripping his riding crop a little too tightly. Apparently Simon's grandfather ('who wasn't homo, just sexual') had a fling with Kitchener, Chief of the British Forces during the First World War.

So I continue to take his calls.

*

Sorry to hear about your cat. And even sorrier to hear that the experience means you won't mercy kill me when the time comes.

When I read that this was the first time that you and Alex had cried together it almost goes without saying that I immediately thought that your dead cat – who had had a long life – symbolized yours and Alex's doomed attempt at domestic, lesbian happiness. Cats for queers do have a habit of turning into surrogate children – the issue of a relationship without issue. But then, when I cried at Diana's death I was, like most of this country, almost certainly crying for myself more than for a dead Princess. And perhaps I shouldn't judge Americans by English standards – maybe you don't need something fluffy to displace your emotions into.

Speaking of displacement, I've been reading the great bio of Freud by Peter Gay. In agonies from cancer of the palate caused by his love of cigars, struggling with a huge, nightmarish prosthesis inserted in his mouth to keep his nose separated from his oral cavity, he asked his doctor to honour his promise made several years previously about 'not allowing the others to prolong the torment'. He had in mind his beloved daughter Anna, whom he worried would keep him alive long past the point of sense out of sheer misguided love.

He'd arrived in Hampstead, London (a mile down the road from here) only a few months earlier after fleeing Nazi Austria with his family. Rather like you did San Diego.

But I couldn't help but be struck by the irony that Freud's last years were tormented by and eventually ended by a cancer which attacked the wall which separated his nasal cavity from his mouth, while most of his professional life had been overshadowed, or at least slightly shaded, by his youthful, passionate literary love-affair with Fliess, the batty rhinologist he corresponded with passionately for years before a terrible falling out. After the Fall, he detected the influence of Fliess in everything – or rather, 'the remnants of my homoerotic attachment to Fliess' in everything (including, most notably, his disastrous relationship with the future Aryan New-Age Nazi Jung – his proudly proclaimed 'son').

Fliess was a bit of a charlatan and botched a number of operations, on one occasion leaving a wad of lint in a patient's nasal cavity which festered and turned septic. Freud was present at the emergency exploratory operation when this appalling error was discovered (famously writing in his letter to Fliess, 'that this should happen to *you!*' – when, of course, it didn't; it 'happened' to Fliess's unfortunate patient) and was haunted by the memory of it. I couldn't help thinking that Freud was fated to repeat this scene in his own life, having to suffer numerous mouth operations, infections and pus explosions, as well as wrestling with that prosthesis/wad.

Fliess's most radical theory, apart from universal bisexuality, was the idea that the nose is the seat of the libido. This was considered a very respectable idea at the time. Fortunately for the history of psychoanalysis, Freud appropriated the theory of bisexuality and not the theory of rhino-libido (although, sometimes, when I look at Torquay Lee's perfect nose, I wonder whether Fliess might not have been onto something there after all...).

But it was Freud's love of oral gratification with cigars which almost certainly brought on his mouth cancer. Sometimes a cigar may just be a cigar, but I wonder if it ever was to Dirty Siggy. Isn't it poignant that the disease which finally killed him after so much suffering was one which literally did away with the distinction between the beloved Fliess's organ of sexuality and Freud's mouth?

*

I'm also sorry that you couldn't make it to Sanibel Island, Florida, for my week's vacation there this November. Your company would have been especially welcome, if slightly surreal in a place full of old fat people and beaches.

The flight to Fort Myers was like a long, tedious, slightly demented parable. I sat next to a black couple and their toddler daughter who was playing with a seemingly endless collection of Barbie dolls – coffee-coloured with legs which went on for ever, big hair and the most adorable brightly coloured outfits you ever saw. The little girl, who was doted on by her father (a nice bloke from South East London who was something in printing; following British etiquette, we didn't speak until the eight-hour flight was nearly over), was already modelled on these dolls. When she wasn't playing with the dolls she was busily fiddling with a dressing-up kit involving cardboard cutout people and cardboard cutout clothes.

All this intense femininity was a tad camp – even without the strange gurgling, wailing, banshee noises the little girl made as she clutched one doll in one little fist and one in the other *banging* them together more and more violently – 'AIEEEEEEEEUUURGHH!'

Every now and again, when her cutesy little girl femininity threatened to destroy the plane, mum or dad would be forced to intervene. 'Shush, honey,' they'd say and she'd go back to 'la, la, la' and cooing noises, making her puppets dance and comb their hair, only to get bored with this just a few minutes later and have them beat the shit out of one another again to a banshee soundtrack.

I carried on playing my laptop space war game involving death and destruction on a cosmic scale. When I grew too bored or too guilty with the wastefulness of this to carry on, I pulled out the in-flight magazine and began reading an article about ... computer games. One section dealt with why computer games are so much more popular with boys than with girls. The piece contended that boys are more interested in shooting things and girls more interested in manipulating. 'After all,' the author said, 'playing with dolls is about making *lovely little people do exactly what you want*.'

I think I'm going to trade in my laptop for some Barbie dolls.

The first in-flight movie was *Contact*, starring that famously dubiously feminine star Jodie Foster. This is a film about a little girl whose dad dies at the beginning of the movie and she spends the rest of her life trying to find him again (well, he is rather cute). Which, you'll be glad to hear, she manages at the end of the movie – after a fashion – when she is transported millions of light years to the other side of the universe by an advanced alien race who then speak to her in the form of her dead dad. Of course, they should have called the movie *The Elektra Complex*. Those aliens know a thing or two about transference. Jodie, naturally, is completely unconvincing in this scene of girlish fantasy fulfilment and looks more frightened than she did when she met the TV tanning killer in *Silence of the Lambs*. With just cause.

As if all this adult childishness wasn't enough, the following movie was *Big* – the one where Tom Hanks plays the eight-year-old kid who grows into a thirty-year-old in the middle of the night. This being an American movie, he quickly finds a way to turn his misfortune into a profit and becomes a consultant to a toy manufacturer and teaches all the hard-nosed adult executives the virtues of childishness. As if America wasn't already a country full of eight-year-olds in thirty-year-old bodies playing with toys.

But I can talk. If you remember, the film begins with the boy playing a computer game.

Throughout the flight I kept noticing a young lad in dark trousers and natty green shirt and tie a few rows up from me. He was about 5-foot-10 with well-groomed dark hair and a nice, attractive face. He also had a fantastic, pert arse which curved out from his belt to the top of his thigh. It made for a marvellous sight when he reached up into the overhead lockers on tiptoe, *clenching*. Something he did a lot of. I tried to catch his eye once or twice, accepting finally that he wasn't up for any buggery-pokery and that I was just being an incorrigible letch again.

At Atlanta I filed out of the aircraft and walked along the long and sumptuously wide Olympic showcase corridors to immigration. As I was doing this, admiring the Imperial extravagance of the décor compared to scummy Heathrow, the lad in the green shirt who last time I clocked him was some way behind me suddenly overtook at great speed on my left and then veered right, across my path into a nearby restroom.

I got the hint. I followed, heart pounding. At the urinal a

man stood between us. He left. Looks were exchanged. I was about to move smartly to a urinal adjacent to the lad when more legit pissers arrived. Bloody pests! I headed into a cubicle – one of those killjoy American ones with a door that stops two feet from the floor.

I heard the bolt lock in the next cubicle and then, moments later, a hand with an impeccably ironed green shirt sleeve appeared underneath the partition, the fist half-closed in an inviting and helpful-looking gesture. It was a odd sight, although by no means the first time I'd seen it. But the Puritan cleanliness of this brand-new Olympic showcase airport toilet; the immaculate shirt sleeve and cuff; the thick but not too coarse wrist; the manicured hand with just the right amount of fleshiness to it, just the right curvature to the meat at the base of his thumb and little finger; and the way it jerked up and down, helpfully semaphoring its friendliness. Half stoned on the surreality of it all, I could only think how the green of his shirt matched the pastel coloured partition perfectly.

I knelt before this vision (which also brought to mind Thing from *The Addams Family*: the hand that popped out of a box to light Morticia's cigarettes), and as it instinctively found and moved up and down my shaft it paused every now and again to allow its thumb to play with my cock head. It was just a little detail, but it nearly reduced me to tears. Not because it was so erotic – although it was that too – but because it was so *thoughtful*. That someone could take so much trouble when wanking off an anonymous cock underneath a toilet partition in Atlanta airport seemed to me to be the very definition of love.

Besides, I had been ogling the owner of this arm for eight hours on the plane. Which means that, in homo terms, we had a *relationship*.

Whilst I was in Florida, I made an alarming discovery. I've become the fat of the lover.

Of course, Florida is the place to be fat. A sand bank covered with burger bars and shopping malls full of Hefty Hideaway clothes shops and lots of very straight roads – so there's less energy expended moving the steering wheel – connecting them to motels, condos and beaches: places where you can lie down and rest after all that eating and shopping. This is a place of inconceivable plenty for a European. Even the Gulf of Mexico must be teaming with life, a vast all-you-can-eat 24-hour buffet, judging by the numbers of shells washed up on the beaches every day and the huge birds that sit lazily around on the beach most of the afternoon, obviously satiated. It's funny how you described living in San Diego as like being washed up dead on the beach. In Florida most of the beaches appear to be made of crushed white shells – the bones of long-dead sea creatures.

Next to Florida, Southern California is Athens-with-valet-parking. No wonder Andrew blew his brains out.

It's entirely appropriate that NASA should have its rocket base in Florida at Cape Canaveral. After the vacuum of Florida, space must be a cinch to survive in. And Florida is the home of that most American of luxuries, *air-conditioning* – a place made *inhabitable* by air-con. After all, space travel is really just a form of air-conditioning – frozen oxygen fuels the trip into space while space capsules and space suits with their own mechanically processed and climate-controlled atmospheres keep the astronauts alive while they're up there.

Air-conditioning is not just about heading into the future but also about evading the past – a form of cryogenics. Old people flock here in droves. One day I lunched in a refrigerated diner outside Fort Myers popular with crumblies. The lobby was full of old folks waiting to be seated and enjoy the 'Over 60s Menu'. It was eerie watching them waiting for their name to be called: 'Mr and Mrs Isaacs, your table is ready. Booth 13, Aisle Styx. Your waitress is called Charon.'

During my first trip to Florida, with my parents in the late 70s, I encountered three things I'd never come across before: air-conditioning, obesity and body-builders. The first body-builder I ever saw was sunbathing by the pool in one of the hotels we stayed in. I remember being transfixed by his chest, arms and back, wondering how a man could have enough blood in his body to supply such a volume of muscle, when I seemed to have barely enough *skin* to cover my lanky bones. Of course, he represented something even more flamboyantly, extravagantly American than obesity, air-conditioning or NASA. *Narcissism.*

That holiday was when my ill-fated love-affair with the US really took off.

In Britain in the 70s we didn't have air-conditioning, ice-machines, body-building, space travel, or really, really fat people. In the 90s things haven't changed that much. We have a whiff of air-conditioning in some new offices, but not the sort that gives you goose-pimples. A few American-owned hotels have ice machines in the corridors, but no one seems to have any behind the bar. Fortunately for me, being really very fat is still too expensive, as there are hardly any all-you-can-eat buffets, and McDonalds isn't allowed to feed its customers with milk shakes intravenously here. There is quite a bit of body-building and space travel now – but it is practised mostly by men in gay clubs on ecstasy.

*

Back in Blighty I went to see *Wilde*. Oh dear. Oscar has been done to death by his fans even more than Reading Gaol.

The most irritating thing about this treatment of Oscar Wilde by Julian Mitchell was the most irritating thing about practically every treatment of Oscar Wilde – it was really a ninety-minute apologia for homosexuality in general and Wilde in particular. The film begins with Wilde flirting with some cute half-naked American miners; the script then takes us about five miles underground in a cage of 'sexuality'. The phrase, 'I have to obey my nature...' was repeated *ad nauseam*. Wilde was portrayed by the buffoonish Stephen Fry as a slightly bewildered, basically affable fat old gent incapable of doing anything really bad, browbeaten into making some foolish decisions by his fruitcake boyfriend Bosie.

In fact, if it hadn't been for Jude Law's electrifying performance as Bosie, I would have fallen asleep. Trouble was, this film made it seem that the most interesting thing about Oscar was that he fell for an undergraduate aristo with father issues and serious psycho crumpet tendencies. Which might actually be uncomfortably close to the truth – the snatches of the plays we glimpse seem, unintentionally I think, infuriatingly trite, smug confections. (I've always thought his one novel, *The Picture of Dorian Gray*, is better than all his plays put together.) Probably the best scene is when Bosie loses his temper and slags Oscar off for being vulgar and middle-class and his plays as shallow depictions of a world he doesn't know anything about. '*You don't love me at all!*' he yells. '*You just want to be seen with an aristocrat!*' He then smashes a jug of water on the floor. Reminding me of that saying: 'The best thing about being a gentleman is that you don't have to behave like one.'

After this, my favourite scene was between Bosie and his father, the bugger-bating Marquess of Queensberry (who, naturally, I rather liked). Queensberry orders Bosie never to see Wilde again. Bosie doesn't like this, and shouts at his dad and runs off.

'*Bum boy!*' Queensberry screams after him.

But the point of the portrayal of Bosie and Queensberry's dysfunction (and Queensberry's heavily signalled latent homosexuality) is to naturalize and justify Wilde's relationship with Bosie as one of good daddy versus bad daddy – and make the 'incest' of the good daddy seem preferable to the uptight, pathological frigidity of his bad daddy's love.

As I say, I think that *Wilde* makes too much of Wilde's sexuality. But I suppose this is inevitable – *history* has made too much of Wilde's sexuality.

Funnily enough, Rupert Everett was much more Wilde in *Another Country* – another film written by Julian Mitchell – than Fry was Wilde in *Wilde*, and much more believable as an outsider who wanted to be an insider. Yes, *Another Country* was also an apologia for homosexuality, but a rather better one, I thought.

Interesting, though, that this is the first film about Wilde that has been able to actually show the dynamics of their relationship – chasing rough trade together (although, inevitably, the film makes Bosie the instigator of this and Wilde the reluctant accomplice), with young Bosie romping around with the working classes while the older Wilde looked on from a chair. Wilde was, you see, a watch queen.

To gays this interest in rough trade must look very old-fashioned now, and yet the *dynamic* of their relationship must have looked very modern, very familiar. And how much at odds it is with the hallowed hollow image of the model gay 'marriage' being touted around in our media at the moment...

I found this part of the film especially depressing, though. A few months after Jason disappeared I ran into an advocate of 'swinging' in the Heath car park on a Sunday afternoon. I'd left my lights on (ominously, there'd been a thunderstorm on my way there) and had to call the AA for a jump start. A stocky thirty-something man in the next car who'd been cruising me but whom I wasn't interested in offered me the use of his mobile phone. I couldn't think of a polite reason not to use it so I did. Of course, this meant talking. He asked if I had a boyfriend. I was still in that pitiful post-relationship period where if someone asks you such a question you find yourself saying, 'Well, I *was* seeing someone...' Spotting his chance he then went into this evangelical speech about the marvels of gay swinging, how he's been with his current boyfriend for three years – 'And do you want to know the secret of our success? Well, I'll tell you,' he said before I could tell him I *didn't*: 'threesomes.'

He must have caught my unimpressed look because he added: 'Well, you've got two choices: You either let them leave you or you start going out looking for sex together. There's only two choices. They always leave when they start to get restless.' This was obviously a speech he'd practised many times, and perhaps by now it sounded half convincing to him, even sitting alone in his car in a car park on a damp Sunday afternoon.

'Well,' I said, trying to end to this line of conversation, 'if that's the case, I'd rather they left.'

He was, however, basically correct. Desire of the Other is at the root of sexual as opposed to contractual relationships and if it goes off the boil – as it must when the Other becomes Mother – then the relationship is over unless you can stoke the flames of desire by importing something Other into it again. So why not base your relationship around desire for *other people*? So long as you live in the metropolis, this is an infinitely renewable and fairly reliably anonymous source of sexual interest.

A Military Policeman I know is in a live-in relationship with another man. They have an agreement which is only to have sex with other people with the other party present. He told me that they came to this arrangement because they had seen jealousy and distrust destroy the relationships of their gay friends.

They are genuinely fond of one another, and their system appears to work – in as much as they are still together. I even believe that they continue to have sex together without other parties present. But new covenants bring with them new humiliations. I once rang in the middle of a row they were having. Apparently the other half had gone off to the Heath without the MP. He swore blind that he didn't do anything, but the MP – and this goes to show that cops are cops are cops are cops – *had examined his underpants and found a cum stain on them.*

He felt betrayed and angry. 'I ought to fucking smash his face in!'

They patched it up. Or boil-washed it. But a few days later I came across this interview with Felix Guattari, author of *Anti-Oedipus*, by George Stambolian:

> FG For me desire is always 'outside'; it always belongs to a minority. For me there is no heterosexual sexuality. Once there's heterosexuality, in fact, once there's marriage, there's no more desire, no more sexuality. In all my twenty-five years of work in this field I've never seen a heterosexual married couple that functioned along a line of desire. Never. They don't exist. So don't say that I'm marginalizing sexuality with homosexuals, etc. because for me there is no heterosexuality possible.
>
> GS Following the same logic, there is no homosexuality possible.
>
> FG In a sense yes, because in a sense homosexuality is counterdependent on heterosexuality. Part of the problem is the reduction of the body. It's the impossibility of becoming a totally sexed body. The sexed body is something that includes all perceptions, everything that occurs in the mind. The problem is how to sexualize the body, how to make bodies desire, vibrate – all aspects of the body.

Felix may be right about there being no heterosexuality, that *marriage* is the opposite of homosexuality. Certainly Peregrine Worsthorne would agree. Though, I have to say, this idea of the 'totally sexed body' sounds perfectly dreadful. Not least because, as my academic friend Nick said when I read this out to him, of the 'small fortune you'd have to spend on batteries'.

Predictably I prefer the more pessimistic account of desire Terry Eagleton gives in the current issue of the *London Review of Books*:

> Schopenhauer saw us all as permanently pregnant with monsters, bearing at the very core of our being something implacably alien to it. He called this the Will, which was the stuff out of which we were made and yet was utterly indifferent to us, lending us an illusion of purpose but itself aimless and senseless. Freud, who was much taken with Schopenhauer, offered us a non-metaphysical version of this monstrosity in the notion of desire, a profoundly inhuman process which is deaf to meaning, which has its own sweet way with us and secretly cares for nothing but itself. Desire is nothing personal: it is an affliction that was lying in wait for us from the outset, a perversion in which we get involuntarily swept up, a refractory medium into which we are plunged at birth.

We're all *permanently pregnant with monsters*. So you see, Steve, homosexuals can have children, after all.

*

A posturing magazine that likes to pretend it is the bastard child of journalism and cultural studies called the *Modern Review* has been relaunched here after an absence of two years. It's owned by a celebrity journalist called Julie Burchill. The new *MR* is edited by a female Sussex graduate the papers claim Burchill left her husband, Cosmo Landesman, for.

The current issue includes a piece on 'the gay identity crisis' written by some confused lesbian who lives in Manchester. It was unbelievably dense and misinformed, even for a confused lesbian who lives in Manchester (actually, I hear the author is straight and lives in Brighton, which makes it even worse). She lumps me in with that gay milk monitor, Andrea Sullivan. I can copy it for you if you are still having trouble getting to sleep at nights. I suspect its side-effects will be worst than melatonin, though.

(By the way, do you think lesbians would have ever become obsessed with 'lesbian visibility' if their genitals had been external instead of internal? I recently attended a 'drag king' workshop presented by Dianne Torr. She wore trousers 'packed' with some kind of dildo-beanbag, delivered a sermon in a suit and a faux-deep shouty voice about the threat of 'falling sperm counts' and then humped a hole in the floor. As far as I can see, the crowning achievement of lesbianism has been to turn penis-envy into penis-resentment.)

Meanwhile, *Vogue* – of all things – have just run a long feature about *Anti-Gay*. Of course, the only bit I paid attention to was where it talked about me: 'Articulate and witty . . . for traditional gay fundamentalists, Mark Simpson is the Anti-Christ.' The man who wrote the piece and who was very charming and flattering when he interviewed me was Cosmo Landesman, Julie Burchill's ex-husband.

Should I read anything into this?

*

It goes without saying that I can identify with Tom's disappointment at his experience of gay love after Marine love. And not just because of my experience of it on a lower scale in the TA (and at boarding school). Or my 'complex psychological reasons' which Bersani referred to and which I suspect was polite code for 'self-loathing'.

My relationship with Jason, at least for the first year, before he began to get the jitters, or just got bored, was probably the nearest thing to some kind of combination of the homoerotic and homosocial that someone like me can hope for. I especially remember the long walks we went on together, followed by a pub lunch and a pint. Our first holiday was spent hiking in the Lake District. (I remember that when I told my London gay friends I was going to spend my summer holiday hill-walking they thought I was mad.)

Although Jason could be very affectionate (and brought out an affection in cynical old me that I didn't know – or want to know – was there), we weren't moon-eyed lovey-dovey together; we were casually special. The sun shone out of our behinds. There was a rightness to being together and doing stuff which I've never had with anyone else since I was a kid. I could walk for miles and miles with Jason. To the horizon.

I know I've lampooned others for saying it, but we were like 'brothers' – in precisely that sense people use it when talking about men who very definitely aren't like brothers. I suppose it's that Gore Vidal 'twin' narcissism syndrome. One of the fondest memories I have of our time together, for me, was when we went to the Marine barber's in San Clemente on the way back to LA after meeting you in San Diego. The taciturn stern-faced but cool old man who cut my hair referred to Jason as 'your brother'. Of course, this could just be down to the fact we were both sunburnt, spoke strange English and wore Adidas – or his seasoned diplomacy – but it felt like some kind of Papal dispensation.

The sex was great, but even better than sex for me was the fact that Jason was – at least for the first year – *reliable*. His word was his bond. If he said he was going to be at my flat at 9 a.m., he was there at 9 a.m. on the dot, even after driving 250 miles – the distance he travelled every weekend to come and see me.

And in the novelty-sized Old Country 250 miles is a lot – almost half the length of England. In London it's unthinkable. If someone takes a two-mile bus ride to come and see you, it's heart-warming; although you can't help wondering if they want to borrow money. No matter that he'd been out in the field all week on exercise, only catching a few hours' sleep in a tent or under a basher. No matter that he'd already been driving twelve hours in a Land Rover back to base from the exercise. He'd be on his way to see *me*. Or getting up at 6 a.m. the next day to get to my house for 9, letting himself in with his own keys, opening my bedroom door quietly so as not to wake me (but I'd already be awake an hour or two gone, listening for his key in the lock) slipping off his clothes with barracks-speed and easing himself into bed with me for some dozy cuddles.

Stupidly, I once asked him why he slept so much when he came to stay: 'Because I feel *safe*,' he explained, matter-of-factly, but in a soft, little boy voice instead of his usual Glaswegian broken-bottle brogue. But best of all, Jase was someone who always spoke his mind – to everyone. If this wasn't always comfortable to be around, it certainly made life a lot livelier. Once we were trying to hire a motor boat at

Coniston Water in the Lake District, and the boatman was being especially officious and unhelpful even by British service standards. I was trying to reason with him, testily. Jase, who had said nothing, suddenly spat out with practised but heartfelt Glaswegian venom: 'Yoo're a WANKERR, yoo arre!' The man looked as if he was about to burst into tears. He gave us no more trouble.

Or the time when, noticing that a woman in a pub had taken a bit of a shine to me, he growled, loud enough for her to hear: 'That woman cannae take her eyes off yoor muscles. The *bitch*!'

Who wouldn't fall for someone like that? Even if they didn't have Jason's bonny blue eyes, dazzling, cheeky grin, and fucking gorgeous meaty man-arse?

I'm telling you all this because I don't think I ever properly explained Jason. You just got the moaning, which must have made my relationship with him seem completely masochistic instead of only mostly. By the same token, I don't think you ever really explained Alex. Are you ready to do that?

Or maybe my unhealthy sentimentality is just because tomorrow is Jason's birthday and, after promising myself that I wouldn't send him anything, I posted him a card and, anonymously via a mail-order company, a bottle of Bollinger champagne. Was this an act of generosity or hostility? Probably the latter, as the fact that I still think the world of him doesn't mean that if I ever actually see him again, I shan't cheerfully kick his fucking head in.

I should learn something from Tom's remark about his sad personal ad suitors: 'I wouldn't respond, and they would keep writing, and keep writing. You'd think after a while they'd get the point. But they were like pit-bulls. They wouldn't let go.' Well, of course not. They thought they had themselves a piece of something that money and success and all the gay bars in the world couldn't get them. Besides, as Mr Sartre might have said himself, for Platonist-Nominalists (Sartrean for 'fags' – see below) there's only one thing better than a 'Marine' – and that's a *mute* 'Marine'.

Nevertheless I'm haunted by the sad, lonely image of Tom the Celtic ex-Marine cruising AOL's USMCM4M chat room. Not least because I felt that much of Tom's interview sounded like a conversation I might have with Jason in five years' time. In a parallel universe. By e-mail. Under a false screen name.

*

I've been dipping gingerly into a fairly predictably boring Routledge book called *Changing Bodies, Changing Meanings: Studies on the Human Body in Antiquity* edited by someone called Dominic Montserrat (whose own contribution, 'Unidentified Human Remains: Mummies and the Erotics of Biography' suggests that Wilde's *The Picture of Dorian Gray* was inspired by an exhibition of mummy paintings. He should know: like many of the contributors – and indeed most cultural studies writers – his prose style is its own kind of embalming).

But the book has its moments. Jane Stevenson writes a piece called 'Nacktleben' about the role of 'Greekness' in late Victorian and Edwardian society and the place of nudity in this. She gives an account of Henry Scott Tuke, a member of the Royal Academy who spent most of his career painting and selling images of nude adolescent boys, which were enjoyed by Wilde and his contemporaries, but managed to evade the disaster which befell Wilde because he was able to appeal to the notion of the essential chastity of the nude male body – something which was not an entirely cynical pose as interviews with the young Falmouth boys he liked to paint in the nuddy later confirmed (apparently they were 'emotionally charged' but not 'physical'). His pictures were also chaste in as much as he always managed to find some jutting branch or billowing piece of cloth cover the young man's genitals. He was, in other words, no David Lloyd.

She quotes from the poem 'The Call', by The Revd E. E. Bradford which is, she suggests, 'a verse Tuke'. In it Eros, we are told, is 'up and away', marching along 'erect and free' while calling to the men:

> *'Turn away from the wench with her powder and paint,*
> *And follow the Boy who is fair as a Saint.'*

Sometimes this 'manly love' thing can be too embarrassing, even for me.

*

Torquay Lee, fair as a saint but flaky as rent, is staying here at the moment. He was recently turfed out of his flat in a Soho brothel by his effeminate Italian prostitute boyfriend (which is exactly what I called him when he rang at 1 a.m. asking in his huffy voice: 'Eees Lee there?'). I've agreed to help him out for a while because he seems to be making an effort to get his shit together, because my flatmate's away for a few months, and because he's very decorative. He comes and goes as he pleases and pays no rent. But he makes this place look like a home, or at least a hostel.

The other night I found myself cooking spaghetti bolognese while two failed projects of mine watched *Carry on Nursing* – 'Oooh! Matron, nooo!' – on telly in the living-room. One was Torquay Lee, the other was Sydney Charlie. My own Tom and Blond Boy, even if I never managed to get as incestuous-ma-tear-nal as Wormcan did with his puppies (but then, I'm not a filthy rich ex-rockstar).

Charlie is an Australian twenty-four-year-old on walkabout. He looks like a rugby player – *''e 'as thighs you could crack nuts with!'*, as Michelle shrieked, excitedly stroking his legs in the back of my car – has red hair, blue eyes, big hands, meaty forearms and a chin with one of those sexy bum-cracks in it.

In fact, he is a rugby player. A very good one. And Irish – Irish as in: put on this planet to be fancied by Mark Simpson. 'Are you Irish?' I asked him a little too eagerly the first time I saw him.

'No, Australian.'

'Oh, come on!' I scoffed. 'You've gotta be Irish. I'm never wrong about these things.'

'OK,' he sighed reluctantly, 'I'm third generation Irish-Australian.'

'Thought so!'

Unfortunately, Irish or not, he wasn't interested in me sexually. Of course, that just made me more keen. If Lee was my failed project of 1996, Charlie was my failed project of 1997. I took him to the pub. I took him to dinner. I even *cooked* him dinner. I drove him to the South Coast and showed him Bournemouth, Brighton and Beachy Head on a beautiful English Summer's day. *In my convertible.* I made him laugh until he cried. I flattered him. I stimulated his brain with Platonic dilemmas and intellectual puzzles. I gave him more attention than even a vain rugby player could handle. But I didn't get anywhere. Amazingly and rather pointlessly, this Australian is a snob. When I twigged this, I said: 'Charlie, you're looking for a man you can introduce to your mother. Which rules me out, of course, because I look like a thug.' Charlie didn't disagree. When he found out I attended Oxford University, he perked up a bit; he glazed over again when I told him I ran away to sea after a term.

The last time Charlie was round my place for dinner I think I scotched whatever chances I had with a disastrous culinary *faux pas* – I served pizza topped with tinned tuna. He seemed to take this as a personal insult (tinned tuna is white trash food in Oz). All night the phone kept ringing off the hook. As I inched closer to the poor lad on the sofa, my arm creeping slowly around the back of his neck, like one of those old-fashioned cads (my smoking jacket, though, was at the dry cleaners), Charlie kept asking pointedly: 'Aren't you going to answer that?'

'Oh, no,' I'd purr, 'it can wait. Have you ever had your feet massaged?'

Eventually, Charlie grabbed a magazine that happened to be lying near him, opened it and began to study it very intently. Suddenly, happening on an advert for aftershave featuring one of those fashionable shiny black-haired Italian boys with shaped eyebrows and pneumatic breasts, he jabbed his finger at the image and said, a tad too emphatically, '*That's* the kind of man I fancy!'

'Oh, right,' I said through thin lips and tightening jaw. '*That's nice.*'

'Well, I'd better be heading back,' he announced briskly and getting up. 'Can you run me to the tube station?'

'*Of course.*' (In fact he'd missed his train and I had to drive him across London to his empty bed. And then alone back to mine.)

Playing my messages when I got back, I discovered that the frantic caller was a Northern lad I'd met a couple of weeks previously who was even sexier than Charlie, but who hadn't returned my calls. Apparently he was just down the road from me that evening and wanted a good seeing to. Needless to say, this turned out to be my only opportunity to shag him.

*

My friend Stéphane called me from Paris recently to tell me that he was fed up with being a top. He got into a scene with someone he'd picked up, was encouraged to be really brutal with them, and was revolted by the experience (after he'd come). 'I don't want to be turned into someone else's *bête*, you know?' he said. 'I think that is what 'appen when you are a top. You become someone else's fantasy.' I told him that I thought that it was an inescapable element of all gay sex, this being for others, but I agreed that it was probably worse for tops. I've lost count of the number of times I've felt like a pre-warmed dildo with legs. Mind, that straight French expert on buggery, Sartre (in *Saint Genet*), seems to think that there is only one kind of homosexuality and that the 'top' is merely a dishonest and cowardly bottom:

> The inflexible male homosexual seeks in the girl queen only himself. He wants to coincide with the image he has glimpsed in submissive eyes. And when he thinks he has succeeded, the image dies as a result of being attained, and the desire with it: this is the orgasm.

Which maybe explains my desire to split and run after coming. Funnily enough, I'm more inclined to give value to his explanation of the fickleness of bottoms:

> The homosexual does not know, in the griping ache of his pain, whether he is expelling excrement or opening himself to a foreign body. Rejection and acceptance are intimately mingled in the most immediate impression.

Moreover, he appears to have been reading your books, Steve:

> The notorious 'maliciousness' of homosexuals is due in part to their having at their disposal, simultaneously, two systems of reference: sexual rapture transports them to a platonic climate; each of the men they seek is the passing embodiment of an Idea; it is the Sailor, the Parachute Trooper that they want to embrace through the husky who lends himself to their desire. But as soon as their desire is satisfied, they re-enter themselves and con-

sider their wonderful lovers from the angle of a cynical nominalism. Goodbye to essences, farewell archetypes, there remain only commonplace and interchangeable individuals. 'But I didn't know,' a homosexual once said to me, pointing to a little Montparnasse hoodlum, 'that young man was a MURDERER!' And the following day: 'Adrien? A dull little faggot.'

So, Steve, are we Platonists or cynical nominalists? Or the queasy admixture Sartre describes all too well? Whatever, it makes you wonder what Simone de Beauvoir did to him in the privacy of their *salon*.

Stéphane went to the same sauna sex club I did when I was in Paris, looking to meet someone who would fuck him. Well, you can guess the rest. The place was heaving, but he couldn't find any tops; everyone wanted him to fuck *them*. He's aware that this might have been because he can't escape people's expectations of him as someone who is masculine and tough-looking. I told him that he ought to go to America, where there is this officially recognized national institution called the butch bottom (though I didn't tell him he'd have to go to boot camp to join it).

Which reminds me of an anecdote recounted by my friend Michael, the organ builder, when he was working in Detroit recently. He went to a sauna there and after the usual brief silent courtship ended up with a guy who, the moment the cubicle door closed, announced: 'Number 1: I don't get fucked. Number 2: I couldn't take anything that big!'

Returning home afforded him no escape from American fag madness. Popping into the sauna at his council-run gym in Victoria, he heard someone leaning up against the wall murmuring appreciatively in an American accent, 'Mmmm, *nice ass!*'

'Oh! Thank you,' Mike said, somewhat embarrassed at the man's forwardness.

'Not *yours!*' retorted the American irritatedly. '*Mine!*' And carried on feeling his own buttocks.

*

Last week I was in Leicester Square standing in front of the Warner West End with a hundred or so other people trying to decide what film to see. The choices we had were: *Wilde, The Full Monty,* and *GI Jane.* What kind of choice is that? Roll up, roll up! Come see a famous fat bugger cavort with rent boys, or a bunch of ex-steelworkers who get their lunch-packets out while dancing to Donna Summer, or how about a woman who joins the Navy Seals, shaves off her hair and tells men to 'suck her dick'?

This queering of the mainstream has gone too far, Steve. I think my next book will be called, *It's a Straight World.*

I won't bother analysing *The Full Monty,* which is too self-consciously 'masculinity-crisis' to bear. But there is a curious token homo sub-plot tacked onto it, where two of the troupe members get it on unexpectedly. When they started puckering up I was about to groan, 'Oh no!', but three or four women in the cinema did it before I could. So instead I had to go, 'Oh YES!'

At this the audience was noticeably subdued for the remainder of the film.

As you discovered at his gig, military boys are in some ways a poor substitute for the kind of footballing, window-cleaning bequiffed timeless archetypes of cheeky-chappy laddishness Morrissey is in love with. Actually, thinking about it, military boys in the US, even those with arses fatter than their heads, are the nearest thing you can get over there to British 'ordinary boys'. All the American civilians I've met – OK Californians – are just too *spoilt* to be sexy. I suppose that the military is the closest you can get to being British in America: the repression, the tradition, the hierarchy, the resentment, the overdeveloped sense of humour, the bad food and third-rate dentistry – it's all there. Perhaps this is why, with the exception of my Scottish Marine, who anyway originally chased me, I haven't really done any military chasing in Britain.

Moz's 'Maladjusted' tour takes him to dizzy London soon, and I'll report on that in my next letter (hopefully seated behind someone dwarfish with no hair).

Love,

Mark

I've Changed My Plea to Guilty

Seattle, January 1, 1998

Dear Mark,

I'm giving up public sex.

Well, sort of. Really this isn't a New Year's resolution. It's more that I've given up hoping that anonymous public sex will ever again be worth the bus fare. Leaving San Diego, I thought I was maybe burned out on the military thing. Now I realize the truth. I was just burned out. My secret plan to eroticize civilian men has failed. Every time I visit the University of Washington tearoom over the course of three to six hours I have something resembling sex with three to six college boys. But I have an ever harder time concealing my boredom.

Still, I haven't yet lost my capacity for passion. CD shopping a few weeks back I happened to glance at a young man who did not even look necessarily military, just some short white boy in ball cap and jeans with a nice butt. Mark, words cannot convey the vertiginous heart-pounding arousal that enveloped me as I tagged after him about the store and out into the parking lot – where he met up with three obvious Army buddies and left.

It appears that I'm a lifer. And I thought I was half joking when I accepted that invitation in your first letter to join you in the House of Marines.

*

I was touched by your memories of the good times you had with Jason. You're only too right: I supposed you and Jason had good sex, and that he satisfied certain complex psychological needs of yours, but I never stopped to think about whatever else you might have shared.

So yes, I'm ready to say some nice things about my good times with Alex. It's tough to get started, though. Here and now, the easy opening sentences are: 'I remember how adorable Alex looked, cocking his head like a puppy dog that first time we had coffee together – calculating exactly how to manipulate my every thought and emotion,' or, 'I, too, would pretend to be asleep as Alex turned the lock to my apartment and crawled into bed beside me in the early morning hours – reeking of bars, bathhouses and other men's bacteria.' But that is unfair. And not altogether accurate. From the beginning, Alex made it clear that he was not looking for a lover.

In my four years in San Diego I met between three and four hundred sailors and Marines. For a month, I was smitten by Ted, the straight Marine whose photo I sent you with my first letter. For a week, I had a crush on Tim, the Melville-quoting lieutenant friend of Andrew's. But not since the boy I followed to Germany did I 'click' with anyone like I did with Alex. I stopped writing, quit socializing, and for wonderful long months was blissfully, stupidly happy simply being with him.

We talked. And talked and talked and talked. Bizarrely for a gay boy in San Diego, Alex sometimes asked questions about my life, and actually remembered the answers. I joked that it seemed as though we were scripting our own private Woody Allen movie, superficially analysing ourselves in two-hour stretches.

Of course, Alex was a Marine. Even now, I still I find him too cute. But the first time I saw him I was not especially attracted to him.

Alex and I met on the Fourth of July – on your twenty-eighth birthday. At 3 a.m., after yet another multi-bar drinking binge, I said good-night to Seaman Anthony, my star interviewee from the Navy book, marvelling that for once it appeared he would actually sleep alone. When I stopped by the next morning for mimosas, I found him sitting in the living-room with a young man in a blue and white striped shirt. This was Alex. At 4 a.m., Seaman Anthony explained, he was feeling hungry and had stepped out to a convenience store.

Seaman Anthony and I were supposed to meet up with some other members of the gay-Navy social group we belonged to, which three months after its formation was falling apart. Alex rode along to a party that wasn't. On the beach, I told him about my project. He nodded thoughtfully, met my eyes, and pronounced:

'There are times when I like to play the bottom, and there is a naturalness to it that I attribute to being in the Marine

Corps. In the breakdown phase of recruit training, they totally debase you. The drill instructors talk down to you, call you "maggot". They make you feel worthless, subhuman. They totally strip you of your identity so as to build you back up as a Marine. Even outside of basic training, the Marine Corps still debases you. As a Marine, you always strive to please your higher-ups. There is a craving to serve, to win approval, or even love.'

I wrote it down on picnic napkins.

We left the beach. At another sailor's *Melrose Place*-like apartment, Alex dived into the courtyard pool with the other guys. I sat on the patio furniture drinking more beer. Something like every thirty seconds Alex made eye contact with me. Finally he suggested I throw coins or other objects into the pool so that he and the sailors could compete to retrieve them. He won every time.

Alex, the day Zeeland first met him, 4 July 1993 (Mark's birthday)

That night at Club West Coast (which, at Seaman Anthony's urging, I frequented three or four times a week, even though it was in a remote neighbourhood and I didn't have a car), Alex took me aside and made a confession. There was one man in the bar he was strongly attracted to, and it wasn't Seaman Anthony.

Alex pointed across the room to a thirty-something ex-Special Forces body-builder. I introduced them and said good-night.

Seaman Anthony had the keys to my apartment and hung out there whether I was at home or not. One night I returned from the video booths to find a message on my answering machine. 'Uh, hello. Um, Steve, this is Alex. I was thinking about you tonight and – BEEP!!!' I asked Seaman Anthony about the message he had intercepted. 'Oh,' he said, 'Alex was calling for me.'

That summer I paid eight dollars' admission to attend San Diego Gay Pride and drink bad watery beer in a fenced-off area of Balboa Park overlooking the approach to Lindberg Field. I amused myself picturing more interesting queens with shoulder-fired rockets shooting down killer-whale-painted Southwest 737s. Suddenly Alex was there, tagging after me, asking me out to coffee. He said he needed some advice.

Dropping me off at Casa de Las Pulgas, the Spanish court-yard style apartment complex where we would later end up living together for two years, he asked me which service branch I liked best. He said he realized that it was a personal question, and that I didn't have to answer. I considered and told him that each branch, with its own haircut, uniform, and traditions, had a distinct image and even a culture and range of physical types that held a different erotic appeal for me. Even the Air Force. He waited, expectantly. I offered that, because I like short hair, I found Marines especially attractive. 'Do you?' 'Mmm.' I touched his bristles. 'And, Marines really do seem to have the nicest butts.' 'For real?' 'Yes, yes. It's a generalization, but any amount of casual observation confirms that it's true. It must be all that running they make you do, or something.' Alex asked, 'Do you think I have a nice butt?'

I patted him on the head and said good-night.

There were other meetings – including dinner with his Texas Marine buddy's wife, who resembled a female version of Alex; they had those same Japanese cartoon eyes. But it wasn't until another night at Club West Coast that Alex told me he was no longer comfortable visiting Seaman Anthony's barracks room and wanted to spend the night at my place. As I understood it afterwards, he felt he should reward me.

Soon after, Alex called me up and said that he was on leave for a week. He wondered if he could use my apartment as his Hillcrest headquarters. 'All I need is a little corner.' I told him flatly that I wasn't looking for another Seaman Anthony. But remembering my sage editor's advice ('Everything's ne-gotiable'), I made him a proposal. I wouldn't mind having another kind of buddy.

Alex was more than comfortable with this understanding. We slept, ate, drank beer, horsed around, watched videos, and masturbated together. I could have entered my Marine into any barracks contest and won. Once, when I left the window open, his ejaculate struck the windowpane of my old dyke neighbour Rachel, in the next wing of the building, a good yard beyond the sash. More commonly, Alex splattered the wall behind our heads, or, grinning with tight-lipped embarrassment, his own face.

'I fell in love with that man right there,' a construction-site-owning military chaser in my book-in-progress says (in regard to an Army Ranger who, on a construction site, tore out a wall with his bare hands, thinking it a test).

*

This being Southern California, Alex and I took long drives, not walks. North, or more often, east. As he didn't want to go to Mexico, those were the options (like other of my military acquaintances in San Diego, Alex said that Tijuana was too painful a reminder of the poverty he had witnessed in Southeast Asia). At the peak of our lesbian bonding phase we bought some maps of the back country, and soon were goading his Nissan Sentra down all-terrain-vehicle trails cruelly strewn with jagged rocks. An hour's drive into the desert took us to the celebrated Well of Seven Echoes, which turned out to be a coffee-can-sized hole in the ground; a dropped coin yielded a lone faint plop. Another trail disappeared beneath a 50-foot-wide pool. Miraculously, Alex's little car negotiated the waters. It was leaving here that we passed a small farmyard. I said, 'Big cows.' Alex said, 'Little cows.' Turning our faces towards each other, in the style of the Bergman movies I had already begun forcing him to watch, we intoned in perfect synch, '*All the cows.*' Which was not a reference to anything.

Alex and I had a lot of laughs together. That summer I was living with a sweet, developmentally disabled man named Ken. Despite my 1970s high school immersion in almost every available form of substance abuse (I was too conceited to sniff glue, and no one I knew used heroin), it took me months to notice that my roommate was taking street drugs. True, I was a little suspicious the night I brought home Ted, Keith and Seaman Anthony. The latter two were preparing to have coitus on my living-room floor when Ken emerged from his room and insisted on scrubbing the hardwood floors surrounding them with bleach. But I didn't recognize the scope of the problem until a neighbour pointed out that Ken was washing his car, at night, in the rain.

Ken was in the habit of rearranging his living-room

furnishings daily. It was like living with a tornado. It didn't help matters when I invited Bart to live with us. This skinny grey half-Siamese, named after Bart Simpson, wasn't actually a stray, but belonged to a chunky Casa resident named Wendy. He was personable but strong-willed, and didn't like it when you tried to dissuade him from, for example, rolling in the street. When Bart disappeared, we feared the worst. But months later he reappeared. The unforgiving Wendy refused to let him back into her home. After watching him just barely escape getting run over on University Avenue, again, I locked him in my apartment. Bart would be turned into an *indoor* cat, I resolved.

One night Ken and I awoke to a crash. Investigating, we found a vase in pieces on the bleach-stained parquet floor.

'Maybe you shouldn't place fragile items where they can fall.' I observed. 'You know how Bart is.'

Ken was hysterical. 'Yes, I do! And I know other people who have cats! Other cats aren't like Bart! I'm not going to let Bart control where I put my stuff!' He purposely repositioned another vase on the edge of the mantel.

I shrugged. The disintegration continued.

One day I attempted to cook for Alex. Sitting at the dining-room table while I heated store-bought spaghetti sauce and frozen garlic bread, he examined one of Ken's knick-knacks. It was one of those oriental glass dioramas with wood carvings and tiny storks. Ken had found it on someone's curb. Alex pointed out that all the storks were headless.

We laughed so hard and so long that I didn't notice the smoke from the oven. Using Ken's oven mitt, I transferred the Pyrex bread pan to Ken's glass table, which shattered.

Alex was impressed at my lack of reaction. 'Oh,' I told him, 'It's no problem. Ken owes me hundreds of dollars.'

This was very true. Ken's crystal problem seemed to be getting worse. Passing his open door in the night, I often saw that he had fallen asleep, clothed, with lights and radio on. The next morning he would still be lying there in the same improbable position. Friction increased in the household – and not just between him and me. I returned from a week's vacation to hear him spout, 'You said that Seaman Anthony would be staying over some nights. But I didn't know that he would be over here *every night*. With a different guy here *every night*. Or more than one guy here, *every night*.'

(I met more than one military boy who told me, 'I haven't read your book. But I've slept in your bedroom.' Seaman Anthony and Ken would gossip to me about seeing each other in especially compromising positions – drugged, trussed, being beaten – at San Diego orgies, allegedly sometimes on camera.)

Things came to a head on one of those strangely hot October days in San Diego. I had a cold. It was an oddly pleasant feeling, being all hoarse, stuffed up and in love in that dry, eucalyptus-scented air. Sitting in jeans on the gay nude beach I watched Alex dive into waves. On the way back up the cliffs, Alex laughed at my routine about queens negotiating the treacherous incline. One of them plummets. A companion screams, 'Oh my God. Becky's still alive. She's suffering,' and bludgeons him to death.

Back at the Casa, Alex and I wrestled, watched some more porn and then a video of the British comedy *Eat The Rich*. Along about the time the queeny black lead, 'Alex', is phoning someone declaring that he is homeless, asking if he can just sleep in the cupboard under the stairs, we heard someone banging at the door. I investigated to find a hurt and angry Seaman Anthony. He had been knocking at the door for at least five minutes, he said. He was sure that we had heard him knocking; he could hear us laughing. And, in a way, of course, he was right. The Navy was sending Seaman Anthony to Japan, but Alex had already pushed him out of the nest.

Ken was cowbird-Alex's next victim. Alex found him creepy, he told me. (In retrospect, I wonder whether this means that Alex, too, was implicated in a videotaped date-rape drug gangbang.) I immediately gave notice and moved to a one-bedroom apartment. My new landlord didn't permit pets. Wendy welcomed back Bart, who, effectively graduated from my 'indoor cat' boot camp, continues to torment her to this day.

*

Sleeping with Alex was the warmest and fuzziest feeling I've known in my adult life. He didn't toss and turn or snore. Oh, every now and then he would scream out some post-traumatic stress syndrome threat in the night, ripping us both from sleep. And then there was the night of the Northridge earthquake. My posh new place was set on stilts, and was shaking that morning at 4 a.m. But as Alex had been uncharacteristically restless all night, I assumed that the tremor was just him hitting me with his butt.

As I have already written you [see page 147], it was a drive to LA and the sex club with the two-headed rabbit that ended our physical intimacy, or gave Alex an excuse to kill it off. But even after that he still asked me to shave off his body hair the time he did drag. And when he got out of the Marine Corps, we made our home together – in Ken's and my old apartment at the Casa.

Alex took more than he gave emotionally, but not financially. I loaned him money a hundred times, but he always paid me back. When I was poor, he bought me groceries from the Marine Corps commissary. Alex gave me his dog tags. *He asked me to look at his pus plug.* But I never particularly wanted to tongue down with Alex. And even on the occasions when he had sex with enemies who got off on imagining that they were humiliating me, I never really cared who he was fucking.

People found this strange.

I don't think I'm very Marine-like. But I have to wonder whether my own sexual needs aren't more barracks buddy than lover.

*

Alex declared that he was not observing Christmas this year. We didn't exchange gifts, but did give presents to Samantha. Christmas, after all, is for cats. I'm sorry, Mark, but human reproduction is a sorry substitute for animal companionship. I just don't share your view that having children somehow makes people more natural.

Lately, as my own benzodiazapine consumption has begun to escalate, I've been thinking about giving up writing. My last, credibility-destroying book will be titled after a quote from you. *Boys Are Like Cats.* I hope you'll let me include your story about Caesar. I think I've reversed your coming-of-age replacement of your loyal Manx with a boy. Alex has observed that if I didn't have Samantha, I'd probably have found another Alex. But Sammy's my pal. And Alex is still a buddy. And I'm still not sure that a thoughtful touch in an airport men's room isn't better than a boyfriend.

*

I have yet to read the copy of Pat Barker's *Regeneration* you kindly sent me. I want to read it, and I will. It's just that normally I read fiction as I'm going to bed, and last summer when I started to read that novel the wartime flashbacks were too much for me.

Last night I had a dumb melatonin dream. I was with Sapphie from AbFab, my last girlfriend from junior high school. I explained why, when I tried to kiss her at that 1976 Who concert at the Pontiac Silverdome *and missed*, I never tried again. She was shocked at the news that I was gay, but almost instantly converted, screaming that she was lesbian, lesbian, lesbian. And *you* were there, too, Mark, shirtless and looking very shaved-chest gay muscleman, making blackly humorous comments passing out postcards of some kind. The key to the dream was on the postcards. When I woke up, I remembered them clearly, but now of course it's gone. What was on your postcards?

I think I'm better off with Andrew's prescription.

Did you happen to see this news story last week?

Nation IN BRIEF, FLORIDA

Boat Where Versace Suspect Hid Sinks
From [LA] Times Staff and Wire Reports

The houseboat in Miami Beach where suspected serial killer Andrew Cunanan took refuge and killed himself last July has sunk. The two-storey boat sat on the bottom of Indian Creek with water lapping half-way up its street-level front door after a leak developed overnight.

The year really is over. Happy new year.

February 14, 1998

Please forgive the tardiness of this letter. Brooding about Alex took some of the piss out of me.

I've since spent time at both the university tearoom and at

the Army post. I logged five and a half hours at the UW before finally touching and being touched by a beautiful, blushing peroxide-blond boy no older than eighteen wearing red silk boxer shorts. When at first, brazen and desperate, I peeked my head over his stall door, he shook his head no. But I stood on the other side of his peephole to the urinals, and he changed his mind.

The climax of my talk-show confessional exhibitionism is probably the disclosure that while my penis is not small, my *glans penis* has often been likened to a doorknob. Ever the poet, Troy compared me with a toilet plunger. 'You got a big head' are the words my public sex partners typically shatter the silence with. That's why public sex suits me. Unbuttoning my fly is usually all it takes to, for example, change a blond boy's mind.

Maybe I've relied on this a little too much.

It didn't do me much good last week at Fort Lewis, where I wound up kneeling under the stall partitions with a rough-looking Army boy in a green shirt and Hanes underwear who without invitation aggressively jabbed me with one extended finger, snarling, 'I wanna FUCK, FUCK, FUCK you.' Like you, afterwards I asked myself why I resisted. At least he knew what he wanted.

The most exciting part of the trip happened on the ferry ride to Bremerton. The captain announced: 'The killer whales are right in front of us!' The passengers, me included, ran to the bow as one, oohing and ahhing like little children as a pod of orcas breached and splashed, making their way back to the open sea.

Now and again snacking on seal.

Somewhere deep within me, I still have the capacity to feel awe at something other than dick. But what else will anyone ever pay me to write books about?

Love,

An Abstract Insight Wakes

London, 6 March 1998

Dear Steve,

> *When shall we learn what should be as clear as day*
> *We cannot choose what we are free to love.*
> — W. H. Auden, *Canzone* (1942)

When I was a kid I used to walk past a plaque saying 'W. H. Auden, poet, was born here in 1907' twice a day: once on the way to school, once on the way back. That plaque has a lot to answer for. I think it explains everything that has gone wrong in my life.

It encouraged me to think that being a writer or even a poet meant something (after all, you got a plaque on the wall of the house where you were born – so imagine what they give you when you're still alive, my oh-so-naïve reasoning went). Worse, I became obsessed with W. H. in my final years at school, feeling I had some kind of personal connection to him and scribbled reams of sub-sub-Auden poems involving stopped clocks and emotional storms in cracked tea-cups and read out one of his own in the school reading competition in my final year. I won, and my name was read out twice at school Speech Day, but I didn't appear to collect the £15 book token and a firm handshake from the headmaster and the visiting retired General/Archbishop dug up to inspire us callow youths with enthusiasm for the challenges of adult life with a speech so jawbreakingly dull that none of us were left with any doubt that the greatest challenge of adult life was keeping your eyes open.

I was lolling in the park, drunk on cheap cider. This was to make an empty juvenile protest at the 'fascist' school state and the fact that the reading competition was judged by the schoolmaster who frustrated my first experience of oral sex by unexpectedly inspecting the changing rooms one afternoon. So off I went in a sulk to get pissed in the park. Where I've been ever since.

The poem I read out (over-dramatically) in the competition

was *Lullaby*, which begins: 'Lay your sleeping head my love/ Human on my faithless arm...' But it was the second verse that chimed:

> Soul and body have no bounds:
> To lovers as they lie upon
> Her tolerant enchanted slope
> In their ordinary swoon,
> Grave the vision Venus sends
> Of supernatural sympathy,
> Universal love and hope;
> While an abstract insight wakes
> Among the glaciers and the rocks
> The hermit's carnal ecstasy.

The hermit's carnal ecstasy. I was moved by your description of sleeping with Alex as 'the warmest and fuzziest feeling I've known in my adult life'. And not only because it reminded me of my own loss. It is one thing to be a hermit, Steve; it's quite another to be a lover – and that's what you were, regardless of all your 'buddy' talk – and then try to be a hermit again. Abstract insights, or even Platonic Idealism, don't quite hit the spot any more after you've experienced the ordinary swoon of supernatural sympathy.

*

I came across the *Canzone* quote at the head of this letter in the essay 'One Hundred Years of Homosexuality' by David Halperin. Mark Vernon, a journo friend of mine and a correspondent of Halperin's, contacted me to let me know that David was in town and wanted to meet me. Having agreed, I thought I ought to read something of his. Fortunately the essay is a minor classic of its kind. Probably the best gay studies essay I've ever read. It's a very elegantly written and intelligently persuasive argument for the social constructionist position on sexuality. It also contains another quote that I thought I ought to share with you:

> ...political aspiration in women and (at least according to one expert writing as late as 1920) *a fondness for cats in men* were manifestations of a pathological condition, a kind of psychological hermaphroditism ... expressed by

the preference for a 'normal' member of one's own sex
as a sexual partner. [My italics.]

David turned out to be a tall, handsome, thick black moustachioed, middle-aged leather guy (in a dark greatcoat instead
of a leather jacket). He was very amiable and sharp, with
something of a naughty streak; I liked him a lot.

I decided to be nice to our august guest, but he did succeed
in provoking one exchange.

'I like straight people,' he said at one point. 'But don't you
just want to round them all up and put them in a camp?'

Silence.

I had to bite my lip to stop myself saying, 'I like gay people
– because they've already rounded themselves up and put
themselves in a camp.'

Sensing that he may have made something of a *faux pas*,
David tried explaining himself: 'When you meet straight
people,' he said, 'don't you feel like there's something
missing?'

'It's funny you should say that,' I said, no longer bothering
to bite my lip. 'Because I often feel that about gay people.'

David laughed louder than anyone else at our table.

*

Also at that lunch was Steve Kokker, the Canadian contributor to your *Military Trade* collection, who has spent the
last year chasing cadets in St Petersburg. Steve is such a
lovely guy; so, so ... *poetic*. I can understand why he feels
at home in Russia. He has too much soul for the West in
general and gays in particular. And I can also understand
his enthusiasm for some of the natural assets of the former
Iron Curtain countries. He brought with him his twenty-
year-old Russian Estonian, Pasha, a solidly-built, tall, beautiful, blond, blue-eyed Slav with hands the size of Siberian
open-cast coal mine steam shovels. In short, Pasha looks
like a Stakhanovite to die for. He certainly raised my quota.
Pasha, however, is an intellectual – he is studying Law at
Talinn University. But he also loves to put those big hands
to good use and wrestles. Poor Stevie, who is tall but not
exactly what you'd call a jock, has been thrown around his
flat by Pasha for the last year (though I don't notice him

complaining). Apparently Pasha – who is straight, of course – was looking forward to wrestling me, but had second thoughts when he met me: he thought that I might win. I should have made it clear that for someone as beautiful as Pasha I'd be happy to lose and pay the forfeit, *whatever that may be.*

'You know,' said Pasha in that rich, deep accent, lying on my curvy 70s hotel lounge sofa, gazing up at me through his long, curling, batting eyelashes, 'you would make great phee-losofurrr.' I'd just been lecturing him and Steve about the fate of the former Eastern Bloc after the end of Central Planning. I can't remember what it was I said, but I do recall it was a crock of bullshit. That's why I have to emigrate to the East – because boys like Pasha live there and they don't just want to talk about football and women; they also love, in between wrestling bouts, to listen to charlatans like me talking through our beards into the night.

Which, of course, is exactly why their country is in ruins.

*

I seem to remember talking a lot about being pregnant with monsters in the last letter. Perhaps I had a touch of indigestion. Anyway, shortly after posting it to you I went to see *Alien 4* – with Michelle of course.

This sequel takes the pregnant-with-monsters premise of the original to the max – Ripley, now with her genes mixed with the alien creature, even gets to see a laboratory full of aborted half-alien/half-human foetuses that she's given birth to. Most of the time I had to look away from the screen, so queasy were the images.

Michelle, on the other hand, never removed her gaze from the screen once, staring at it with wide, unblinking eyes shining in the darkened auditorium, a look of religious ecstasy on her face.

During the climax, when Sigourney's monstrous nephew-alien is running amok, some guy behind us stood up and started shouting 'FUCK YOU!! FUCK YOU ALL!!!'. It was a bad film, but not *that* bad. It was a curious experience, not really wanting to look in front at the screen which was horrifically demanding my attention, and not wanting to look behind either at the schizo man behind me doing the same thing. Eventually he was escorted out of the cinema, still shouting at his own monsters.

*

I got rid of my cat-monster Torquay Lee before Xmas. Unfortunately, I didn't have him euphemized. I just told him to go. Perhaps this would have been a heartless thing to do if I hadn't known that he was back with his effeminate Italian prostitute boyfriend and just using my place as somewhere to store his baggage and as a vague but empty threat of independence. And I didn't quit the post of Jase's unpaid landlady just to become Lee's unpaid Left Luggage Dept. Besides, Lee is more than capable of rubbing himself up against some other legs if needs be.

Before I booted him out, I took him to an *Attitude* party in Soho, along with Sydney Charlie. After several G&Ts too many Charlie, who, like most living creatures, fancies Lee, decided that he was going to sort Lee's life out. Unfortunately this involved collecting Lee's shit from his Italian boyfriend's flat in a brothel around the corner – and taking it to *my* place. We had to carry the bags and boxes down the brothel's sweaty staircase past swaying stinking drunk businessmen in creased suits being led into dimly-lit rooms by women in corsets and rubber skirts asking, 'Is it full sex you wanted, love?'

In the minicab home an interesting conversation developed with the driver, who was African. As we drove past a queue of gays outside a gay taxi firm, Charlie asked, 'What are they queuing for?'

'Oh,' replied the driver, irritatedly. 'They are queuing for "Freedom", a gay taxi company. They can't take any cab – it has to be a gay one. It is a cult, if you ask me.'

My ears pricked up. 'Yes,' I said, nodding vehemently, 'you're absolutely right, it is.'

The driver continued: 'The other day I was flagged down by some people outside Trade, which is a gay club, and they asked me, "Are you gay?" I said, "No, I'm not gay. I'm a taxi driver." They said: "Well, we don't want you if you're not gay! We have to have a gay taxi driver!" Why do they have to have a gay taxi driver? This is stupid, no?'

'Well, you see,' I explained, 'gays must never knowingly come into contact with a straight person, and must never,

never, *never* pay a straight person any "gay" money. Only other gays are allowed to take money off gays.'

'It is crazy,' he said. 'Why should I have to answer such questions as "Are you gay?" when I am driving a taxi? Will they want to know what religion I am next?'

'Well,' I replied, 'I think the gay question sort of covers that.'

Back at my place we unloaded Lee's shit from the taxi into my hallway. I was so drunk I just went straight to my room to lie on my bed and watch the room spin round. Charlie, meanwhile, wasn't getting off with Lee as he'd hoped. In fact, as I think I mentioned before, Lee doesn't fancy Charlie and had only lured him back to my place in the hope that he would sleep with me. Charlie, in other words, was intended by Lee to keep me sweet; Charlie was to be his rent.

Charlie spent the evening on the curvy 70s sofa, keeping nobody sweet and paying nobody's rent, while Lee and I slept alone in separate double beds.

Now, is it just me or is there something really, really *impractical* about these sleeping arrangements?

*

There's no accounting for taste. Michelle had a run-in with a Glaswegian recently. She has an ad in one of the local papers 'Stunning pre-op male-to-female transsexual seeks rugby players' etc. Apart from the occasional builder, she complained that all of them were 'lying fat mongs' (mongoloids) as she calls them, in her Christian manner. Until last week when she met Tommo, a twenty-five-year-old Glaswegian.

'Oh!' Michelle enthused. 'I really think he's *the one*, Mark! He's so handsome and so keen. We shagged three times the first night. He sucked me off and everything! He calls me every day and is coming over tomorrow night. I can't stop thinking about him. I think I'm falling for him. He wants to stay over, but I'm not sure that's such a good idea. I don't think I'm ready for that.'

The morning after Tommo's second visit I get a message on my ansafone.

'Hello, *lover*, it's Michelle. Ohmigod! Last night was a *nightmare*! 'E turned out to be *mad*! I had to *throw* 'im out in the middle of the *night*. *Call me!* Love you. By the way, are you coming to Jerry's birthday party tomorrow?' (Michelle's Chihuahua is called Jerry.)

I called her back: 'He came over, I cooked him dinner, then we shagged wildly *three* times,' she trilled. 'I came in his mouth twice; he wanted me to fuck 'im *up the arse*, but I refused and then went to sleep. About two hours later at *three o'clock in the fucking morning* he woke up and started pacing the room, saying to himself over and over: "*What have I done!*" Then he had a panic attack and almost *fainted* on my bedroom floor! When he recovered, he started saying that I'd *made* him do it, that he wouldn't have done it if I hadn't been so *beautiful* and *deceptive* – he said that I was a witch and a *devil-woman!* "I've got a *wife* and *kids!*" he said. "What would they think!" "I don't know," I said. "But I'd have to charge them *extra!*" He just kept on saying, "What have I done! I've had sex with a man!" I said, "Where's this *man* you've been having sex with?" "It's *you!*" he said. "You seduce innocent young laddies and turn them gay! Make them do things they don't want to do!" Well, after that I just lost my temper with him completely and told him that he was just another SICK HOMOSEXUAL and no use to me WHATSOEVER! I threw my portfolio at him, you know the one with pictures of me when I was Mitch the tattooed male stripper and body-builder, and made him look at them. *Mark*, you should have seen his face. He was so *shocked!* I said, "*Yes!* that's what you really want, *isn't it?*" and slammed the book shut on his fingers. Then I threw him out. "YOU CAN'T DO THIS TO ME!" he shouted. "OH YES I CAN!" I said, shoving him out the door and slamming it behind him. He got the complete Myra Breckinridge treatment. Poor Rusty! I've still got his gloves and scarf. From *Next* [a mass-market designer clothing store for office workers].'

Michelle has a way of talking that doesn't allow for paragraphing.

I told her what she already knew – that all of this, including the gloves and scarf from Next, were occupational hazards for pre-op trannies.

*

Just before Xmas I went to see Julian Clary at the Vaudeville theatre. He's a camp comic who likes to spell out the filthiness of the single entendres his mostly straight audience flocks to hear him make. At one point in the show he talked about 'passing a baby in the street'. The audience laughed. 'No,' he said. 'I don't do surreal jokes. Just buggery jokes. When I said "passed" I didn't mean "pass" as in a bowel movement that produced a baby. Buggery jokes – that's what people come to see me for. Buggery jokes. Nothing else.'

And indeed this is precisely what he supplied his audience with. All night. And they loved it. Occasionally he'd stop to explain in pornographic detail the buggery joke he'd just made, literally rubbing the audience's noses in it. Which only made them laugh more: 'I came over Queer. That's Steve Queer, my butler. I came over him. I came over his face. He was dripping with it. *Sperm.*'

Just before the interval he told us that the management had asked him to make an announcement. 'Apparently a glory hole has appeared in the men's toilet in the foyer. In case any of you don't know what a glory hole is, it's a hole in the partition between cubicles in a public toilet through which men put their bits to have them attended to by their friend on the other side.' Then he went on to sing a song to the tune of *The Battle Hymn of the Republic* which made me think of you, Steve: '*Glory Hole at Euston Station/Glory Hole at St Paul's Cathedral...*'

What a terrible trick to play on straight men with bursting bladders before the interval. Of course, they loved it.

Even the four or five working-class blokes with suspiciously/institutionally tidy short hair in the row in front of me who went very quiet every time Julian made a bent squaddie joke seemed to like it. However, on my way back from the bar I overheard the oldest of them, a fat man of about forty, insist to one of his mates very loudly: 'I'm *not* threatened by 'im, I'm not...' (He literally had his back to the wall as he was saying this.)

*

'Why can't we just stop hating ourselves so much?' weeps Michael at the end of *Boys in the Band*, which I saw at the Aldwych the other week. Of course, today such a play would have to end with, 'Why can't we just stop *loving* ourselves so much?'

I enjoyed the play. No one is content: neither the 'closet-queen' Alan nor any of the 'out' homosexuals. There is no happy ending. No parades and no epiphany in a gay bar. No rousing political speech in the final act. Mercifully, the play was written before Stonewall and gay politics poisoned the Martinis. So it's a play about the human condition in general and the homosexual condition in particular rather than a play with a message. Perhaps this is why the audience looked like they had probably seen it the first time around – in the 60s.

There's also a lot of discussion of the 'Christ, was I drunk last night!' syndrome. But since this is a play about the evils of denial, no one advances the Simpson–Zeeland line.

The telephone game Michael forces them to play as the party masks begin to slip was great fun: 'You have to call the person whom you love and have always loved, tell them who you are and that you love them. Bonus points are awarded if they don't hang up and they tell you they love you too.' Sure, it's melodramatic, but what's wrong with that? Nick, who accompanied me, didn't like this scene at all. But then Nick isn't very good with any demonstrations of emotion, let alone the kind of histrionics that follow this game. Which is one of the reasons why I like him so much. I remember that during Diana Week he practically had to go into hiding, so appalled was he by the mass emotional incontinence he saw washing the streets.

Of course, I found myself practically shouting out *à la Rocky Horror Show* the lines in that climactic moment, when Arnold delivers his crushing speech to Michael, even though the fantastic, mad intensity of the moment was fluffed in this production. In the movie it's marvellous: Michael staring straight ahead, sweating like a man facing a firing squad, Arnold relentless, pitiless: 'You're the unhappiest creature of all: a homosexual who doesn't want to be a homosexual. You may very well know a heterosexual life if you pursue it with the fervour with which you annihilate, but you'll always be a homosexual Michael. Always. *Until the day you die.*'

And then the perfect touch. Arnold makes to leave and says casually: 'I'll call you in the morning.'

There is no escape, you see: you're a homosexual and I'm

your homosexual friend. Always, Steve. Always. *Until the day you die.*

*

My friend Justin called me last night to tell me about a recent experience of his – an alternative Xmas Carol. Picture the scene: a bitterly cold night in Pimlico. Justin is hurrying back from the petrol station with his and Jack's 24-hour ration of nicotine. He spots a laddie outside the hostel opposite his housing estate. The kind of young man you see in the street and want to spend the rest of your life with but who doesn't even know you exist.

'All right mate?' the lad calls out. ''Ave you got a light?'

Justin runs across the road without even looking both ways as his mother taught him and begins rubbing sticks together, striking flints and trying to conduct lightning. Justin can't believe his luck: 'dark-haired, with velvet smooth, *smooth* skin and big *big* hands. Even better – he was really, *really* drunk'.

Apparently John, as he introduced himself with a firm grip, was waiting for a mate of his in the hostel to open a window and let him in. 'I'll share 'is bed,' he confided with a wink, 'but if 'e asks me to pick 'is nose, I'll use me elbow!' (Justin had no idea what the lad meant by this either, but laughed loudly anyway – as you would.)

Justin desperately wanted to be a Good Samaritan, take the poor boy upstairs to his flat and 'warm him up'. But Jack wouldn't approve. Jack is Justin's full-time, live-in ex-boyfriend. They've been ex-boyfriends for two years. They stopped having sex and started rowing a lot instead and then Justin, following the convention, moved out. But then Justin moved back in again because, as he put it, 'suffering from homosexuality is bad enough when you have company but too much to bear when you're by yourself'.

So Justin tried to manoeuvre the lad towards the alleyway. But it didn't work. John kept saying, 'I like you Justin – you're a nice bloke!' Then, just as they were looking into one another's eyes in the way they do in the movies before they kiss, *'the frigging window opened'*. John's 'mate' stuck his head out. He was thirtyish and looked like an alkie. John whispered to Justin: 'Just say you're my brother's mate.' Justin decided it was time to leave.

Back home Jack was shouting. 'Where the fucking hell have you been? I'm sick of you taking *two hours* to get a packet of cigarettes with *my fucking money*! You've been slagging around again, haven't you? You've been *having sex* with some *bum* you picked up off the streets, *haven't you!*' (Just because the relationship is over doesn't mean you have to give up the joys of jealousy.)

'No!' protested Justin. 'I've just been talking to someone. I wouldn't have minded shagging him. But we only talked. He was really, really, *really* cute.'

'Oh yeah!' snorted Jack. 'I bet he was some homeless trash – like you'll be if you don't watch out! I'm going to bed!' And with that Jack retired for the evening, slamming the door behind him so hard that the jumble-sale cutlery rattled in the kitchen drawer/and last year's male stripper calendar fell off the wall.

Justin sat in the living-room pondering his options. Should he smuggle John in, who he could see from his window is still standing outside the hostel in all his gorgeousness (his 'mate' obviously hadn't managed to smuggle him in after all), and chance having his throat cut by Jack? Or should he just forget about him and go to bed, turning down the opportunity of a lifetime?

As he was about to go out and fetch the boy, he glanced out of the window again. *John wasn't alone any more.* 'The dodgy alkie had joined him outside in a doorway with a big, blue duvet, under which they were *huddling together.*'

Cursing his indecision, Justin tried to soothe his nerves by rolling himself a joint and switching the telly on. Five minutes into *Prisoner*, he heard a knock at the door: 'But I didn't give John my address,' he thought. Going over to the door, he looked through the letterbox but could only see a checked jacket: 'But John was wearing a bomber jacket. Perhaps he wore a check jacket underneath, or something?' Suddenly the checked jacket crouched down and looked through the letterbox back at Justin. Justin stood up very quickly. The checked jacket belonged to a middle-aged big black man with *big round eyes.*

'Please, you must let me in,' said a strong African accent. 'They won't let me sleep at the hostel. You must let me in. I am from Somalia. It is very cold here. You must let me in. I will sleep in your hall. It will be OK. *Let me in.* I have my papers – *everything is in order.*'

Justin felt he was being hypnotized by those big round, reasonable eyes in his letterbox: 'Yes, you are right. I must let you in. You must sleep in my hallway. I must give you my biggest carving knife...'

'No, I can't let you in,' he said, getting a grip. 'Go back to the hostel. Tell them it's cold. Let them deal with it.' Just then he heard someone else coming up the stairs. 'Who's that?' he asked through the letterbox.

'That is my cousin. You will also let him in.' Justin was now convinced that he was being punished with bad karma for his lack of gratitude for the gift of John: 'OK, I know that John might have murdered me in my sleep as well – but at least I would have been killed by someone I *fancied.*'

Then the telephone rang. It was Steve, Justin's straight student neighbour. His voice was trembling. 'Can I come over and stay with you tonight? There are some strange Africans shouting through my letterbox. *I'm really scared!*'

Steve waited until the Somalians wandered off downstairs and tip-toed across the landing in his dressing-gown to Justin, who was waiting with his door open and a cup of warm milk ready. Just as Steve reached Justin, a loud 'HO, HO, HO!' erupted from the landing below, like the sound of Lucifer roasting Christian babies. Stuart blanched and bolted into Justin's flat like a bunny that's just caught wind of a wolf. Justin peered gingerly over the landing balustrade and saw the two Somalians on the next landing huddled together, wrapped up in an old curtain.

'So,' said Justin. 'Steve spends the night on the sofa with my teddy. John spends it in a doorway with a thirty-year-old lush. And the Somalian and his cousin spend it on the land-ing wrapped in a curtain. And what I want to know, Mark, is: What does it all mean? You're the writer. Write a conclusion to *that.*'

'We-ell...' I drawled, stalling for time whilst I adjusted my platitudes. 'Maybe it means that we're all – gay, straight, Somalian – "suffering from homosexuality" as you put it. After all, homosexuality is just a form of loneliness and homelessness. Maybe we all need to hug our neighbour, our cousin, our ex-boyfriend, our old lush and his big, blue duvet, for whatever warmth we can get...'

'Or maybe,' interrupts Justin flatly, 'it means I should petition the housing association to fit an electronic door to the entrance of these flats.'

'Yeah. That as well.'

*

Saw *The Invention of Love* last night at the National. Stunning. Travelled home in a daze which still has not quite worn off. I've always been a bit of a fan of Stoppard's, ever since we studied *Jumpers* for English A Level and I tried to stage it as our house play (with me, of course, playing the lead role as the middle-aged Professor of Moral Philosophy having an emotional/philosophical crisis in the wake of the moon landings.)

Invention may be Stoppard's best work. Usually his plays don't combine their showy intellectualism with emotions very well, and come across as clever but cold – but *Invention* does it near-perfectly, producing a play which, in the Greek style, combines learning and culture with love and passion in a way that I've never seen before. It tells the story of A. E. Housman, a classicist, poet, contemporary of Wilde's and a fellow lover of the male form (who lived much of his later life in Highgate, around the corner from my flat). Housman is being ferried across the Styx, glad to be dead at last, but the river connects Hades with the Isis of Oxford during Housman's student years and we see Housman's life played out as a struggle between the 'live each moment for each moment's sake' voluptuous philosophy of the Aesthetics, such as Wilde and his mentor Pater, and the manly stoicism of the High Victorians.

Housman strikes a strange compromise between the two – devoting his life to the study of pagan/classical poetry, eliminating corruption and distortion in the texts, and an unconsummated lifelong love affair with an athlete by the name of Moses Jackson. When the elderly Housman sees, from Charon's boat, Jackson through the mists of time he cries out: 'Oh, Mo! I would have died for you! But I never had the luck.'

Another flashback scene, where a *sympathique* friend tries to tell Housman that Jackson 'will never want what you want', is especially memorable:

HOUSMAN. [*Watching the runners*] What do I want?
CHAMBERLAIN. Nothing which you'd call indecent, though I don't see what's wrong with it myself. You want to be brothers in arms, to have him to yourself . . . to be shipwrecked together, [to] perform valiant deeds to earn his admiration, to save him from certain death, to die for him – to die in his arms, like a Spartan, kissed once on the lips . . . or just run his errands in the meanwhile. You want him to know what cannot be spoken, and to make the perfect reply, in the same language.

'You want him to know what cannot be spoken, and to make the perfect reply, in the same language' – isn't that the best formulation of 'Greek' love as opposed to 'Gay' love? Isn't this is your 'all the cows' moment with Alex? It's almost as perfect as a line from one of the Ancients, quoted in the play – the only surviving line from Sophocles' *Loves of Achilles*: 'Love feels like ice held tightly in the hand by children.'

*

The day after I saw *Invention* I went bar-crawling with Mr Justin, a very funny chap called William, and his new boyfriend Andy, who handed out ecstasy tablets like they were anti-depressants or something. Being the clean-living narc I am, I refused. When I got home I discovered this message on my machine from Justin: 'Don't ever, ever, *ever* let me take a so-called "E" from some boyfriend of William's ever again. I have got the most *incredible*, incredible – hang on [*a loud clanking noise*] – the most *incredible* diarrhoea you've ever fucking witnessed in your entire *life* [*a loud flushing noise*].

'I'll call you tomorrow.'

I guess Justin is my Arnold. (While you, Steve, are my Sophocles.)

*

Steve, if you don't manage to summon the interest to do anything else in 1998, please see *The Butcher Boy*. I've never liked any of Neil Jordan's movies – but *The Butcher Boy* is fantastic; the best movie I've seen since *The Cable Guy*, which it resembles in some odd ways. There's a streak of authentic Irish madness running through it. Eamonn Owens, who plays the young lead, turns in a breathtaking performance.

Based on the Patrick McCabe novel of the same name, it tells the story of a troubled young teen called Francie Brady, whose father is a wasting wino and whose Mother is cracking up. It begins with Francie and his best pal, Joe Purcell, in Indian headdresses whooping to one another across a gorge, a lake glittering impassively behind them; a beautiful world of adventure and comradeship in waiting. We see them discussing what they would do if they won a 'hundred trillion million dollars'. But the beautiful world begins to tilt against Francie, as his harried Mother commits suicide, and his good-for-nothing father, who drove her to it, blames him. Francie gets into trouble with the law and is carted off to reform school; as he's being taken away, Joe clasps their hands together and shouts out, 'Blood brothers, Francie!'

Shouts Francie back: '*Until the end of time, Joe!*'

Of course, time has other plans. Joe, as they say, moves on. Joe makes new friends. Francie doesn't.

On his release (after a priest attempts to kiddie-fiddle him at reform school in a hilarious scene) he pursues Joe to the boarding school his parents have packed him off to. He breaks into the dormitory in the middle of the night and is collared by one of the priests. Francie explains that he's come to see his 'good friend Joe'. This is how this scene plays in the book:

> Joe said to me: What do you want?
>
> No he didn't. He said: What do *you* want?
>
> It was no use me trying to say I wanted us to ride out, Joe, I wanted us to talk about the old days and what we'd do if we won a hundred million trillion dollars, maybe go tracking in the mountains, I don't know, Joe, it was no use me saying that, for I knew it wouldn't come out right, so I said nothing, I just stood there looking at him.
>
> He asked me again: What do you want me for? Are you deaf or something?
>
> Then he said: Do you hear me? What do you want me *for*?

Shortly after this Francie goes completely berserk and kills Mrs Nugent, mother of Joe's new best friend, firing a slaughterer's bolt into her head, and then chops her up with an axe. (Well, you would, wouldn't you?)

Francie's madness is to take everything literally – especially love. He refuses the vague degradation of everyday life and his place in it. Francie, like all psychopaths, is an idealist.

Or should that be: like all idealists, he's a psychopath?

*

Before Xmas I saw Morrissey, the greatest living refuser of the degradation of everyday life, at his only British gig of the *Maladjusted* tour at Battersea Power Station. 'As soom of you may know,' joked the Lancashire dandy of desolation before starting his set, 'I used to be the drummer in a band called The Smiths.' (A reference to *that* lawsuit filed by his former rhythm section stalwart, Mike Joyce.)

I enjoyed the gig, even if it had little of the magic of the others I've attended. Perhaps this was because I found it difficult to lose myself in the bitter-sweet funny-sad lyrics of frustration and loneliness because throughout the show, a lusty young man had his hand down my flies squeezing my cock. (It did however lend a special poignancy to the line 'you touched me at the soundcheck' in 'Paint a Vulgar Picture', but probably not the right kind.) I worried a little that some of the people standing around us might realize what was going on – not because I was afraid of causing offence or denounced as a pervert, but because I was afraid of being called a fraud.

The lad in question was somebody I'd met through AOL a couple of months earlier and had a quickie with. I hadn't seen him again since, but he was the first person I saw when I entered the auditorium.

He tried to entice me to the toilets for another quickie. But even I – even I – thought that sex in a portaloo at a Morrissey gig was a bit too tacky.

*

There's nothing quite like the death of another year to put people in a party mood. I spent New Year's Eve in the company of Michelle, Justin, his live-in ex-boyfriend Jack, Tony the Irish butcher turned scaffolder turned (London's only legit) masseur, Michael the organ man and Torquay Lee the failed project turned albatross around my fucking neck (with impeccable timing he called me that evening to tell me that he'd been kicked out by his boyfriend yet again). We commandeered the pub across the road from me, which tends to be full of Jewish Princesses and their boyfriends. A few of them were dancing drunkenly, imported beer bottles in hand, and kept asking me to join them; so I did, grinding my hips against theirs to the strains of the Lambada. Michelle meanwhile was regaling another group of girls – who hadn't rumbled her; bizarrely, people very rarely do – with a story about Justin, whom they *had* rumbled as being gay on account of his orange sunbed face and Bette Davies cigarette movements: 'He's a female-to-male transsexual. You mustn't mention the word "gay" around him,' cautioned Michelle with a serious look. 'He gets very upset. It reminds him of his former sexuality that he wants to forget.'

Then she started telling them that she was a prostitute and that I was her pimp. I was taking her out for New Year's Eve as a special treat, but she'd be back to work on the streets within a couple of hours. 'No!' the girls in Prada black dresses and fur coats exclaimed, shocked, fascinated and very credulous.

'Yes!' said Michelle, realizing excitedly that she was dealing with people who had led very protected lives. 'You know, I'll do anything for money. I've eaten shit, I've been whipped. I'll even dress up as a man and fuck them up the arse with a strap-on!'

'No!'

'Yes!'

Come midnight I was standing on the table shouting. Something I tend to do whenever I get drunk; it's just that on New Year's Eve it doesn't result in me being thrown out on my arse. Michelle had her tits out and it seemed everyone in the bar, male and female, was queuing up to lick them. A harried waitress walking past our table carrying a tray of empty glasses clocked the scene and turned away hastily. 'Now I've seen everything,' she muttered under her breath. But it was *New Year*, so she couldn't object. Justin meanwhile was chatting up a cute young bloke who had been sitting with his pretty girlfriend at the end of our table. She was nowhere to be seen. Apparently, Justin related later, the lad was complaining that he wasn't getting anywhere with her: 'Been seeing her for months now, and she still won't put out. She's no fun. She doesn't even like coming out. So she's gone home, the cow.'

'Well,' said Justin, edging a little bit closer, his orange face catching the light fetchingly and his perfectly coiffed wedge wobbling invitingly, 'you know what you need, don't you?'

'Don't tell me,' he said. 'I should find myself a bloke. Then I'd have more fun. A geezer wouldn't mess me about the way she does.'

Justin didn't have anything to say to that. (Well, he did, but he didn't want to spoil the moment.)

After the whooping/mourning was over, we trouped back to my place and sang karaoke to my neighbours until 4 a.m. 'Back For Good' was a favourite. As was 'YMCA'. Michelle, of course, sang Abba. The whole back catalogue. My personal choice was 'Suspicious Minds', which I think I sang about five times, or at least until the taxis had arrived and everyone had hurriedly piled into them and left.

Except Lee.

I'm caught in a trap. I can't walk out.

Welcome to 1998, baby.

*

I'm glad to hear that you're giving up public sex in the New Year. Well, sort of. Sex with several blond college boys of an afternoon must be a terrible imposition. My heart bleeds for you, really it does. But, I suppose, if you are a lifer and there is no chance of parole from the House of Marines, it probably makes sense for you to live somewhere where they can at least reach your doorknob.

On the other hand, there's something to be said for *not* following your appetite, at least from my selfish point of view. After all, if you did, would you have the time or the inclination to write letters to me?

I have also well-sort-of given up public sex – and not just at Morrissey gigs. At least until it gets a little warmer; and until some of the bushes they've recently cut down on the Heath to discourage sex pests like me grow back. As for following my appetite, I did a recent bit of reviewing my sexual history and realized that far too many of the lads I've had a thing for/have been either Scottish or Irish, or some combination thereof. My next book should be called *Celtic Trade.*

Lately I've been thinking seriously about marrying Michelle and moving to Dublin where she will be Violet to my Sebastian in an Irish remake of *Suddenly Last Summer.* Mind, I suspect that Dublin has become far too fashionable for me of late. And anyway it's much too likely that Michelle would end up playing Violet *and* Sebastian to my bath-chaired Hepburn.

Thanks for your phone message about your impending trip to Germany. I can appreciate your dilemma about whether to come to London or visit the jagged glory hole you've heard about in the mens' in a Burger King restaurant on a forgotten American base in Vilseck, Southern Germany. Mind you, while it is undoubtedly your fate to die haemorrhaging from a snag on a glory hole in a lavatory somewhere in Central Europe reverberating to the crash of ten-pin bowling and re-dolent of Whoppers With Cheese, I think you should forget Vilseck and come and see this jagged old glory hole in London.

I may not hold as much promise, and my edges may be even rougher, but I do at least have lots of tea and sympathy to offer. We shall draw the curtains on the world and watch over and over again Mozza's favourite film *A Taste of Honey* – the one about poor Rita Tushingham falling for a sailor, dreaming big dreams and planning big plans but ending up preggers and abandoned with only faggy Murray Melvin to turn to.

I notice that A. E. Housman's old cottage round the corner is up for sale. Shall we put in a bid?

Love,

PS Those weren't postcards I was handing out in your gay dream. They were flyers promoting a new nightclub: 'Come home to Planet Uranus, where all your friends are waiting for you.'

PPS I finally gave into temptation last Wednesday evening and called that pager number I've tried to forget. I left a message asking: 'Are you still alive??' Two days later I got a holiday postcard from Germany. From Jason. Dated the same day I left the message. It began, 'Long time no hear!' and ended, 'Keep in touch!'

His pager doesn't work outside the UK. Another paging system, however, obviously does.

I think it's called the Death Instinct.

Text references

Page 3 — Leo Bersani, *Homos* (Cambridge MA, Harvard University Press, 1995).

Page 22 — Oscar Wilde, 'The Ballad of Reading Gaol' (London, Leonard Smithers, 1899).

Page 34 — Walt Whitman, 'What Think You I Take My Pen in Hand?' *Leaves of Grass* (Philadelphia, McKay, 1894).

Pages 71–2 — George Chauncey, *Gay New York. Gender, urban culture and the making of the gay male world, 1890–1940* (New York, Basic Books, 1994).

Pages 108–9 — P. P. Hartnett, *Call Me* (London, Pulp Books, 1996).

Pages 109–11 — Edmund White, *Genet* (London, Chatto & Windus, 1993).

Pages 116–8 — Jean Genet, *The Thief's Journal* (New York, Grove Press, 1987).

Pages 120–4 — Charles Isherwood, *Wonder Bread and Ecstasy: The Life and Death of Joey Stefano* (Boston, Alyson Publications, 1996).

Page 132 — Patrick Higgins, *Heterosexual Dictatorship: male homosexuality in post-war Britain* (London, Fourth Estate, 1996).

Page 133 — Montgomery Hyde, *The Other Love. An historical and contemporary survey of homosexuality in Britain* (London, Heinemann 1970).

Pages 156–7 — Maximillian Potter, 'Her fate was SEALED', *Details*, May 1997.

Page 178 — Flannery O'Conner, 'A Good Man is Hard to Find' in *Flannery O'Conner: Collected Works* (New York, Library of America, 1988).

Pages 183–4 — Gore Vidal, *The City & The Pillar* (London, Deutsch, 1996 edition; originally published 1948).

Pages 185–7 — Edmund White, *The Farewell Symphony* (London, Chatto, 1997).

Pages 189–90 — Gabriel Rotello, *Sexual Ecology: Aids and the Destiny of Gay Men* (London, Penguin, 1998).

Page 242 — 'A Liberation of Desire: an Interview by George Stambolian' in Garay Genosko (ed.), *The Guattari Reader* (Oxford, Blackwell, 1996).

Page 243 — Terry Eagleton, 'Enjoy', *London Review of Books*, 19:3, 27 November 1997.

Page 250 — Sartre, *Saint Genet*, (London, Heinemann, 1963).

Pages 263–4 — W. H. Auden, *Collected Poems*, ed. Edward Mandelson (London, Faber, 1994).

Page 264 — David Halperin, *One Hundred Years of Homosexuality* (London, Routledge, 1989).

Page 277 — Patrick McCabe, *The Butcher Boy* (London, Picador, 1993).

Photo credits

Page 4:	Steven Zeeland/Seadogphoto.com.
Page 7:	Mark Simpson.
Page 8:	Steven Zeeland/Seadogphoto.com.
Page 13:	Steven Zeeland/Seadogphoto.com.
Page 21:	Steven Zeeland/Seadogphoto.com.
Page 26:	David Lloyd. Private collection.
Page 53:	Bart Snowfleet.
Page 58:	Steven Zeeland/Seadogphoto.com.
Page 60:	Steven Zeeland/Seadogphoto.com.
Page 65:	United States Marine Corps.
Page 68:	Steven Zeeland/Seadogphoto.com.
Page 68:	Steven Zeeland/Seadogphoto.com.
Page 81:	Private collection.
Page 90:	United States Marine Corps.
Page 96:	Bart Snowfleet.
Page 149:	Steven Zeeland/Seadogphoto.com.
Page 152:	Tony Hutt.
Page 152:	Mark Simpson.
Page 178:	Steven Zeeland/Seadogphoto.com.
Page 204:	Michelle Graham.
Page 255:	Steven Zeeland/Seadogphoto.com.

New Fiction from Arcadia Books

THE ANGELIC DARKNESS

Richard Zimler

San Francisco, 1986 – a city where Dionysian liberation is beginning to pall beneath the first shadows of a strange new darkness. Bill Ticino's fruitless and numbing marriage finally breaks up. Plagued by insomnia and spiritually lost, Bill finds a lodger as the solution to his problems: a handsome, charismatic Portuguese man named Peter, whose pet bird is a hoopoe named Maria. Bill finds himself drawn into a world of kabbalistic storytelling, charms and ritual. Peter ignites Bill's repressed obsessions by telling him emotionally charged tales of hidden meaning.

One night they venture together into the Tenderloin district, a dead-end world of prostitutes and transvestites. Bill begins to see that his new tenant has plans that will force him down a perilous sexual and spiritual path, with the power to both redeem and destroy.

Praise for *The Angelic Darkness*:
'A heady mixture of the mythical, the mysterious and the earthy. Above all, it affirms the power of fiction and makes the world seem a more complex and wondrous place'
– Michael Arditti, *Daily Mail*

'His serene and calm prose probes with a fine scalpel into emotions and sexuality. Zimler is an exciting writer and *The Angelic Darkness* is an ambitious novel, full of mystery'
– *Times Literary Supplement*

'A moving homage to outsider cultures both ancient and modern' – *Scotsman*

'A taut suspense story . . . compulsively readable'
– Alannah Hopkin, *Sunday Tribune*

New Fiction from Arcadia Books

EASTER

Michael Arditti

'Arditti writes about Western Christianity with
pungency and satirical frankness' – Muriel Spark

WINNER OF THE MARDI GRAS & WATERSTONE'S BOOK
AWARD 2000

The parish of St Mary-in-the-Vale is preparing for Easter. In his
Palm Sunday sermon, the Vicar explains that Christ's crucifixion
and redemption are taking place every day. He little suspects that,
before the week is out, he and his entire congregation will be
caught up in a latter-day Passion story which will tear apart their
lives.

Michael Arditti's magnificent novel is both a devastating portrait
of today's Church of England and an audacious reworking of the
central myth of Western culture. Taking the form of a traditional
triptych, it is at once intimate and epic, lyrical and analytic.
Shocking events unfold against a backdrop of meticulously observed religious services. High Church ritual, evangelical revivalism
and the ancestor-worship of the English gentry are all subjected to
merciless scrutiny.

In a fictional climate dominated by materialism, *Easter* stands
apart in its bold exploration of the nature of God, the problem of
suffering and the existence of evil. With an unforgettable gallery of
characters ranging from a Holocaust survivor and an African princess to Aids patients and Queen Elizabeth II, it provides a dazzling
and panorama of contemporary society. In its radical fusion of the
sacred and profane, *Easter* throws down a challenge to believers
and non-believers alike.

'A masterpiece that – if there is a God, and provided He's
Christian and gay – could easily end up on the Booker
shortlist. Even if He's not, you should read it' – *Time Out*

New Fiction from Arcadia Books

MOE'S VILLA & OTHER STORIES

James Purdy

'An authentic American genius' – Gore Vidal

In this new collection of short stories, James Purdy produces the same 'magnificent simplicity' that Edith Sitwell extolled when reviewing his earlier collections. 'There is never a sentence too much, a word too much.'

From the great opera star and her talking cat to the young girl with her fire-breathing dragon; from two black ladies in retirement and their mysterious tenant – a world-renowned film star – to two young illegal Mexicans and their 'cracked' landlord, James Purdy shows himself once again to be a master of the short story. In the words of Dorothy Parker, 'Only Purdy could make you think as you read: My God, these people happened! Those who read him are his for life.'

'A writer of fantastic talent. His books take one by the throat and shake one's bones loose. The American language at its best' – George Steiner, *Sunday Times*

THE HITE REPORT ON SHERE HITE

Shere Hite

'Beautifully written . . . women everywhere owe
Shere Hite an enormous debt' – Bel Mooney, *The Times*

'The cultural icon Shere Hite' (Jon Snow, Channel 4 News) has
changed how we view sex, relationships, friendship and the family
in the twentieth century. Her work remains at the cutting edge of
contemporary thought.

Shere Hite's ground-breaking Hite Reports have had a profound
and lasting influence on generations of readers – countless millions
all over the world. Hite writes here for the first time about growing
up in rural Missouri, the early feminist movement, her private life
and sexual identity. She left America to live in Europe because of a
fundamentalist political backlash, renouncing her US citizenship
in 1996 to become German.

Hite's initial research grew out of her involvement with a feminist group in New York, and it was with the publication of *The Hite
Report on Female Sexuality* in 1976 that she shot to international
acclaim.

The four Hite Reports, showing an increasing depth to her controversial theories, have been translated into fifteen languages and
published in thirty-five countries, receiving numerous academic
and professional awards and honours. The initial *Hite Report* was
named as one of the 100 key books of the twentieth century by *The
Times* in 1998.

'A revolutionary whose theories on sex and love ring true
with so many women' – Joan Smith, *Guardian*